"Policemen tell such wonderful stories . . . memorable cameos of pathos, foolhardiness, depravity, ragged courage, grief, astonishing stupidity and instant genius."

—*Chicago Tribune*

"Alarming, funny, moving, sometimes all three at once. . . . Compelling."

—*Newsweek*

"Fascinating . . . *COPS*' language is raw, blunt, bitter, profane. . . . What the cops face eight hours a day is graphically told. . . . crammed with shocks."

—*Philadelphia Daily News*

Their Lives in Their Own Words

Killing

All the guys are making jokes about the poor bastard. Taking bets about when he's going to die over in ICU. I didn't feel good, I didn't feel proud. I was glad it was him and not me; otherwise all I felt was empty. It still makes me swallow hard to think about it.

Their Lives in Their Own Words

Smooth Talk

We got a call one day, a jumper. He's hanging from the fire escape. I say, "Hey, stupid. Get your ass up here." And I walked away, right? A couple of minutes later he comes back in through the window. I said, "That's psychology and it worked." That was cute.

Their Lives in Their Own Words

Fear

A cop is scared all the time. He's scared of looking
like a fool, of being weak, yellow, of being a coward.
Afraid he's going to say the wrong thing and get in
trouble with the department. Fear is a policeman's
life.

Books by Mark Baker

Cops*
Nam
Women*
What Men *Really* Think About Women, Love, Sex, Themselves*

* Published by POCKET BOOKS

COPS

THEIR LIVES IN THEIR OWN WORDS

MARK BAKER

POCKET BOOKS

New York   London   Toronto   Sydney   Tokyo   Singapore

POCKET BOOKS, a division of Simon & Schuster In.
1230 Avenue of the Americas, New York, NY 10020

Copyright © 1985 by Mark Baker
Cover photo copyright © 1986 Magic Image Studios, Ltd.

ISBN: 0-671-68551-1

First Pocket Books printing May 1986

15

POCKET and colophon are registered trademarks of
Simon & Schuster Inc.

Printed in the U.S.A.

Fenway Cooey has been a friend of my family since before I was born. He has always been an example to me of what it means to be a gentleman, because he is a truly gentle man. This book is dedicated to Cooey, a good police officer and a fine human being.

Acknowledgments

I WOULD LIKE to thank all the men and women who were willing to take the time to talk to me about their experiences. Obviously there would be no book at all without their generous participation. I hope I have repaid their trust by presenting an honest account of the world they live and work in.

I owe Bob Bender, my editor, many thanks for his hard work on this book and for making it as good as he believed it could be. My agent, Esther Newberg, is always there when I need her, which is usually when I run out of money or spirit. My friends Frank Fortunato and Gary Smolek, as well as my father, Bob Baker, read the manuscript. All three of them gave me their honest criticism and their suggestions, and that has made a positive difference in the book. Bruce Margolius kept asking me questions that made me think. Mark Dickerman reminded me that my initial impressions were probably the right ones.

Special thanks go to John Davis, who taught me to operate his home computer and then let me use it to generate the final manuscript. Every evening as I finished for the day, John was there to read the chapter fresh out of the printer. He offered encouragement and a keen eye for what was important and what was not.

David Lindzian and his Blues Patrol provided technical, ballistic and procedural information that was essential. Tom Trepcyck helped me get the proposal for *Cops* off the ground in the first place. Bob Leuci spent a lot of time and some of his best material helping me understand the way police officers think. Ed Donovan, president of the International Law Enforcement Stress Association and head of the Boston Police Stress Program, has been more than generous with his connections and his insights.

As I collected these interviews and traveled around the country many people gave me a place to stay, an introduction to the local police or some other assistance. I'd like to mention them here and say thanks: David and Mary Ann Baker, Captain William Johnson, Andy and Irene Crichton, Tim and Cracker Conaway, Raoul Robino, Martin Perlman, Peggy Grossman, George Moon, Peter and Cathy O'Sullivan, Judy Collins, Judge Marvin Romanoff, John Morgan, Linda Roule, John and Cindy Davis, Joan O'Sullivan, Helen Pantzis, Hope Katcher, Stephanie Phelan, Anya Cvikevich, Eve Zeigler, Marvin Bevans, Kathy Pohl, and Cheryl Weinstein.

I would like to thank my mother, Gloria Baker, for reading to me all those years of my childhood. She sparked my interest in language. Then she and my pop told me I could be anything I wanted to be and encouraged me in whatever I did.

Veronica, my wife, imposes order and sensibility on the chaos of my life. Without her intelligence, foresight and vitality I'd never get a book finished. She manages our partnership with patience and grace and I love her very much.

Contents

Contents

Introduction

"MY HUSBAND, the cop. Always has to be the big man. One of the neighbors gets a ticket, they show up on our doorstep. 'Hey, Jimmy, old buddy, can you fix this for me? I swear the light was yellow. Can you fix it?'

" 'Don't worry about it,' he says. 'No problem.' "

The wife of a police officer, a thin, conservatively well-dressed woman in her fifties, was trying to explain to me the gulf between illusion and reality in her neighbors' perception of her husband, as well as in his perception of himself. He is a patrolman in a large metropolitan area and has worked in the same precinct on the same assignment for fifteen years.

"The big, important policeman. Do you know how he fixes tickets? He goes downtown and he pays them, that's how he fixes tickets."

She was angry about his behavior, but in telling me this story she wasn't trying to belittle her husband. She wanted to give me a glimpse of the man inside the uniform—not a hero or a Fascist, a gunslinger or a centurion, just a mere mortal like everyone else.

1

Cops and crime are a national obsession these days. America has more police officers per capita than any other nation in the world; yet the specter of violent crime still terrorizes the public consciousness. Every evening at six o'clock we sit transfixed before our television sets waiting for the bad news. The day's police report is dramatized with videotapes of the sensational aftermath of the crimes: confiscated plastic bags of cocaine, a table laden with exotic automatic weapons, hand-cuffed youths hiding their faces in windbreakers, chalk outlines on the pavement splotched with dark stains. We shake our heads and lock our doors.

Then, for the next few hours we try to relax and forget the jungle out there in the streets. We tune in to prime-time television drama and watch cop shows—good cops, bad cops, private cops, secret cops, ex-con cops, jiggly and feminist cops, straight-arrow and rebel cops, fantasy and "real" cops. And it's not just television. American popular culture is permeated with images of the police as saviors or monsters, peace officers and pigs.

Most Americans believe they know how a police officer does his job and lives his life because they read the newspapers and watch "Kojak" on TV. We see police officers riding around in their cars and we avert our eyes. Unless a cop is writing us a ticket, we never talk to the police, not even to say hello. In fact, we get very little realistic information on exactly what police work is like and even less insight into the day-to-day existence of police officers—the human beings, men and women, good, bad and mediocre.

I wanted to go beyond the crime statistics and sociological studies, beyond the flat cardboard characters of most fiction, behind the stone wall of press releases police administrators pile between the public and the cops. I wanted to find out just who these people are, why they become cops and how they do their jobs. Does our image of the police square with their reality? How do they see themselves? How do they see us?

I interviewed more than a hundred cops for this book. They work and live in a variety of settings—urban, suburban and rural—in a dozen states scattered all across the continent—the North and South, the Midwest and the West Coast. I traveled from communities with no more than a few hundred souls to sprawling cities with millions of residents.

I talked with police officers in locker rooms, briefing rooms and squad rooms. I took every available tour of holding cells and drunk tanks, helicopter hangars and communications centers. I visited the kids in the academies and saw the stiffs in the drawers of morgues. I walked with officers through red light districts and posh apartment complexes. I rode in police cars on patrol on different shifts around the clock, watching cops make car stops and settle family fights—and I felt that little grip of fear in my guts every time the radio blurted out the number of the unit I was riding in.

Although I worked my way through official channels to get some of the interviews included here, most of my contacts were quietly unofficial, without the knowledge of or sanction from the bureaucrats and bosses. I met cops in their bars and in their homes. We talked in coffee shops, on front porches and standing around in parking lots. Sometimes an officer and I just found an interrogation room that no one was using in the back of the station house.

I promised the men and women I talked to that I would not use their names regardless of the circumstances of our meeting. Police officers live in a closed society—"hermetically sealed" might be a more accurate description—under incredible pressures from their peers and their superior officers to conform. The consensus among them is that conversation with anyone outside the police department can only be trouble. In-

Introduction

terviewers with tape recorders remind them of prisoner
interrogations and internal affairs investigations where
anything the subject says may be used against him. They
feel constantly vulnerable to recriminations from the
public, the press, the department and their fellow officers.

I wanted them to relax, to feel safe to talk frankly
with me, as though I were a trusted partner. Further
than that, in the relatively short time I spent with each
officer, I hoped to establish a sort of neutral ground
with this confidential, off-the-record approach. I wanted
them to feel free to tell me things they might not discuss
even with a partner or a spouse—things they might not
ordinarily admit to themselves.

This is not a very scientific approach. I had no control
group with which to compare my interviews. I did no
aggressive fact checking to authenticate the veracity of
each story. I trusted my instincts and relied on the belief
that the majority of people will not deliberately lie when
they have so little at risk. It takes too much energy and
concentration to lie consistently for no purpose. My
experience has been that once a person makes up his
mind to talk to me and takes the trouble to keep an
appointment, he will usually be quite candid. People
want to be understood. They want a chance to explain
themselves to the rest of the world. Many of the cops
I interviewed were hungry for a little recognition for
the job they do.

Of course no individual sees himself in a totally ob-
jective light. The reader must exercise some judgment,
as though he were studying the conversation of someone
he had just met. There are exaggerations, embellish-
ments, perhaps even lies in these personal accounts.
They do not contain the truth, the whole truth and
nothing but the truth. But I do not believe there is
anything here which would subvert the basic honesty

of the book. Granting cops anonymity did more to reveal the truth than to disguise it.

Even with a guarantee of anonymity some officers could not break the habit of John Wayne taciturnity. Some cops could not overcome their xenophobia for anyone outside the police department. They remained suspicious of my motives. I had limited contact with truly bad police officers. Lazy, criminal or rogue cops see anyone asking questions as a danger to them. And a few individuals who did agree to talk to me would only recite pro-police propaganda.

However, the unwritten code of silence I had heard so much about was not the obstacle I had expected it to be. Maybe they were not entirely representative, but most of the cops who consented to be interviewed were gregarious. A number of them were downright charming. They seemed to enjoy talking. That's not to imply that they ever let their guard down completely. A cop could stand drinking with me at a bar, regaling me with one funny story after another, but he still kept one eye on the door and everyone who came and went. He wouldn't put his back to an aisle where strangers were passing back and forth. I realized this watchfulness carried over to the officers' relationship with me. A cop might be friendly and open, but that didn't mean that he really liked me or that I had been accepted. Even with those men and women I felt closest to, there was always one more layer of suspicion cloaking their inner selves.

This artless amiability coexisting with a skepticism that borders on paranoia is not the only contradiction I observed in the lives of police officers. They work in the middle of the raw, unadorned reality of the streets. It would seem that they should have a finger on the pulse of American society. Instead, they seem to be slightly out of touch with day-to-day existence. Like someone recently returned from a long ocean voyage, police officers have missed many of the cultural points of reference the rest of us take for granted. They know what criminal activity is going on in what part of town; they can recall license plate numbers of suspicious vehicles for months at a time. They are obsessed with their work, consumed by it, and it is fascinating to hear them tell about their experiences. But sometimes it is difficult to talk to them about anything else.

Police officers deal with very adult situations. They are constantly bearing witness to birth, death and the full range of human passions. The job must be a sobering experience. Yet cops have an aura of adolescence about them, something youthful and slightly silly. They tease, bicker and pout, run in cliques and gossip behind each other's backs like high school kids. All police officers, no matter what their ages, refer to their job as "playing cops and robbers."

Generally speaking, police officers lean to the right politically and morally. They advocate the straight and narrow path to right living. They believe in the inviolability of the marriage vows, the importance of the family, the necessity of capital punishment. Some of them are unyieldingly dogmatic—right is right and wrong is wrong and they are the arbiters of which is which. On the other hand, cops are masters of the compromise. It's a job requirement. Laws can't solve the complex human problems cops see every day. A police officer spends each shift negotiating his way through one thorny situation after another. He's seen people literally get away with murder while the innocent cry vainly for justice. Sometimes his personal sense of right and wrong begins to warp. After a few years on the street, he may acknowledge a hierarchy of wrong: dead wrong, wrong but not bad, wrong but everybody does it.

Even though a cop will hang onto his conservative dogmatism, he will apply situational ethics to his own behavior. At least 50 percent of the married male police officers I interviewed had a mistress or a couple of girl-friends and had very little trouble making mental accommodation for the relationships. They reveled in the fact that they almost had to kill somebody to get in any real trouble on the job. Off duty, a cop's greatest joy is the freedom he has to live above the law in minor ways—ignoring red lights when no one is coming, never having to look at his speedometer, getting away with all kind of trivial offenses by flashing his badge.

Similarly, cops are cynical people; yet they cling with tenacity to the ideals of Superman. Even though his sneering heart of hearts tells him there is only falsehood, iniquity and death in the world, a cop will still claim that he stands for truth, justice and the American Way.

One last contradiction is that for all the mixed motives that draw men and women to the job and for all the personal and professional impediments they must contend with once they are police officers, there are some really good cops. I met people who are selfless, larger than life, honest-to-God heroes. And I met many average men and women who earned my profound respect for performing their duty, day in and day out, year after year, with honesty, integrity and imagination.

I should admit that I like cops more than I thought I would when I started this book. Having tasted the casual violence and bone-numbing boredom they experience, I am better able to understand their point of view. I don't fear the police as a group as much as I used to, because I now know a good number of them as individuals. When I see a police officer today, I look at his face, not at his uniform.

CHAPTER 1

School of Hard Knocks

"I KNOW IT sounds corny as hell, but I really thought I could help people. I wanted to do some good in the world, you know?" That's what every cop answers when asked why he became a police officer. He'll probably say it with a laugh or a touch of bitterness. That doesn't mean it isn't true. He just isn't a rookie any longer. Experience has kicked a lot of gray onto his black-and-white, turned him cynical and suspicious. The naive egotist who was going to save the world may look pretty silly to him now.

Here's how it begins for the typical young aspiring cop. A white male from a working-class family, he graduates from high school and serves in the military or spends a couple of years in junior college. When it is time to get a job, he forgoes the heroic and takes a position selling women's shoes or life insurance or auto parts. He might become a baggage handler, a Xerox machine repairman, the assistant manager of a fast food joint. If he has an inside connection he may join a construction or industrial union and learn a trade.

He gets married. Within a year or two there is a child to feed. The most heroic thing he does is to put food on the table three times a day. That's an accomplishment in itself, but there's not much of a thrill to it. This is the life he sees stretching before him for years and years—pulling the same lever, twisting the same screw, pushing the same papers from In box to Out box, forever and ever.

One day he signs up to take the Civil Service Examination. He tells his wife, his family and himself that he's after higher salary, job security and better benefits. That's not the whole truth. He doesn't want to be a mailman or a garbageman or even a fireman. Those jobs are too much like the one he already has. He's looking for a little excitement with his opportunity of advancement. He wants some action as well as a good credit rating. He wants to be Superman with a pension plan. He wants to be a cop.

Not every candidate approaches the job with a confusion of unrealistic expectations and noble impulses. Some calculating individuals hope to use the position for personal aggrandizement. The opportunist hopes to gain influence. The greedy choose police work thinking graft and bribery will make their fortunes. The power and authority of wearing a uniform and carrying a gun attract more than a fair share of bullies to the profession, men and women looking to get even with the world or to get a leg up on the rest of us.

That these kinds of selfish motives exist among a percentage of the members of all police departments shouldn't be surprising. What is surprising is the honest idealism that the majority of the men and women who become police officers bring to the job. They really mean it when they say, "I thought I could help. I wanted to make a difference." I heard variations of those words over and over again. I came to believe them.

Of course every police officer breaks this mold in one

way or another. There is the college graduate from a very wealthy family who had the world spread at his feet and decided to become a cop: "Being a cop was not one of the things you talked about over dinner while you were sipping your Beaujolais. It just was not an acceptable profession. The only one in my family who approved was the guy who really earned all the money in the first place. He was the only one who was not a snob."

There is the man who grew up in the ghetto with no options at all: "Most of the guys I grew up with in the barrio didn't do much but become drug addicts and go to jail. It was the luck of the draw that I ended up a cop and not a drug addict. Lo and behold, some of us just had to become cops. The job was held in some awe. You got respect. Hey, it meant a legal gun."

And the jock who grew up in suburbia, got a sports scholarship, dropped out of college after three years because he couldn't see himself coaching basketball at the YMCA the rest of his life. This is the cop who started out as the small-town high school hood. He spent his educational career smoking in the boys' room and skipping class, but he did have the native intelligence to realize that his talent for getting into hot water would just boil over someday. He chose law enforcement over reform school.

There is also the talented flautist who left her prestigious music school because she found the camaraderie of the police force more attractive than the competition in the concert hall. And the black woman from the inner city who saw her neighborhood burned down around her and decided that the only way to change the system is from the inside. She sued the government, forcing them to allow her to become a police officer.

Once they've made it through the rituals of psychological questionnaires, polygraph tests and physical examinations, they spend approximately six months in the police academy. For many of them it is a less than memorable experience.

"You have all the instructors up there teaching you the penal law, the study of minority groups. You dabble in a little psychology, a little sociology.

"Then you got the guys downstairs in the gym who're telling you, 'That's all bullshit. It's either you or him out in the street. Go for the eyes. Kick them in the groin.'

"You say to yourself, 'What the hell is going on?' It's the same thing as being in high school. The English teacher is telling you one thing and then you go downstairs to the gym and that teacher is saying, 'Well, the English teacher is a fag anyway.' "

Some trainees take their instruction more seriously than others, but most of them see the time spent in the academy as a formality they must put up with in order to get out on the streets where they can really find out what's going on: "I got in a lot of trouble while I was in the academy, clowning around and what. I wanted to study to know the laws and be a cop, but I didn't want to pick up all this other bullshit they give out. I never took it serious, the discipline part. For punishment like, they had you carry bricks. I used to carry three bricks in one hand and three bricks in the other hand.

"One time the patrol chief came out to the academy after we'd been there for a few months to do an inspection of the cadets, as they called us. The chief would come down the line, ask each cadet a question—something about police work—and you had to give him an answer. Then they'd all eyeball you up and down to make sure that you looked sharp. I was standing in ranks with my six bricks. He come up to me and saw the three bricks in each hand and he said, 'What's your name?'

" 'Cadet Johnson, sir.'

" 'All right, Cadet Johnson, what's the definition for fornication?'

" 'Sir, the definition for fornication is, uh, I guess that's two people of the opposite sexes in the backseat of a '57 Chevy having fun.'

"He walked on and he had a big grin on his face. The lieutenant from the academy stopped and said to me, 'Johnson, that's why you're carrying six bricks.' "

At graduation, they raise their right hands and they swear a solemn oath. Each one is presented a shiny metal badge, which is never quite as heavy as he expects it to be, and a pistol that drags down on his belt like Fate itself. They are congratulated by the mayor and the chief of police, their families and friends. Now they're cops.

DIFFERENT FRATERNAL groups come by graduation day and talk to their ethnic group. So you have the black guy come in from the Guardians. He'd grab all the black guys on the side and tell them, "These are the problems that are peculiar to the black cop." The Irish guys would come from the Emerald Society and Columbians talk to the Italians.

When it was over, we all got together and said, "What'd your guy tell you? What'd your guy tell you?" It was hilarious.

Clearly the Irish cop would say, "Our problem has been and continues to be that we can't get an Irish cop that doesn't drink. An Irish guy who doesn't drink at all before he becomes a cop, becomes a cop and all of a sudden he's a major drinker. He gets all his drinks for nothing, so you can't get him to walk past the bars. We got alcoholics. We got guys with serious problems because of drink."

The black guy says, "The black cop could live in any middle-class mixed neighborhood in the city and has never been to Harlem, but as a recruit they'll send him to Bedford-Stuyvesant or Brownsville or Harlem for sure. He's there and all of a sudden he finds cousins everywhere. We can't keep you guys on the street. You're always running up in a building and getting laid all the time."

The Italian guy's speech was pretty much the same thing. "You guys can't keep your pricks in your pants. You walk by the bars all right, but you're all looking to get laid. It's all right. We know you're going to do it. But be careful and try not to."

Then you have the chaplain coming in to tell you how important the marriage vows are. "Maintain a discipline for yourself. You're going to run into temptation."

*

I was out with my training officer the first night. We'd been riding around about ten minutes when he slammed on the brakes, ran around the car, grabbed this guy and threw him up against the side of the car. He started shaking him down.

I get out of the car and start practicing my patrol techniques that they had taught me at the police academy, which consisted of watching my training officer while he's shaking down this guy and putting him in the backseat.

When we'd sat back down in the car, I looked over very casually and said, "What'd we get him for?"

"He just robbed that man over there."

"Oh, really?"

Talked to the man and, sure enough, that's what happened. "Yeah," the man said, "he held me up at knife point. Took my $26 I had and put it in his left pocket." We felt in the guy's pocket and there was the $26. We arrested him and took him to jail.

So that was what a trained eye will see and an untrained eye will not see. I thought I was looking around pretty good, but I didn't see him rob the guy. I began my real education in the department.

*

My first night out on the street, I went out with a guy by the name of Charlie. Charlie had about twenty years on the job, maybe twenty-five. I don't know whether or not he resented the fact that I was with him. He said, "Come on, let's go." We had Tremont Street from Oxford Crossing down to Camden where Slade's Restaurant and Estelle's were located. They were places that a lot of people come to after the regular bars closed down.

So we walked from the station to Slade's. After that we walked right to the firehouse which was right on Fremont Avenue. We went up to the third floor. Charlie opened a locker and began taking off his uniform.

"What's this?" I said.

"It's all right," he said. "You go over there and lie down. I'll wake you up when it's time to go." He took off his uniform and put on his pajamas.

I had this big, long overcoat on and I went over and I laid down on the bed at attention. I was so afraid of being caught in this situation, I laid there for six hours, eyes like silver dollars, waiting for something to happen.

Come six o'clock or so, Charlie got up and said, "Come on, let's go." Put his uniform back on and went downstairs. We checked all our doors and windows on the beat, went back to the police station and checked out.

The next shift I worked I got the same beat again only by myself. I must have walked it 250 times. I would not get off the street.

*

I found out early that there were some rough characters around Bay Street and Main Street. The first night they

15

put me with an older fellow, one that had experience. He started to naming different men on the street who was real bad. He called one of them by name and he says, "Now, he's bad. He'll try to put a fellow in a damn trash can the first night."

"Could he put three of us in there?" I asked this officer.

"What do you mean by three?"

"Me and Smith and Wesson."

We hadn't walked three blocks before we saw the man. The man come up and the older officer introduces me and tells him, "He's going to be the new officer on the beat and this is his first night really. But you got to watch him, because he will give you trouble sometimes."

The man kind of sized me up and down. He was a pretty husky fellow, too. He says, "He looks to me like he would fit in a trash can."

I just backed up one step and put my hand on Smith and Wesson. "You won't get all three of us in there," I said.

"What would you do?" he says.

"If you laid a hand on me, I'd kill you dead," I says.

He looked at me and then he looked at the older officer and he says, "By God, I believe he means that." After that I didn't have no trouble walking the beat.

*

They made a big deal of it when I first started. The first day I got interviewed by the local newspaper. In the first four days, I was interviewed twice and photographed three times, which did not set well with the guys, of course. "How do you like being a female officer?"

"Shoot, guys, I don't know. Give me a chance."

One of my first duty shifts, I was partners with this guy whose first words to me on the way to the unit were, "Don't even think about driving, because you're not going to." Other than that, he didn't speak to me. He was macho man and he refused to speak to me. He did not want this woman in a uniform, doing the job he was doing. For five hours we sat in the same car and didn't talk.

*

You come brand spanking new out of the academy and you think you're going to save the world. You'll make the streets safe for everybody. There won't be any more crime out there after you get done. Takes about two weeks to burst your bubble.

The first fellow I rode with said to me the first thing, "Have you ever ridden Midland before?" That's a black ghetto part of town.

"No, sir," I said. "I don't even know where Midland is."

He turned his head and rolled his eyes. I could see him thinking, "Oh, boy, that's just what I need. Not only is he a rookie, but he knows less than a rookie."

We get out there on those calls and he says, "On this call, I want you to do all the talking."

"Okay, okay." I'm chomping at the bit. I get in there and I start talking to these people like I was having a regular conversation. They look at me and look back at my training officer, and then they look back at me. They scratch their heads, lean over to the training officer and ask, "What'd he say?"

He would translate for me: "He said that if you don't shut up, he's going to kick your fucking ass."

"Yes, sir. We understand that."

I looked at him kind of amazed and said, "Did I say that?"

"You did that time."

After a while you realize that you can't educate everybody you come in contact with, so there is only one other choice. Go down to their level as far as your verbalizing. You have to learn a whole new language.

My first wife was a teacher. After a month or two, she looked at me and said, "Your English is really becoming atrocious." You begin to talk the same way all the time. You don't even realize you're doing it.

*

It happened to me. You go into the diner with your uniform on and all the girls are looking at you. All of a sudden I thought I got better-looking. People are starting to pay attention to you. They want to talk to you. There's a whole ego trip that goes with the job. You start saying to yourself, "Am I special? They have been telling me that I am."

*

Walking down the street in that uniform and seeing blue-haired old matrons turn to look at you like, "Thank God, you're here," it really is a wonderful feeling. It's like Dodge City and you're the sheriff. This street is mine and ain't nobody going to fuck with it. That's a great and professional feeling. You've done something, you're important. Up until then in your life you may have done absolutely nothing. Now all of a sudden, at the ripe old age of twenty-one, there's a whole lot of people looking to you to protect them from the madhouse around them. That's a wonderful thing.

*

I suddenly found myself standing on the streets, a thread still hanging out of the sleeve of my uniform, wondering what the fuck I'm doing in this blue suit. It's funny, I thought I knew a lot about the streets and about crime. Most of us, including a lot of policemen, are educated to think that we do. But we know about as much about crime and the streets as a fisherman knows about the bottom of the ocean. We paddle around in the sea, but we are largely ignorant of what actually goes on down there.

*

It's a shock to everybody when they first come on the job to find out that everybody does not think like you think. That's one thing that I learned. That's what makes me crazy about the peace demonstrations that I see with "Ban This and Ban That because we're all Brothers," and all that stuff. Jesus, go down ten blocks from here and you won't find your brother down there. The whole world isn't your block and your neighborhood ball team and your bar. There's a million other people out there who think completely different from you.

*

The street is very seductive and very sensual. You may take it home because you want to take it home.

There used to be a place in Manhattan between First and Second Avenue on 100th Street that was like Bombay. Eighteen thousand people in one block and 17,500 had criminal records. The place was a zoo. Thousands and thousands of people were outdoors on the street. The one block had four cops. The guys who worked it regularly stayed on the corners. I came into the precinct and we were going to take over the patrol. I asked one old-timer, "You going on that block?"

"I ain't going on that block," he says, "and I don't give a shit if they all kill each other."

I had my partner and a couple of other guys I worked with and I said to them, "Come on. Let's go in there and see what's happening." I was very young.

It was hysterical. What went on in that block in one night was more police work—if you wanted to participate in it—than most cops would experience in a lifetime—stabbings, shootings, fighting, gambling, prostitution—on one street. I came on post one night and they were having a cockfight in the middle of the street.

I would go home at night and think to myself, "What a world! What a place! What an experience! It's really exciting." The smells were even very special. It was smells I'd never smelled before, exotic.

And the girls. If a guy is fairly good-looking and has anything going—anything at all—and he works in the ghetto, he can fuck himself to death if he wants to. That's no bullshit. It's just so available. It's so easy to get laid. Even the shy guys, guys who would never think of hitting on a certain type of woman in civilian clothes, would hit on a woman in a minute in uniform, because you can just walk up and say anything you want to her. She feels secure and she'll respond. You're not going to get turned off immediately. You have a shot. If you're ballsy and you've been around a little bit, you can get laid as much as you can stand.

This is a single man's job, because you meet literally thousands of women. And you meet them in unusually stressful situations. You come in as the knight in shining armor. Some guys will take advantage of that. There's this ethic that says you don't do it, but we all know that everyone does it. I don't think I locked up a guy the first year on the force without fucking his wife, girlfriend or mother.

*

I got my first call to a domestic dispute. On the way over, I was thinking maybe I'm going to be a hero and save some woman.

First, I bang on the door and this voice says to come in. I walk in and there is this guy sitting there, crying. Now what do I do? He's mumbling something. Now another guy walks into the room with his hair in curlers. I thought, "I'm in the wrong area here."

The guy with his hair in curlers walks up to me and

puts his arm around me and says, "Trooper, I really love that guy. I don't know why we can't live together."

Now, I'm destroyed, I don't know what to do. I took his hand off of my shoulder and slowly backed out the door.

I found out later that every new trooper is sent to that house. I didn't do a thing, I didn't help them at all. Too weird.

*

I was on my first post. A young fellow walked up to me—he had his load on—and made some snide remark to me. I deflected it. He came back again and made some very personal remark about my family and I started to ignore that, too. I looked around and I was aware that everybody was watching me. I realized that if I didn't take this situation in hand right away, there would be nothing I could accomplish.

I pretended to walk past him, but before I had gotten by, I kneed him right in the balls and dropped him to the ground. I picked him up gently, very gently, sat him on the stoop and walked away.

I never had a problem again on that post. I didn't beat him up or leave any scars. I didn't enjoy it. I didn't put myself in a situation where people would feel I was getting my rocks off. I just made my point. I had given him the opportunity to get his rocks off and leave. He didn't take it and that was that.

*

The very first call I got as a patrolman was a head-on collision between a tractor trailer truck and a Datsun pickup. In the wreckage both the driver and the passenger in the Datsun were killed. The driver of the semi was not injured, but he was very shaken. He was being treated for a heart attack by the rescue unit when we got there. The other people were totally destroyed. You didn't have to check for vital signs; you just had to pick up the pieces and load them on a rubber stretcher.

As the wrecking crew and the other officers arrived to help clear the street, everyone was kicking the sharp glass and metal pieces to the curb of the road. The passenger had no identification on him so we were looking through any paper blowing around. It was raining. I picked up a piece of paper that was folded up and I unfolded it. It was a suicide note written by the driver. He was taking his buddy with him. That was a real freaky experience. I read it and then read it again not really putting two and two together. That really brought me down to earth.

*

I'd just been on the job about eight months. I wanted as much activity as possible. I wanted to get my feet wet. They stick me with this older cop who had the glassy eyes and the ruddy complexion, you know what I mean. I'm a little perturbed. This guy, his glory days are long gone. They also gave me a sector where nothing is going on. I'm really disgusted.

I'm driving the car and all of a sudden a job comes over the air: "Youths in the water." This is the winter. Boom! I go down because it's our sector. There's a bunch of people standing on the pier and they're pointing. It's maybe fifteen feet, twenty feet down to the water. I go out onto the pier and I see this guy floundering around. I hear yelling underneath the pilings of the pier. My brilliant mind said that this guy went in to save the kids. He's hurt.

We open up the trunk. I don't know why, but we had life preservers. Generally, there's not even a spare tire in most of those cars. They're supposed to put life preservers in cars on patrol bordering on the water, but they were actually in there—I couldn't believe it. There was probably no jack.

I get to the end of the pier and I fling one of the life preservers to this guy. It lands near him, but he couldn't get to it. I think to myself, "Here's a chance for a rookie to get a little notoriety." So I strip off my coat, take my shoes off, take off my gun belt. The older guy is looking at me now like I'm probably nuts. It was February. I jump off.

I'd done some lifeguard work before and I'm thinking as I go off this pier that there could be anything stuck under the water that would impale me and that's the end of my career. So I take a shallow water dive. When I hit that water, I thought my heart was going to stop. I said to myself, "This was a mistake."

I swam up to this guy and got the life ring to him. I couldn't tell him what to do. If you've ever been in very, very cold water, you know that you can't talk, because you get very short of breath. In the meantime, another radio car came. I'm assuming that they called the harbor guys, which is what they're supposed to do. Yet there's no other cop in the water, just me, this jerky kid.

While I'm down there with this guy, Emergency Services gets there and they throw a harness down and take him up. Then they drop the ring down again. I'm looking around and I see a guy holding on to a piling. There's ice on it. I go get him. He's in the harness and they hoist him up.

They throw the ring down again. Now, I'm starting to hurt. I go underneath the pier looking for this other guy. I can hear him yelling, but I can't find him. This guy has climbed up a piling and got on a cross beam. I'm in the water trying to say, "Come on, come on. Get back in the water." He looks at me like I'm crazy. He just got out of the water. He's thinking, "It's too cold. I ain't going back in that water. This is safer." But there was no way you could get the guy where he was, unless you cut a big hole in the pier. The city would never do that.

I said to myself, "I went in for three, I'm going to come out with three." So I climbed up with this jerk, tried to talk to him and then threw him in the water. I got back in. They pulled him up.

I'm getting scared, because I can tell I'm getting ready to go out. They throw the harness down to me and yank me up. Just as I get to the top, the harness breaks. I say, "They're trying to kill me." Finally they get me out and they take me to the hospital. The other three guys are screaming because they are cold. I was never so cold in my life.

The embarrassing part comes when they take you in and they strip you down. There ain't nothing there, you know what I mean? It's gone. Not that I was hung to begin with, but you ain't nothing now. Some old sergeant comes in and he's throwing scotch down me. I was a young guy and I wasn't taking my scotch neat in those days, so he's almost killing me on the table with the scotch.

Finally, the reporters and all come down. This guy, my "partner," has the moxie to say that he was in the water with me. I found this out when I read the papers. The captain was writing me up for a medal. He just wanted in on the medal. The guys in the command knew that this guy wasn't involved in it. I got a civilian award, dinner on the town and a $500 check. But that wised me up to a different personality on this job—a guy that didn't want to get in on the shit. But that's life. People are like that. I haven't seen the guy since.

*

After three months on the street, I began to realize that it's not what I expected. The big thing that hit me is I'm a social worker. That just blew my mind. I was looking for car chases and shoot-'em-ups, all the things

24

I saw on every cop show for twenty years of my life. Now I come on the street and they expect me to fill out a bunch of forms and mediate family fights, child abuse, people OD'ing on the street.

You never see a guy handle an aid case on a cop show—pick up some psycho that's stepped in front of a bus and get him registered in the local hospital mental health ward—but you do that more than shoot your gun at people.

At twenty I'd hung around with teenagers all my life. Now I'm dealing with forty- to fifty-year-old people who have problems which I didn't even know then what the problem was made of. I didn't know what a family fight was or a child abuser. I was brought up in an all-white neighborhood. Suddenly I'm in the ghetto and a woman comes up to me and says, "My husband took the check and the kids can't eat and he's going to come back and beat me up." People come up to you and explain things to you and you felt stupid. You wanted to help them, but you didn't really know what to say to them.

*

I'd been a police officer for six days. Just got my uniform. I was riding with an experienced officer. He was actually a year younger than I was, but he had a whole year on the job.

This was a Sunday afternoon, a real nice, sunny day. We get a call up in a very expensive residential neighborhood: "Crime against nature." What's that? Somebody chopping down a tree? We're looking in our penal code. It's some kind of sex crime, we figured out. We go driving up. There's another unit already there, so I walked up and said, "Hey, what's going on?"

"You won't believe this," they said. "There's a naked lady up there fucking a dog."

"Nah, you're kidding me. That can't be."

"Well, go back and look for yourself."

We go back behind this house which is a $200,000 home and there's this naked woman screwing a Great Dane. And it's not even her house. It was her dog as it turned out. The resident is saying, "There's this lady in my backyard and I don't know what she's doing there. Well, I know what she's doing, but I don't know why she picked my backyard."

Obviously we had to do something. It was beginning to draw a crowd. People were coming around. All these little kids from the neighborhood are showing up. She was quite oblivious to what was going on. She was really into it, orally copulating this rather large Great Dane. So we decided we were going to separate her from the dog. They said to me, "All right, Dave, you grab the dog." I was the new guy.

I didn't think that was a real good idea, but I come up to the dog and tried to grab him. Naturally, he tried to bite me, bared fangs, "Raw! Raw! Raw-raw!"

"No, that's not going to work. Let's back off." We got on the radio and called up animal control. While we're waiting for the dogcatcher to show up, she's continuing with this thing. She was crazy.

This man comes up to me. He was about forty. He says, "You know, I am a visitor to this country. I am from Denmark. We have nothing like this in Denmark."

"I don't think we have much like this here in our country either, buddy."

One of our guys runs back to his car and gets one of those little Instamatic cameras. He says, "I'm getting pictures of this." He's crawling up on hands and knees getting some crotch shots of this gal. She wasn't bad-looking. She's chewing on this dog and sticking flowers up her twat. A few minutes later the animal control guy shows up. "Oh, yeah," he says. "It's Jane. She's always with her dog."

He put the noose thing on the end of a stick over the

dog's head and started pulling the Great Dane away. We got hold of her by the heels and we're dragging her the other way. Her point of connection with the dog is his testicles. We're pulling in both directions and the dog is going cross-eyed, yelping.

Finally, we break her loose from the dog. She turns as we grab her and she wraps her arms around this one officer—it wasn't me—grabs him by the nuts and gives a big squeeze. He's yelping. We're calling, "You got her, Joe. You got her. Hang on."

We managed to get her down to the unit, wrapped her in a blanket and got under way to mental health to see if they knew what to do with her.

As we're starting to drive down to mental health, she crawls up into the back window of the car and all you could see was this big, white butt sticking to the window. We drive her down the street laughing as hard as we can. She's mooning the entire city.

I'd only been on a week and I thought, "This is really going to be strange."

*

My first winter on the street, they sent me on a run for this death. If you can't get a doctor to sign a death certificate, you got to take them to the morgue. The call came from the Eastside where there's a row of rest homes. It was a real nice, prominent neighborhood at one time, but it kind of went down.

It was some old lady. We had to haul her. My partner took the front of her and I took the back. We were going to pick her up, bedsheets and all, put her on the stretcher and take her to the morgue. I lifted her up and everything had let go, bowels, bladder and everything. She'd been dead for six or eight hours. I started heaving. I went to the window and the windows were nailed shut. I stood there, just swallowing it basically.

27

It was bad. That was my first experience with a dead body.

*

I was patrolling a desolate highway in a rural part of the state when I get a call that there's an accident. There's injuries involved, so naturally, being out of the academy not too long, your adrenaline gets pumping. You're going to try to do good and help people out.

I get there relatively quickly within three or four minutes' time. It was a head-on collision right dead smack in the middle of the median in the middle of the highway. The cars weren't burning, but there was smoke and steam rising up from them because the engines had been compressed on both vehicles.

I looked inside and I just stood there for a second. I'm looking at this woman who had no nose on her face. The nose had been severed off. This is shocking to me because without that appendage on the front of your face, you're really looking down the throat of the individual. I had my first-aid kit with me and the best thing for bleeding which we had in there was a Kotex. So I got that on her face and got her on the side of the highway.

A couple of cars were coming by—do-gooders—but they were getting sick because as it turned out five people died in this accident. This woman was alive at least, but she was in shock. She was walking around, asking if anything was wrong with her. I'm trying to calm her down. I'm hearing the moans and screams from other people. I get her down and get one of the passersby to help me out by holding direct pressure on her face. There was extensive bleeding.

There was a small child in the front passenger seat of that car. I walked over and looked at the child. The child was not severely lacerated, but it was obvious that the child was dead. This young girl was two or three years old and died of massive internal injuries caused by the impact of the collision. I could do nothing for her. That was all, in that one car.

I walked over to the other car and there happened to be four people in that vehicle. I went up to the driver's side and realized that we had a problem here because the driver had no head. He was decapitated by a piece of flying metal from the car that he had struck— I later found out it was a he. He was in his early thirties. That turned out to be somewhat humorous, because it took six troopers nearly two hours to find his head. His head had gone out through the front windshield and actually landed over three hundred feet from the point of impact.

The driver's wife, who was sitting next to him, was killed. She bled to death before I even arrived. One child in the backseat was alive. He was a twelve-year-old boy. He had severe compound fractures. He had bones sticking out of the right side of his body. His right wrist was protruding from his arm. But he was saved.

There was another child in the backseat who was about nine or ten and she was alive. She was talking to me. She was crying, asking me how her father and mother were doing. I went to her first because she was the only one conscious and that I could recognize as being alive. I brought her out of the car and was holding her and telling her she would be okay. She was going into shock. I was trying to keep her awake and keep her going. As I'm talking to her, she looks at me and said, "Oh, you're a policeman." I felt so good about that—that she recognized that I was there to help her.

Then a little bit of blood began to come out of the right corner of her mouth and she died. I'll never forget that child dying in my arms as long as I live. I knew she was dead, because when she died she urinated. It sounds crazy to repeat this, but her warm urine, the last warm part of her body, was dripping all over my uniform.

The ambulance didn't arrive until about twenty minutes later. All this activity transpired within fifteen minutes. You experience death and do all these things you've been trained to do, and you say to yourself, "Wow, I'm here."

The cars are being towed away and I've called in some information and we're getting some feedback. Somebody had recognized the car that had been involved in the collision, but he didn't stop at the wreck. The family, in which everybody but the boy was killed, lived in the next town over and were coming from a relative's house. They were known in this area and had only traveled about five miles to the point of impact. This person who recognized the car went back and told the relatives. So the relatives showed up on the scene about twenty minutes later. They were in shock and they're saying, "Where's the baby?"

"What baby? There's no baby here." The time of the accident was about nine o'clock. It was a winter's day and it had been dark since five o'clock. So we can't find the baby.

We look around the whole area. We finally find the head three hundred feet away. So we figure the child was thrown from the vehicle, too. We start at a 300-foot radius and work back into the area. We looked and we looked and we just couldn't find it. Then we went back and we went out a little bit further and looked and looked again. We realized that it would have been impossible for the child to have been thrown that far with the trees and everything.

Right next to where the wreck had occurred, the road was forested on both sides, lot of pine trees and evergreens. They were actually sort of hanging over on both sides of the road. It was only a single lane each way and there was very little shoulder next to the highway.

I don't know why I did it, but I just turned around and flashed my light up in the trees. There's this child, dead, impaled upon a pine tree branch about twenty feet up in the air. The child had been catapulted out of the vehicle and speared through the left side of his torso and was hanging like an ornament on a Christmas tree.

What do we do now? I had to climb up there and cut this kid down. Take it off the branch. So now for the second time in a period of a couple of hours, I've got another dead kid in my arms.

An adult death you can accept. We're programmed to accept that, but a child and an infant . . .

That was my first day I was on my own and I faced that reality. I went back to the barracks and I thought I'd handled everything pretty professionally for being a brand new trooper. All of a sudden it hits you. I got sick to my stomach.

*

I was working with this rookie. Officer Pompano was a college graduate from the state university. The first night we worked together he said, "I believe in using handholds to restrain people. I don't believe in hitting people."

"Well, son," I said, "if you are going to work out in this area, you're going to have to get used to using your fist and your nightstick, if not your gun."

"No, I don't believe in that. There's other ways. You can talk to people."

"Okay, you stick with that philosophy."

We were cruising and we pull up on a black male subject who was trying to break into an old gas station on Main Street. The subject tried to get away. Officer Pompano grabbed him and tried to put an arm hold on him. He thought he had the guy real good. The guy flipped him. So Officer Pompano grabbed him again with his world-famous handhold. The guy twisted away again. I watched a few more seconds, then I went up and cracked the guy on the head with my nightstick and he went down. I handcuffed him.

"Now there," I told Officer Pompano. "You can use your handholds if you want to dance with them. But you've got to realize that you just want to take this guy into custody. On the other hand, this guy doesn't want to go to jail. He's got more to lose than you've got to gain. You can lock all the handholds on him you want, but this son of a bitch is not going to stay around. You've got to get his attention first, because he wants to get the hell out of there no matter how he has to do it."

After that he got the message.

*

I get there and a trooper says to me, "We got a call. It's a bar, a real shit-kicking bar. There's going to be a guy sitting by the jukebox. As soon as he gets off the chair, he's going to get right in front of you. Hit him. Just hit him hard enough to make him double over. Make sure you give him a good whack, because he's going to try to hit you after you hit him. If he can muster up enough strength to knock you backwards, he gets drinks for the rest of the night from everybody at the bar. If you hit him so hard where he can't react and he doesn't come up after you, he has to buy the rest of the bar a drink. This has been going on since I've been stationed here. It's a game. You won't have a letter of complaint; nobody is going to say anything. It goes on here every Friday night. You're the new kid, so we'll put you through it."

I thought, "You've got to be kidding me. I'm from a pretty big town and they don't hit people for no reason at all."

"Kid," he says, "I'm telling you, this is going to be important to your reputation. If you don't really whack this guy, the next time you get into a confrontation with one of these fellows, you're going to have problems. These are hillbillies, and these people have a different image of police work."

I hit him. As soon as he stood up, I punched him. It was a very strange thing. He looked like an alcoholic, long hair, maybe thirty-nine years old. Luckily, he doesn't come back and hit me. Everybody in the bar starts clapping. The guy shakes my hand. It's a shit bar, nothing on the walls. The stench of the beer is terrible. I didn't even believe we were in the United States. This is like the Twilight Zone.

*

I wasn't naive enough to believe there wasn't corruption on this job. It was no big deal to me. I might have been young, but I wasn't a fucking sick idealist expecting to go out there and lock up all the Mafia and stop all the narcotics and make everybody realize that they shouldn't kill each other.

I got assigned to a precinct where there wasn't a guy that had less than fifteen years on the force, which is to say they were all hairbags and I was a rookie. I had the first case of corruption almost immediately. They assigned me to a Golden Gloves match at an Irish parish on the Upper West Side. It's three old hairbags and myself. They're already drunk when we come on duty. We have this wonderful job of watching the lads beat the shit out of each other in the ring and it's going to be a fun fucking night. No dealing with violent crime out there, we are going to drink beer and eat all night long. They're going to do this. I didn't.

I get there and I'm pissed off because I'm being taken off the street. What is this hokey shit? What am I doing in a church watching guys fight? For Christ's sake, I want to get out there and lock up bad guys. They thought they were doing me a favor.

Well, it wasn't so much that as they wanted to use

me. Somebody had to stay on duty and watch. I was the rookie. When we got there one of the guys says, "Lad, do you want a beer?"

"No," I said, "I don't drink while I'm working."

"That's very good, lad. You're going to go far in this job. Now, I'll tell you what you're going to do. You're going to go out there and just walk around the ring. You see, there's more fights that happen outside the ring than in. They're not bad boys; they really just get a bit carried away because there's a wee bit of drinking that goes on."

All of them were seventy-year-old Irishmen and they call them boys. "And if there's a problem, lad, we'll be in that room over there. Feel free to come in and get a sandwich if you want one."

I worked a straight eight, I never left the God damn ringside. My bladder's bursting. I figure I got to do it right.

The end of the evening, these guys come out and they can't even walk now. The monsignor is a very outspoken and drunken monsignor. He is shaking all the cops' hands, "Goodnight. Thanks, lads, you did a fine job this year." These guys must get this post every year. He gets up to me and shakes my hand. I feel there ain't something right in my hand. It's a twenty-dollar bill. A priest has just laid twenty bucks on me. He had paid me off to do my duty. So I turned around and I say, "What's this?"

The old-timer looks at me and says, "It's a twenty-dollar bill, lad."

"I know that. What's it for?"

"Ah, the monsignor is a good guy. Every year he does this. It's just his way of thanking us for keeping the peace."

"I don't want it."

"You don't want it?" Whup, it was out of my hand so quick and he's splitting it with the other guys.

What that whole experience did for me was get me catching dead bodies almost every night of the week, because they didn't trust me. When somebody dies in an apartment or something, you got to guard the body until the medical examiner comes and says that it wasn't a homicide, it was just a normal death. This can go on sometimes for eight hours straight. He's a young cop and he didn't take the money. Better not have him exposed to too much shit.

*

I was with a senior guy who'd been on the job for quite a while, but he'd been passed up for promotion, probably because he had a bad drinking habit. The guy drank a lot, but he was a good cop so they overlooked his weaknesses. But he was a drunkard.

We got dispatched to a suburban setting. The houses were spaced on roughly 100-foot lots. We pulled up on the driveway. I got out of the car. We walk up toward the front of the house and he says, "No, let's go to the back of the house." We get to the bottom of the back steps and he said, "You got this one, kid."

"What do you mean, I got this one?" What's this guy talking about?

He stood at the bottom of the steps and he stayed there. He said, "Is the door open in the back?" It didn't appear to be open. It was a screen door with one of those hook latches on it. "Break it," he says. "Just break the lock off." So I broke the screen door latch. He says, "Open the door." The wooden door was not locked, so I walked into the kitchen area.

"Wow," I go. "Something doesn't smell right here."

"You got it," he says again and he stays off the back porch at the bottom of the steps. "You'll find out," he says.

There was nothing on the first floor. I walked up the steps and the odor is getting stronger and stronger. I get to the second floor. There's a bathroom directly at the end of the hallway and there's two other doors, off the right and left. I went into the bathroom—there's nothing there. I turned back. Went into the left door and there's nothing there either. So I opened the last door and—Oh, my God!—the odor was unbelievable. It was the odor of rotting flesh, decaying human bodies.

It was a murder/suicide. This was a couple in their late fifties. The man had murdered his wife and then killed himself. But they had been dead for over a month. They were maggot-ridden. Maggots had eaten out the eyes. I just stood there and I shook. I forgot about the odor for a second and I shook. Then the odor hit me and I shook again, went out into the hallway and was gagging. This was early June and it had been warm. I looked again.

I couldn't wait to beat my ass down there to tell the other guy. He's standing down at the bottom of the steps with a cigar in his mouth. I said, "How the fuck did you know?"

"If there's one thing you never forget," he says, "it's the smell of rotten flesh."

So we called the first-aid squad. They came, went upstairs and came immediately back downstairs. "We're not going to touch it."

We called the coroner's office. They came with their wagon and pulled the stretchers out of the back. One of them walked up to me and gave me two plastic bags. Bodybags. It was my responsibility to pile the bodies into them, close them with a twisty like a garbage bag, then pick them up, carry them downstairs and place them into the coroner's vehicle. They would not help me.

How the fuck am I going to go up there and handle this situation? I know what's happened, so there's nothing to be frightened about, but it's sickening. You say to yourself, "I don't care how much they're paying me, it ain't worth this." But then if you analyze it objectively, it's either going to be you or somebody else who has to do this thing. So I go up and I do it and I bring them down and put them in the van.

CHAPTER 2

Police Work

DR. RUTH Westheimer, a popular AM-radio sex therapist, was saving a marriage, instructing her first call-in couple of the evening in the methods of combating vaginal odor and on the fine points of cunnilingus. As we pulled out of the department parking lot, the patrol officer I was riding with told me, "Nobody comes up on the air much the first hour of the night shift. Everybody's listening to Dr. Ruth." But that night was not an ordinary night. It was Mother's Day.

"Mother's Day is always the same. A bunch of people who basically hate each other's guts get all dressed up, sit down to a big meal and aggravate the hell out of each other pretending they're one big, happy family. Then they start drinking to take the edge off. Nine o'clock rolls around, they're all liquored up and the gloves come off. 'I don't like you. I never liked you. The only reason I'm in this house is because of your daughter. But if you think I'm going to sit here and take that, you're dumber than I thought you were.' If they make enough noise long enough, somebody calls us."

We drove almost immediately to the first family dispute of the evening. We were the back-up car on the call. No one was fighting. An inebriated Mexican woman, a very muscular matriarch, stood on the sidewalk in front of her home and demanded with operatic profanity that the ten other people living with her in that tiny tract house get out and stay out. Her sisters and female cousins, their children and their children's children stood around her wringing their hands. The overgrown lawn was full of mothers of all ages.

One of those mothers—it was never clear which one—had called the police. But they did not want their matriarch arrested. They only wanted a small miracle: They wanted everything to be okay again. They wanted someone—anyone—to say the words to this drunken, waspish, foul-mouthed woman that would make her gentle, good and calm. Or at least make her shut up and go indoors.

She cursed us all, especially the police. After being cajoled, shamed and threatened for about twenty minutes, she suddenly took it upon herself to perform the miracle. She released her grip on the chain-link fence, marched up the walk and disappeared inside the house. All three patrol cars left the scene. In retrospect it was clear that she simply made the shrewd decision to go back inside where the liquor was. The stamina of that woman was remarkable. We were to return to her house and her screaming three more times before the night was over.

The police department is a service organization, open for business twenty-four hours a day, seven days a week. Dial their number and somebody has to answer, no matter what it is you want. As one officer put it, "People'll call us for everything. If their toilet runs over, they call the police before they call the plumber." A police officer deals with the desperate, the disturbed and all those people out there who are just plain lonely in the middle of the night. His duties put him on intimate terms with the bizarre things people are doing to each other and to themselves behind all the closed doors and drawn shades in the community. While the rest of us look the other way, he carts away the societal offal we don't want to deal with—suicides, drunks, drug addicts and derelicts. We call it keeping the peace, but the policeman often thinks of himself as humanity's garbageman. Every smart cop carries a pair of rubber surgical gloves in his car for handling dirt, disease and death. He uses his gloves much more often than he uses his gun.

A policeman on patrol does not solve crimes. For the most part he spends his time with victims, not criminals. Something bad happens and someone calls the police. By the time the police arrive, the incident is usually over and the officer at the scene can only try to pick up the pieces. It's not his job to put the jigsaw puzzle back together again. He is off to his next call, which could range from a misunderstanding to a major catastrophe.

If a policeman actually catches a criminal it is usually when the cop is protecting property. He is a town's night watchman, answering burglar alarms, checking windows, rattling doors. An alert patrolman knows where the potential high crime areas are on his beat—the isolated all-night gas station, the poorly lighted parking lot, the rowdy bar. He also knows most of the petty criminals, thieves, dope peddlers and prostitutes. Habitually, he will check these places and people between radio calls on the off chance that he may find someone in the act of breaking the law.

This doesn't mean that patrolmen don't crack big cases. The fact that they are on the street in the places crimes are committed and with the people who commit them means that they are the best sources of information on criminal activity. But they are rarely in a position to know where their information fits into the bigger picture. The lead that resulted in the arrest of David Berkowitz as the Son of Sam killer came from a cop on the beat where one of the murders was committed who remembered ticketing a car the night of the killing.

A policeman on patrol mainly talks to people, and he writes. He writes tickets, fills out arrest forms, writes detailed descriptions of traffic accidents. He must make a note of everything he does on his activity chart or in his memo book. He writes reports on everything imaginable, from lost dogs to lost children to lost lives. His superiors judge his performance and productivity largely by the amount of paper that he churns out. The cop sees all this writing as bureaucratic rigmarole that prevents him from doing his "real" job, which he describes as "getting the bad guys off the street."

After a while on the job a policeman will do just about anything to keep from putting pen to paper. So when he is called on a complaint or a disturbance where no clear evidence of a crime exists (he is sent to many more family fights than armed robberies), he talks to people, reasoning with them, browbeating them, cajoling them or berating them—whatever it takes to put things in order, if only temporarily. If he has a choice he'd rather use his mouth than his pen and he'd rather use his pen than his fists.

Police work may be dull, monotonous and dirty, but that doesn't mean it isn't dangerous. Whether he's smart or stupid, kindly or mean, a cop has to sometimes use his body to enforce the law. A fight between family members always has the potential to be a life-threatening situation for an officer.

"The woman who opened the door for me was just a medium-sized black female. The thing unique about her was that I could not see either one of her eyes. Her nose no longer existed. And she had a cavernous opening where there would have been a mouth and teeth. Her cheekbones were broken. In my entire career, I had never seen anybody who was so thoroughly battered. I asked her what the problem was and she said, 'My husband beat me up.'

" 'Well, what do you want me to do with your husband?' I said.

" 'I want him in jail.'

" 'If that is what you want, then that's what you'll get. As bad as you're beaten up, he needs to be in jail,' I told her. So I arrested him and I started to take him out and down the stairs. I'm holding him by his left arm, escorting him down in handcuffs. As we stepped through the front door of the building, she tried to bury a twelve-inch butcher knife right between my shoulder blades. Kachunk! She hit me right in the old bulletproof vest.

"It's human nature. When I walked in there she was upset because he beat her up so bad. When she saw her true love going out the door with the big, bad police hauling him off, then no longer is he the villain. The police is the villain. It just tears your mind up. In spite of all that damage he did to her, she still loved him so much that she wanted me dead as opposed to taking him away.

"The end result was they both got to go to jail. He went for a misdemeanor for beating her up so bad. She went for a felony for trying to kill me."

So it goes, each shift ticked off by one stomach-curdling cup of coffee after another, enlivened only by the knowledge that something hairy just might happen. In those dead hours on the underbelly of the night when the orange glare of streetlights slowly gives way to the dawn, when the worst bar brawler is home in bed or sleeping it off in a cell and the ugliest hooker has made her quota, the hardest part of the job is staying awake until quitting time. By then a cop is running on residual adrenaline alone, struggling to remember that the next wife beater might have a deer rifle, that the next empty warehouse might not be empty after all, that the next underaged driver he stops for speeding might just be crazy enough to poke a pistol in a policeman's face and pull the trigger.

"Any policeman who says that he's not afraid is a fool. I've only met one or two policemen who have ever said out and out, 'I ain't afraid of nothing.' They were very foolish individuals. There is fear involved and it can't help but work on your mind. Police work is basically 99 percent pure bullshit, because there is just not that much going on. But it is punctuated by one percent of just sheer terror. And it happens just that quick. That's the reason a lot of policemen keel over from heart attacks, because of all that adrenaline pumping all of a sudden all of the time. Ulcers, too. You ride around for five or six shifts in utter boredom, worried to death about when that next time is going to happen."

When by chance or design something does happen and an officer has a clear opportunity to "get the bad guy," the maddening seesaw between boredom and terror engenders in him a burning enthusiasm. This is what he's been waiting for—good guy versus bad guy, hero against creep, right against wrong, a little action to offset all those hours spent wearing out his kidneys in the front seat of a patrol car. The pent-up energy bursts out. This is why he took the job. This is police work.

When a cop apprehends someone especially after a chase, the satisfaction of a job well done lasts until he gets his prisoner back to the station. Then the man of action faces his greatest challenge—keeping his patience, his temper and his sanity during the hours and days of wrangling and waiting that precede the application of justice, such as it is.

The prosecutor will berate him. The defending attorney will insult and embarrass him. His colleagues will treat him to a round of Monday morning quarterbacking. His superiors will grill him on his motivation and methods. There will be no recognition in most cases unless a citizen actually pipes up with a "thank you" at the scene of the crime. And that is rare indeed.

At 2 A.M. when we made our final visit to the home of the elderly Mexican woman, an exasperated police officer sent the drunken firebrand to her room with a sizzling scolding as though she were a little child. As soon as she lay down, she passed out. As we left, the entire shift silently cursed the officer who had been the first on the scene for the original complaint because he did not arrest her while she was on the street and fair game for a charge of public drunkenness and disorderly conduct.

I'VE LIVED in this area most of my life. Quite a few people here have, I guess. But people don't realize the things that are going on around them that a police officer sees. A district attorney was explaining to me once about jury trials and he said, "There are times when you're going to go to court to testify and the guy is stone cold guilty—no doubt about it—and the jury will return with an acquittal. It's not because people don't believe you. It's because they can't believe you. They can't believe that someone would go and do the stupid things that they do to each other."

We've got a guy in jail right now, sewed up his wife's vagina for kicks. He sewed her breasts together.

I mean, that's sick. But it's not really shocking. It doesn't just totally blow me away and make me stand with my mouth open. I've seen crap like that before. But you go up and pick sixteen people from those houses lighted up on the hills out there and they're not going to believe that somebody could actually do that. That they do that to their kids. The mother who's tired of the baby shitting his diapers, so she sews his asshole up. It's not frequent, but it happens. People amaze me sometimes, but they don't surprise me anymore.

*

We're not a real big department. There's only five of us. One's the chief and one's the sergeant, so there's really only three of us.

We only cover three square miles. Do you know how boring three square miles can get on a ten-hour shift? It's sick.

Something you can do—one of the more conservative things—is to find a place and read a book. Perhaps more conservative still is to fall asleep. Or you can go find parked cars and sneak up on them. Shine the light in and everybody comes unglued.

You can run up the dune roads and then wait till people walk by. Turn your PA on and make strange noises. If you key your two radios together at the same time, it'll make a squealing high frequency squawk. You do that for just a second. They hear it and get really hinky. Then you wait a minute and growl. When you growl, that's when they really haul ass.

One night we couldn't find anything else to do, so three of us were racing up and down the beach at night. We had those low-powered BB gun rifles and we'd shoot at one another. Usually nothing happened. But this one time, I guess that little BB hit just right and one of our back windows just shattered.

The station bought our story—they bought the story, but they didn't believe the story—that I'd been driving down the street, it was real hot and the back window just shattered. It's actually happened that way before. But usually it only happens in the daytime when the sun is beating down real hard, not late at night.

Of course, we get to back up the county if they got a fight in progress, which in the summer happens with some regularity. Now at The Full Moon, it's a fight a night. Evening shift you could park your car there and wait for the call. We got so many calls there, we didn't even talk to them anymore. Usually fights would be between twelve and one in the morning—the good ones were. They'd really get worked up. Your basic cowboys were in there and they love to fight. If there was only one of them, he'd beat on himself. They're going to beat on something.

What we'd do is, we'd meet outside and get together, then walk in through the crowd milling around. The place was kind of small and when they fought it always seemed to be in this one area and there was a clear wall there. Each one of us would pick out the ones we figured we could get a good grip on, because there was usually three or four of them going at it. It was like routine. You grab one however you could grab him and throw him against the wall as hard as you can. They'd hit the wall, bounce off and fall down.

That usually caught the attention of the others. Then they'd stop. By the time the two we'd thrown up against the wall hit the floor good, we'd have their hands behind them and have the cuffs on. We'd take them out to the car without saying anything.

We'd put those in the car and then walk right back in. If they had gone back to fighting, we'd get two more. The more the merrier. We'd take as many as wanted to go. By the time we came back out the second time, the first ones we put in the car would be asking questions like, "What's going on?"

"You're going to jail."

"Why? What'd I do?" would be the first thing out of their mouth.

"What do you mean, what did you do?" I'd just shake my head.

"I wasn't fighting." They'll say that and expect you to believe it.

*

So the mayor decided it was time once again to clean up Times Square, which means, "Arrest hookers." Which isn't such a bad idea. Street hookers have a tendency to bring crime. The danger is they'll fuck you or they'll fuck you. There are some very hard-core cases who go out with these girls and the girls are working for horrendous pimps. What they do to try and get out from under all of this is to earn the legitimate dollar from you, which they have to turn over to their pimps; then on the side they try to scam so the pimp doesn't know and they can keep the bucks for themselves. If they can fuck you out of your money without really fucking you, they prefer to do that, because they don't really dig what they're doing to begin with. They'll take you off, rip you off.

We turn out on Forty-second Street, at least thirty cops just between Seventh and Eighth Avenue. We work in partners, so you're talking about two cops every eight to ten feet on both sides of the street. With all that, crime still took place. The crowd was so big, my back would be turned and a woman's purse would be stolen and I didn't even know it until she started screaming and the guy is booking.

You can't of course arrest anyone for prostitution. There has to be a lot of things that take place to constitute a prostitution charge. What you're getting them for is loitering for the purpose of prostitution. That is a weak charge. You're supposed to say, "For X period of time, she was in the same area just walking up and down and chewing bubble gum, straightening her panty hose. On several occasions I saw her confront unknown males. I then had the opportunity to be within hearing distance and heard her, for a sum of money, offer this man, you know, some gash." That's the true way you get loitering for prostitution.

We were told, "You guys are cops. You look at a woman, you should be able to tell if she's a hooker." What a godforsaken, God damn deal. Who the fuck am I to be able to look at a woman and say she's selling her ass, constantly on the verge of getting my ass sued for false arrest.

Then the powers that be go one step further and say, "Not only that, but don't think you guys are going to rack up a lot of overtime on this deal by bringing in one girl at the last minute. Minimum is three hookers per man." I couldn't just get one. I had to get three. Well, what do you do when you grab one and you don't have the other two?

To add to the confusion, the mayor wants to increase the productivity of the cops. So along with our nightstick, our blackjack, our bullets and in some cases two guns, our radio—a big, antiquated radio that you have to have two hands to carry at that time—he bestows on each of us a fucking Polaroid camera, and he says, "We're going to build up a gallery of hookers; therefore you guys take pictures of hookers while you're out there."

The average cop can't chew gum and walk at the same time around certain things. One of those things is taking pictures with a fucking Polaroid camera. You're supposed to press a button somewheres and the thing pops out. When it didn't, he started banging it and prying it and then he had a broken fucking Polaroid camera. The wise cops who figured out right away how to make the thing pop right out, like me, got bored and thought the whole idea was bullshit anyway, so I started taking pictures of my buddy. Like here's one of him standing in front of Nathan's, here's one on Forty-second Street for the wife to see how we are at work. Consequently, tourists from Minnesota would see us and say, "Isn't that nice. Could I take a picture with you?" So I got two little blue-haired old ladies on each side of me and my partner takes a picture of that. We take two—one for them and one for me. Now you're spending thousands of dollars on film and you don't have the first picture of a hooker yet.

The truth of the matter is that to make this three-hooker thing work you had to build up a rapport with the girls, which is what I did. They knew the name of the game and so did you. They're working girls. It's an old profession. It's going to be here long after I die. Don't fight the fucking thing. Control it, contain it. So you played the game with them.

I would go out and stop Margie. I knew Margie was generally hanging around with about six other girls. They were buddies and they hooked together. I says, "Margie, we're working the six to two tonight. I need the bust. You got to play. Midnight, you be on the corner with two other girls. I got to have three to make the bust. If you fuck me and don't show, tomorrow night at five minutes after six, you're going in with three or four of your girlfriends. Plus me and my buddies are going to lock up the entire street, so nobody will work at all, all night long. When you end up in court, we'll drag it out so you're fucked for the next day, too."

So what did Margie say? She says, "That isn't a bad deal. The guy's giving us six hours to work. We make our bucks. I'm tired by then anyway. I get to go lay down in a cell and shoot the shit with my girlfriends. The charge is bullshit, so there's no jail time other than the overnighter. What's the big beef?"

We also have to make out thousands of arrest cards. To make an arrest involves so much paperwork, it's unbelievable. When you're operating with the girls, they knew the name of the game with the cards, so you go to each one of them and say, "Okay, what's your name tonight?"

"I think I'll be Janie tonight."

"Janie, here's your arrest card. What are you going to be tonight?"

"I'm going to be Hildegaard."

"Okay, Hildegaard, but don't fuck up with the writing. If you don't know how to spell it, ask Janie. Don't make me look stupid filling out these cards." They filled out the date of birth and address for the new name and we worked hand in hand. But you say, "Now Margie, let me take your picture," and you run into some overt hostility. I mean, come on, they're human beings. Nobody likes their picture taken in a public place by someone they don't really know. Celebrities are constantly throwing beer bottles at photographers. It's a personal affront for someone to infringe on you with a camera.

Then you come to the other end of the spectrum down to the Lower East Side in the Borscht Belt. All these really holy roller Hassids stop on Allen Street prior to going over the Williamsburg Bridge to get the nightly blowjob. It's the funniest sight you ever want to see. They do it in their cars. The streetlight casts a shadow and all you see is this set of side curls coming down from this funny felt hat and they've got this stupid grin on their faces. They're bouncing in the seat of the car because she's down there on the tube. It's like a twenty-buck toll. They get their pipes cleaned and they go across the bridge.

Now what are you going to do with that? Are you going to bust them? Are you crazy? It is one of the areas that is very heavily patrolled by the police, not because of prostitution, but to protect the johns. Make sure the Hassidim gets his blowjob and gets across the bridge. What am I, some kind of private guard?

*

An officer is sitting along the highway watching speeders go by. It's called eyeballing. I've seen motorcycle cops who could stand on the side of the road and tell you how fast a guy is going within a mile an hour. He won't be off 5 miles an hour. Absolutely amazing. "That's 55. That's 60." The guy may have a radar unit. He may have it off. He may even be out of his car, talking to some woman going into a shopping center. A car goes past him.

"That guy's speeding." He's a speeder, what difference does it make how fast he's going? He stops him and gives him a ticket.

They get to court. If the guy pleads not guilty, the cop has to testify. How long did you follow him? Was he caught on radar or not on radar? How fast was he driving?

"I followed him for a mile and a half. Over that distance, I clocked him at speeds ranging from 62 to 68 miles an hour."

If you read ten different testimonies from this guy, they're all exactly the same. It's a protective sort of thing. If he's forgotten any particular incident, he still knows what to say, because he always says the same thing.

In-service training is important, no matter where you are. A guy that's been around awhile will tell you how to testify. Most times it's a set rap that has been inherited from someone else. There's a history to it, almost a tradition.

*

This woman came flying through the neighborhood at a high rate of speed, going through stop signs. So I started chasing her in the police car with the blue lights, the siren and all that. The lady wouldn't stop. She was waving for me to come on around like I was trying to pass her. I finally got her stopped.

She jumped out of her car, ran back and grabbed me by the uniform. "You need to let me go. I've got this hurt animal in my car and I'm trying to rush it to the hospital," she says. Sure enough, I looked in the back-seat and she had a dog in there that had been hit by a car.

"Okay, fine. I'll let you take the dog to the hospital," and I told her where one was right around the corner. "I'll follow you around there, but when I get there I'm going to give you a ticket."

The doctor at the animal hospital was a personal friend of mine. I played racquetball with him. We got in there and he's looking at the dog and treating it. He came out and told me, "Hey, this woman does this about every other week. She's always got some stray animal or other and she's always in hysterics wanting me to take care of it."

"Well, when I get her out of here, I'm going to write her a ticket," I told him. I wrote her one for running a stop sign and one for speeding and she didn't have an inspection sticker on her car. So that was two moving violations and one equipment infraction. She was kind of upset about that. I went my way and she went hers.

She got in touch with the news media. Since it was a holiday, there was no news. Nothing was going on, so a reporter shows up at the police department and wants to talk to the chief about this "incident." The chief makes me talk to him. The reporter said the woman called and complained and he wanted my version of it. I explained to him that taking care of animals was fine, but the woman was putting kids and everybody else in danger trying to get this animal to the hospital. The animal wasn't even her own pet, but some stray that had been hit out on the road. I didn't know if she came to its aid or maybe she hit it, who knows? I just told the guy my feelings.

The next day there was a big article on the front page: GOOD SAMARITAN IS GIVEN THREE TICKETS FOR TRYING TO SAVE AN ANIMAL. This went on for days in the papers. People were calling the vet and driving him nuts trying to see how the dog was doing. The doctor was wondering who was going to pay for this since the dog was fairly messed up. He said, "Under any other circumstances, I'd just put the dog to sleep. But I can't do it because every concerned citizen in the city is watching me." He's performing all this intensive surgery in an attempt to save this dog's life.

The story was picked up by the wire services. I started getting hate mail from all over the country. What killed me was that anybody else probably would have arrested her, as obnoxious as she had been, grabbing me and shaking me. I didn't think I'd been unreasonable. I got a big letter from a national organization signed by famous people who love animals. They didn't like me either. In fact, everybody hated me. Everyday I'd go out and get the paper and flinch before I could look at the front page. This went on for months. People are writing up to tell me I should be run over with a car. People are taking sides. There were editorials in the newspaper, pro and con.

A couple of weeks after this happened I went to a party at a friend's house. There were about forty people there. I hadn't seen these friends in quite a while and most of the people there I didn't know anyway. The hostess pins this tag on me when I arrive that says, "I'm Bob." I just thought she'd had name tags made up for everybody so they wouldn't have to pay too much attention to introductions. I go in and start meeting people and everybody has a pin on, too, but I notice all of their pins say the same thing, which is: "Bob Kramer Hates Dogs."

The woman ended up going to trial. She wanted her day in court. So I show up for my appearance. All the other policemen are patting me on the back telling me to go get her. Reporters roll up from the TV stations with the minicams to film this for the news. I'm sweating bullets. Before the woman goes in to court some people from the Humane Society have a big ceremony out in the lobby of the courthouse and give her a plaque telling what a good job she had done in the face of this ogre of a policeman.

The woman goes into the courtroom and she gives her side of the story to the judge. He's not sure he knows what's going on and is very conscious of the cameras and everything. He hadn't realized it was a national cause he was being dragged into. The judge took my side and found her guilty on two of the charges and dropped one. He fined her fifty dollars. He then gave a lengthy explanation on camera. He didn't want to get his ass in the same sling as mine. He'd already seen what they did to me.

*

We stopped a van for not having any taillights or brake lights or something like that—very minor. When we walked up to ask him for his driver's license, he rolled his window up, locked the door and wouldn't talk to us. So I walked around the front of his van to the right door to try to get it open to get the information from him. He reached over just before I got to that door and he locked it, too.

I'm walking back around the van and he stomped the accelerator and tried to run over me with the van. I felt I had been assaulted with a motor vehicle with intent to do great bodily harm or kill me, which he had banged up my leg pretty good.

"Shall we shoot him?" I said.

"Yeah," Jack said, "shoot him." I shot both the rear tires off the van, which I thought was a handy bit of marksmanship, personally. Instead of stopping, he continued driving on the rims. We followed him with our blue lights and our siren yelping—whoo-whoo-whoo-whoop—for about a mile and a half until he got back to the local Muslim stronghold of a house they called their sanctuary.

We got there and we went up to the van before he could get out. As we're standing there telling him we need his driver's license, a couple of Muslims came out and put flying tackles on me and Jack both. Then the guy jumped out of the van and ran into the house. They jumped up and ran in the house behind him, slammed the door and locked it.

We called the world. Said, "Send us some help around here. We need a sergeant, a lieutenant and God." They send us half the world anyway and surrounded the house. The sergeant tried to negotiate with them to let us have the guy who tried to run over me with the car. They answered that this was a Muslim sanctuary and we could not come in and they weren't going to send him out.

"But you don't understand," the sergeant said. "You've got to send him out or we've got to come in and get him."

"We don't care what you've got to do," they said. "We don't believe in your laws. We believe in the laws of Mohammed and that's it. We don't respect any laws of the United States, this state or this city."

We continued some discussion for about an hour until it became apparent that they were not going to send him out and we were not just going to walk in. So we walked up to the door and started banging on the door in an attempt to knock it loose.

This gorilla answered the door, reached out and grabbed one of the fellows there with us by the front of his shirt, picked him up and threw him from one end of the carport to the other. He then said, "Get out of here, little boy."

This was a mistake, because as he threw Cliff, we grabbed an arm each and passed him down a row of about twenty of us to the car, handcuffed him and in he went.

After some discussion with them, and getting the guy we were after plus half the rest of them that were in there and putting them in the car, we ended up booking the gorilla for assault and we booked the guy who attempted to run over me with the van. We let everybody else go. The ultimate end of the whole thing was this: The reason the guy wouldn't show us his driver's license, rolled up the windows and ran from us was that he didn't have a driver's license. We would have written him a ticket and he would have been on his way. But he was scared and instead attempted to run me over.

My relationship with the Muslims got to be kind of monotonous. I got a call to the Milky Way over on the Avenue. It's a real quiet bar. Just aren't hardly any problems there. But their complaint was my old buddies. The Muslims had set them up a PA system across the street on a grocery lot and were telling all the patrons of the Milky Way, as they came and went, that their time had come. That they were going to die. "You go in there and you won't come out. We're going to follow you home. And kill you."

They were intimidating the man's customers considerably. To the point where he usually had maybe six hundred people there on a Friday night, he now had only forty people in the bar. He was disturbed by this loss of business.

So I got there and he told me all this. I said, "Let me go talk to them." I walked across the street and started talking to the head guy who was talking on the PA system at the time. I said, "Will you turn the PA off, please. I'd like to talk to you."

He was fairly reasonable. He said, "Sure, I'll turn my PA off for a minute."

"Do you have a permit on the loudspeaker out here?" I said, "If you don't, you're going to have to quit. The second thing is, you don't want to incite a riot across the street. What few people are left over there are getting very militantly upset with you haranguing them so severely."

"We don't care," he said, "whether they get upset or not. We mean what we're saying. We're going to kill everybody who goes into that bar."

"You can't talk that way," I said. "You got to be reasonable about stuff."

He turned to his buddy and said, "Take this microphone and go ahead. I'm going to talk to this honky for a little while." The other guy took over the harangue. By this time they had a pretty good congregation there, maybe four hundred people on the block who were members of the church or followers of some sort. I got curly hair, but I started noticing that I was the only light individual in the group and that I was surrounded by all four hundred of these people. There was no place for me to go.

Wanda, my female riding partner, was sitting across the street in our patrol car watching all these proceedings. One of her most profound moments was when she discovered, "They're probably fixing to annihilate my riding partner. He's just going to be a little bloody spot in the middle of the parking lot over there if he doesn't shut his mouth and quit telling them they can't do what they are doing." So she picked up the radio and said, "HQ, why don't you get some more units over to this call."

One of my friends and his riding partner arrived because they were close by. Marv had a little more experience than Wanda. He looked over and said, "Hey, you have misread this. We need a bunch of units and we need them now." He picked up his radio and said, "HQ, this is a 34. Officer in need of help—now."

While they are observing all this, I'm in the middle of all these people. I've figured out that I really need to get out of this situation. I had a really big flashlight, a 26-inch, twelve-cell light that I was carrying with me.

I just barred it across in front of me and started walking. A guy grabbed my flashlight and held on to it. Another one grabbed for my gun. I let the one with the flashlight have the flashlight, but that was in order to not let the one with the gun have the gun. I made an instant decision that if indeed they were fixing to kill me, some of them were probably going to die with me. I didn't know how many of them I would get before they split my skull, but I was prepared to take at least one or two of them with me.

Then off in the distance I heard the sirens getting closer and closer. The first car around the corner just drove into a crowd of four hundred people at about 50 miles an hour, locked up all his brakes and slid up right into the middle. It was like Moses and the Red Sea. They just parted. He stopped next to me and said, "Who do you want?"

"That one, that one and that one," I said. "And that one, too."

*

We had a cop shot on the highway. We came in as backup. We ran this guy into a cornfield. I'm running through there trying to find the guy. The corn is higher than my head and he's got a shotgun. It brought back memories of Nam for me. I'm expecting this guy at any time to pop out of the corn and just blow me away, a fucking ambush. I got my gun out. I'm sweating and it's a tense moment. But we got the guy flushed out.

Got back in the car and get a call to a robbery in progress. We respond with lights and siren at 90 miles an hour. The job turns out to be bullshit.

So I'm coming down the main avenue there and there's a white guy and this woman in a fancy Cadillac. It's two lanes with no room to park on the side. He's stopped, blocking traffic basically in both directions. He didn't care.

I'm still soaking with the sweat from the chase in the cornfield. I'm still a little hyped up. I pull alongside this guy and I say, "Can you do me a favor, please? Move the car. You got the whole lane blocked."

They cut into me, the both of them. She called me every name in the book and then she says, "Haven't you got anything better to do? Is this all you got to do to keep yourself busy?"

I'm trying to control myself, but I looked at that guy and I said, "You better move this car right now or you're going to be the sorriest cocksucker around, I'll tell you that right now."

But people don't know that you just been on two heavy runs—being shot at and running through a field, going to what you think is an armed holdup. I still got to tell these people to move.

They're white middle class and they got a big Cadillac and they don't give a fuck about nobody else. They can park wherever the fuck they want to. Because I told them to move, I'm a cocksucker and I don't have anything else to do. Why don't I go arrest those black people? That's what they say. They always say that. "Why don't you go to the bad area, the ghetto? You're scared of them so you're down here bothering white people. You're scared of them people, so you're here bothering us."

*

Stolen vehicle. The suspects were a good ways away from us, but my partner said, "They don't know the area and they're going to try to get off the main road. Let's go out after them just for the heck of it."

We hadn't started down the road but about a half-mile when here comes the vehicle the other way. We spun around and got behind them in a high-speed chase down a big old twisty, winding country road. No street-lights, no nothing.

We finally ran them to ground. They finally pulled over and stopped. We bailed out. It was a fourteen-year-old and a thirteen-year-old kid. We'd been told they were armed with a .22 pistol that they'd shot at the guy they stole the car from.

We jerked them out of the car and frisked them down. About this time my partner found the .22 on one of the guys. I flipped open the back door and was getting ready to throw them in and this kid—a thirteen-year-old—turned around, looked me in the eye and said, "What about my rights?"

This is three o'clock in the morning, out on a deserted road. These kids held up a man, stole his car at gunpoint, tried to outrun the police and this kid's worried about his rights.

We throwed them in the back. Anyway you look at it, there was a lot of adrenaline flowing. John and I sat there and looked at each other. Then we just busted out laughing. "What about my rights?"

*

Some guy had the bright idea to sell the city automatic gas-dispensing machines. That'll eliminate the guy out there to pump gas. It'll be better for bookkeeping because it'll be a machine.

It was bullshit. Every cop received two days' training at headquarters on how to operate the gas-dispensing machine. A very necessary machine. You're going to have to learn. You're given a stupid little test afterwards and then if you pass they issue you a plastic dispensing card. And every car has a card, so now you've got two cards. This monster has what you desperately need, gasoline. The combination of instructions must be performed exactly right or it ain't going to spit shit out. And your car won't move.

You take one card and you put it in first. Then there is a series of buttons to punch and then a little light blinks on. If you've done something wrong, it's the green light. "AAAAAAHHH, the Green Light! I fucked up and I got to do it again. I don't know where I made the mistake! Why didn't it give me my gas?" At some point the second card goes in and you punch in the odometer reading and at that point the machine's brain registers that, yes, you are due for gas.

The machine is a mess. One of them has written on it in big black letters, "This machine puts out like my wife." They are bent and dented where they have been kicked and slugged. There are jack marks on them where they have been literally assaulted with blackjacks. "You don't want to give me my gas? I'll kill you, you son of a bitch. Give me my nightstick."

They beat the piss out of the machine and then they feel guilty about it. "Look what I've done. It's made me a lunatic. I've just killed a gas pump."

The wife says, "What did you do tonight, Harry?"

"I killed a gas pump. I jacked it and then I stomped it. I couldn't believe I did it."

"Catch any criminals?"

"Nah, I was too busy with the machine. It wouldn't give me gas. Son of a bitch, I did everything right, too."

*

The owner of a car lot said, "One of my Cadillacs is parked in front of this guy's house. It was stolen a couple of weeks ago."

I told my partner when we got there, "I'll get up on this porch next door and watch. When he gets in the car, you pull up and block him in with our car. I'll run up and pull my gun on him from the driver's side." That seemed like a pretty complete plan to me.

About an hour later, this guy comes out and jumps in the car. I radioed my partner and told him the guy was in the car. He pulls up alongside this guy. I run over there, pop open the door and this guy floors the car in reverse. There's cars behind him. He pushes them out of the way, runs me down with the damn car, scoots out on the street and hits about four other cars going backwards.

I'm laying in the street. I said, "Son of a bitch," pulled my gun out and opened fire on him. I put a couple of holes in the car, but I didn't hit him. He got out and away, although they caught him a couple days later.

It would have been better for the car dealer if he'd just got into the car when he saw it, driven it back to his lot and never told us about it. It was a brand new Cadillac. By the time the thief and us got through with it, it was worth about $600. He wasn't too much in love with us after that.

*

I was riding with a young officer in a wagon and we pulled up behind a motorcyclist. He was making a dope deal; we thought it was either heroin or coke. So I hit the beacon. The guy takes off and I started chasing him. My partner is saying, "A wagon has never caught a motorcycle. You can't chase a motorcycle with a wagon."

"Hang on," I said, "cause here we go."

We chased the son of a bitch. He goes down behind this hospital; he must have been doing sixty or seventy going down this alley. As I came around there, two doctors were coming out the back door. The only thing I saw in the rearview mirror was them diving for the ground as I go flying.

The alley goes out onto a street, but it drops off sharply and then there's another incline on the other side. That motorcycle sailed right across the son of a bitch. I told my partner, "Hang on."

We hit and we sailed off the first incline. When we hit the street level, we lost the right rear tire. The whole thing came off and went shooting in front of the wagon.

But the wagon is still moving, because I was still throwing the coals to it. We were just riding lopsided, leaned over to the right.

The motorcycle went between two telephone poles. I went between the two telephone poles. The front end of the wagon made it fine, but the back end of the wagon, leaning like that, was too big for it. So a chunk of the body just ripped right off.

He lost control of the cycle at the next street and laid it down. I went over the top of his motorcycle with the wagon and he takes off running. My partner couldn't move at this point. He was frozen to the seat. I jumped out and I heard him say, "You're never going to catch that brother." I chased that son of a bitch for about five blocks and caught up to him. He was too tired to do anything. I just handcuffed him and walked him right up the middle of the street. I always loved to do that. "Guess who got who?"

My sergeant showed up and he said, "What happened to the wagon? I'm going on vacation tomorrow. What did you do?"

"There was not an accident, sarge," I said. "We just lost a wheel and a little of the wagon on those two telephone poles." They had to junk the wagon.

"For what?"

"I got the drugs and the motorcycle."

"You did all that for a motorcycle and a little bit of heroin?"

"Sergeant, I'm surprised at you. He broke the law and that's what we're out here for, to catch criminals."

"Jesus, I'm glad I'm going on vacation."

*

We used to argue about whether or not the driver of the patrol car would stay with the car when we came up on a stolen vehicle. If the guys bailed out, the driver was supposed to continue to cruise around the area.

The passenger would bail out and chase the suspect. I never liked that part.

We were driving around one time and we spotted a stolen car and we gave chase. The guys pulled up in an alley and bailed out. My partner said, "You stay with the car." But I didn't. I took off and he took off. I grabbed the driver of the car and I handcuffed him. My partner was a little overweight, so he was still running after his man.

I told my prisoner, "Okay, asshole, now you're going to run as fast as I am going to run, because we are going to catch up with my partner and get the other dude. If you don't," I said, "I'm going to club you."

We're running down the middle of the street. This guy is running along beside me keeping right up with me with his hands cuffed behind him. A sergeant drove by and did he ever give us a look, a prisoner and a cop running along, side by side, after another suspect.

We caught the other guy. The sergeant says to me, "I've been on this police department for eighteen years and that's the first time I ever saw a thief run along like that. You do some strange shit."

*

I got assigned to the embassy precinct. It covers the Upper Eastside from Fifty-sixth Street to Eighty-sixth Street. It is known for a lot of women and for fixers. Fixers are embassies and such that they assign a cop to stand in front of. You stand there for eight hours like a doorman. Or you stand in front of the Temple Emanu-El on Fifth Avenue so there would be no vandalism there. Very boring in the extreme.

Here I am all primed to go out and combat crime and I end up in a precinct more boring than you can believe. I once fell asleep propped up in a doorway. Sergeant honked the horn and woke me up.

It got to the point that when I got a fixer on Fifth

Avenue, I'd stand out at the curb and look up the avenue for cars that would run the light on the side streets to make the lights on Fifth Avenue. I could see what color the lights were from the side shades on them. This guy would turn onto Fifth against the red and I'd stand out in the middle of the street, put my hand up, "Stop in the name of the law. You ran a light. Give me your license and registration." I'd give out moving violations, standing on a fixer. The sergeant comes around, "What are you, wacko? How can you give out moving violations standing on a foot post?"

"What do you want me to do? I'm going crazy!"

Occasionally, I'd get a car that wouldn't stop. He'd flash past me. In his mind, he figured, "This guy's on foot, what can he do?" It wasn't that they didn't see me or didn't know to stop. They'd just speed past me. So I started throwing my nightstick.

I threw it at one guy. When it bounced off his roof, he stopped. I gave him a ticket. He went down to court and he told the judge, "Your honor, he shot at me."

"No, I didn't," I said. "I threw my nightstick at him and it bounced off his roof." The judge looked at me like I was some kind of weird-o, but said, "That's not the point here. The point was you ran the light."

A couple of cars went off down Fifth Avenue with my nightsticks sticking out their smashed rear window. They wouldn't stop. I lost more nightsticks in the first couple of months. I wasn't crazy. I was bored for something to do.

The Greek junta took over Greece and I had the unfortunate duty to be in front of that place the day it happened and got caught in a demonstration. I didn't get hurt, but it was my first brush with personal violence.

The people are outside the embassy yelling and milling about. One of the officials was going inside. As he passed, he hit or pushed one of the demonstrators. Then they wanted to go inside and get him, of course.

This one guy confronted me. I didn't know how much force to use, so I just held my nightstick in front of me across my body. He grabbed on and now I'm no longer in control. I'm wrestling with this guy. I'm back to where I was when I was a kid and I was getting into fights and losing. What do I do? How do I react? Do I go for this guy's eyes?

Before I could decide, other cops helped break it up. Before you know it, it's over and he's at arm's length again. It was traumatic in that, even though I'm a cop, people are still going to go for me and not listen to what I say.

*

We're all rearing at the bit. Six o'clock, we turned out of the station house, charging like a football team, "Aaargh!" Hit the bricks, you know.

It was a hot summer night. The streets were crawling, man. We're going to really get the big one. In the back of the young cop's mind is the big arrest that's going to transform him immediately to a suit of clothes and a gold shield. That's first and foremost—The Big Arrest. It could happen and it could happen anytime cause we're in a prime situation. We're looking for the heavies.

Ten of us have got out the station house door. Almost directly across the street in front of the station, there's a dispute going on between a little PR and a black guy. It's a parking dispute. The black guy has scammed into the Puerto Rican's parking spot. The Rican was waiting for that spot, but he parked behind the space. The Spade came up, Johnny-come-lately, but was very smart and said to himself, "Look at this fool. That motherfucker's going to pull out and I got the spot." And he sure did. He slid in there. The Rican said, "No way,

Jose. For a half-hour I been sitting here sweating my ass off with no *cerveza* Rheingold, no nothing. And this nigger comes sliding into my spot." That's using their terminology, but that's the way they feel. They're very prejudiced against these people. They don't like niggers and that's all there is to it. Forget the white/black thing, we're not even prejudiced by comparison with the Spanish guys.

This argument is ensuing and it is bullshit. It could develop into a small little fucking violation. We don't take violations—we take felonies. We're hooking. We're getting the fuck away from these fuckers.

We're about ten feet away from these two dudes who are arguing and we hear, *"Bam! Bam! Bam!"* Undeniable fucking gun shots. We didn't even have to turn around. We know that one of the two has shot the other one. "Oh, God. I don't fucking believe it."

We turn around and the Puerto Rican smoked the Spade. The gun is still smoking and there's the black guy deader than a fucking doornail. Put three right in the fucking locker on this guy from about a foot away. I look at the gun he's holding and it looked like a police revolver. I think, "He must, you know, be a cop." That was my first impression, because I thought, "He's so fucking calm. There's ten of us cops with guns, ten feet away and look at him. He's just looking at the body, holding his gun. Well, he's got to be a cop. I'm very fortunate."

I hesitated and didn't do what I really should have done, which is as follows: That fucker has a gun. He's just wasted this guy. My gun should be out. I say, "Drop the gun." If he says nope, then *"Bam!* You're dead." That's it. That's the smart thing. Totally justified.

What did I do? I hesitated. That was a mistake. But it turned out that I didn't get hurt. He wasn't a cop, but he wasn't a fucking cold-blooded murderer either.

He was an angry fucking man who wasn't too bright and just went the limit, man. Went the limit.

When me and you got mad as kids, you'd say to your friend, "I'd like to kill you." It's in us, the fact that we could conjure up kill. The guys who commit it, they've brought it out and let it surface. But there are a segment of those who're still not considered murderers. They just snap and that's that.

I walked up to him and said, "Give me the gun." The other cops with me now all have their guns out. It suddenly dawns on me, "I got nine guns on my fucking back because they want him. It's a gun collar and it's a murder. This could be instant promotion. These fuckers will kill me to get this son of a bitch. Oh, wow, Jesus." There was a moment of that thought.

I looked at the guy and I said, "Why did you do that?"

He looked back at me and said, "He took my parking space, man." Pure honesty. "He took my parking space, man." He had killed the fucking man. It might have happened the next day and he would have just argued with the guy about the parking space. It might have proceeded to a very violent oral altercation. But this day was just the day that he snapped. I don't believe that he was a killer, that he would kill over any parking space at any time. That was a momentary thing.

*

I really don't have much use for the FBI. I'll give you one prime example why. I was walking a beat downtown around the Greyhound Bus Station one night about one o'clock. Two FBI agents come up to me and showed me their ID. They says, "Now, we're expecting a fellow to come in on the bus from the state capital tonight. He's very dangerous. He usually wears a holstered pistol under each arm." They showed me his picture. He was a little fellow, I'd say about five foot six and skinny, too. "He's supposed to come in at two-thirty; but we got something else we have to do, so we'd like for you to look after this for us."

At two-thirty I'm out there on the alert. I had checked with the dispatcher and found out what slot the bus would go into and I'm standing right at the door as it opens. The people start coming off. There is no one on it by the description or even with his build. So I asked the driver, "Is this all you had?"

"No," he says, "we had so many, we had to put on an extra section. They should be here in about twenty minutes."

I waited and waited and finally the second section comes in. The first man off was him. When he got off, he was looking down the barrel of my .38. He put his hands up. I told them to close the door of the bus and not to let anybody else off until I searched him. I took these two pistols off of him. I put handcuffs on him. Everybody thought that was some show.

I took him inside and I asked the dispatcher to call the police to send the wagon. I didn't want my attention taken away from him. Even though I had handcuffs on him, I held him by the arm.

My wife is expecting me home by eight o'clock that Sunday morning, so she can take the kids to Sunday school by nine-thirty. Time is rushing along. I have to go to the police station with him. First of all, the captain has to know. The sergeant has to know. The lieutenant has to know. And you have to tell each one of them the story individually. By then it's seven o'clock in the morning, see? After I get it explained to all of them, the captain tells me, "Okay, go to the detective bureau and explain it to them. Then write up your reports. Make damn sure that there's not flaws in them. Concise and to the point and everything." I didn't get home until about ten-thirty that morning. My wife went down and borrowed the neighbor's car and took the children to the church, so I went home and went to bed.

Well, when I woke up that evening, she was boiling, she was hopping mad and told me that I had lied about the whole situation. Actually she said, "I got a good notion to run you off." She thought I was lying to hide something else. I had told her about how I had got this fellow and everything. She put the newspaper in front of me and said, "Look here. You're lying to me." There in black and white was a story about how the FBI had captured this notorious criminal down at the Greyhound Bus Station. It had the description I had given her about finding the two guns on him and everything.

I had to get the dispatcher at the bus station to tell her how he made the call for me. Now I'm not dumb. I could see how she thought I was lying to her. Anyway, that's why I don't have any damn use for the FBI.

*

I used to love to ride the midnight shift when you had most of your B&E's. It was a game trying to outsmart the criminal. We would ride the alleys, cruise with the lights out and catch them coming right out of the buildings sometimes. We didn't get paid that much money, but when you caught a burglar you went home with your chest sticking out and you really were a champion of justice.

We had a burglar out there breaking into cars. He had a regular MO. We had a fairly good description of him. He always wore this little knit watch cap. Detective division had a man specifically assigned to try to catch him.

Between calls in a slack moment after dark, we decided we were going to catch that guy. Enough is enough. We were going east on Third Street right at Calhoun. We ease up with our lights out. We look up the sidewalk and here's this guy sticking his head out from behind a tree. I can see the outline of that knit cap. We knew we had him.

I went screaming down there where he was and slammed on the brakes. I let my partner out and said, "I'm going to circle the block." I went screaming around the other side and jumped out of the car. We were driving an extra car at the time instead of a patrol car. It was for accident investigations—one of these Plymouths with the push-button transmission on the dash. It all happened so quick, I couldn't remember how to put the car in Park, so I just jumped out and left it. When the whole thing was over, an hour later, we come back to the car and there is some citizen holding the car from rolling down the street.

I chased the burglar behind the old folks' home there at Second and Calhoun. We're running down the alley and I'm hollering, "Halt, police," and all those things they teach you in the academy. They don't ever work anyway.

Back then you could fire warning shots at your discretion, so I fired a warning shot at him. All of a sudden— Kapow!—here comes one back. From reports, we knew that he had shot at some of the people that had surprised him while he was breaking into cars and he shot at them at very close range. One of the witnesses had said, "I don't know how he could have missed, he was so close." So we figured he was shooting blanks. I thought to myself, "Heck, he's just popping blanks at me. These sure aren't blanks that I'm shooting at him." Still I wasn't sure.

I ran north up to Third Street and when he crossed the street I kind of squeezed one off at him this time and hit him in the leg. He went down in a yard there at Third and Calhoun. When I come around the corner of the house, he's laying on the ground and he pumps a couple more at me. He comes pretty close with those blanks this time. So I shot a couple more back at him and all of a sudden I was empty. It's a terrible feeling. I backed off down the street and reloaded.

By this time he had gone around the corner of the house and was behind a hedge. I got up there and he fired another shot at me. When I fired twice more, he stopped shooting. I shined my light on him and saw he was down and bleeding pretty bad. At least he wasn't shooting any more. We called the rescue and he survived. They patched him all up.

Later on when we went to court, I got one of the lowest blows of my career. The jury found him not guilty of trying to kill me. He had stolen a nine-shot automatic pistol and it wasn't blanks he was shooting. He fired five of the nine shots at me before I shot him. I hit him four times. He would have bled to death if we hadn't got him to the hospital right away.

The jury said, "We don't deny the fact that he shot at this police officer. But we don't think he was trying to kill or hit him, because he would have fired all nine shots at him."

He was also tried for breaking into the car to steal the gun in the first place. The jury and judge were different in that case. The jury found him guilty. All this came out about him shooting at me, so the judge threw the book at him. He got ten years for stealing that gun. That kind of offset the damage done to my morale.

You never know what a jury is going to do. You can't predict a jury. A lot of policemen get discouraged by what a jury does sometimes. But those people, they watch Perry Mason and all this stuff on TV, so they start reading things into everything. There's no telling what they'll come up with.

*

Usually when you go to a burglary, the people have gotten there hours after the house has been robbed.

You're going there strictly for the formality of checking out the house and making them feel more secure. You do it a hundred times and you never find nobody.

Then all of a sudden you go in one that has just happened and a couple of things just make you feel like the guy didn't get out of the house in time. So you start to look a little extra, a little more thoroughly. The first thing that pops into your mind is the attic. Attics are suicidal. The attic has got to be checked. The only way to do it is to poke your head up through that hole. If that son of a bitch has got a gun or a knife, you're a dead son of a bitch and you can't do a thing about it. There's no way to get around it. The only safety precaution I take is, if I can find a hand mirror on someone's dresser in the house, I'll use that to look up there as best I can—to check out the immediate circumference of the hole anyway. You can actually angle a flashlight off it and do some good with it.

But when that's not available and there's two or more of you there, one of you has got to stick your head up there. Most often it's going to be the one who is a little bit more insane than the rest. In my particular situation, it's usually me. I'll go first.

We went to a house and the window was out. I checked the attic and it was clear. None of the lights in the house worked so we had to search it all by flashlight. Although it was daylight, there are a lot of dark corners to be looked into. Everybody searched everywhere and didn't find a thing. But I said, "I just don't feel like the guy got out of here."

I went back and searched everything again and then got down on my hands and knees and looked under the beds. The last bed I looked under, God damn, my flashlight batteries were almost dead. I barely got a little orange light out of the flashlight. I was on my hands and knees and squinting trying to get my eyes adjusted to what little light I had. When they got adjusted I saw a shoe, a tennis shoe down there.

"Shit, I can't see under there." I went back out in the hall and said, "Hey, throw me your flashlight." He threw it to me and I went back and flashed it under there and this son of a bitch had an automatic pistol pointed right at me under the bed and could've had me anytime he wanted to.

"Jesus Christ, motherfucker! Get out from under that bed!" I was ready to start shooting through the mattress. But then I realized he could, too. I was jumping from one foot to the other so he wouldn't shoot off my ankles. I was dancing.

*

I got a call of a burglary in progress. I get there and this woman comes out in the road and she's yelling, "They robbed me! They robbed me! They took my jewels!"

"Lady, lady, who robbed you?"

"The Gypsies!"

"Gypsies? In Southern California?" We get into the house and there are five Gypsy women. The victim says, "I was just sitting there and all of a sudden these Gypsy women are in my house and they're taking my rings and my jewels." So I round up these Gypsy women. I start talking to them and they just look at me.

All of a sudden this Gypsy man drives up in a brand new Ford car. He didn't speak any English, but he spoke a little German and I do, too. So I started talking to him. It turns out they were European Gypsies who had come to Canada. Then from Canada they had come driving down through the U.S. They were going to some Gypsy gathering in L.A. They had lots of cash, but they only spoke a Serbo-Croatian dialect which almost no one knows.

Why me, Lord? This is a real mess. None of them

had any identification on them. I get the sergeant down there. "What are we going to do with this?"

"Take them all down to the station," he tells me. "We'll figure out there what to do with them." We interview the victim and find out what they did. There had been some similar-type thefts reported in the area, so the sergeant told me to book them. "Book all of them."

Two of the five had babies, little babies. Great. I got them into the booking area in the station and I booked them—Jane Doe No. 1, Jane Doe No. 2. No address. I'd put down a little physical description. So finally we get them all ready and we take them out to jail.

The Gypsy men wouldn't take the babies, so we had to put the babies in the pediatrics ward at the hospital in protective custody while their moms are in jail. So I load all the Gypsy women into a paddy wagon and I take them to the hospital to do all the paper work.

Mama's holding her baby and I get her out and into the emergency room. There's a lot of people in there. I get the baby from her, and the nurse comes toward me. About that time the Gypsy woman figured out what's going on here. She's trying to get her baby back and she starts chasing me. I'm running round and round the emergency room. The nurse is standing there slack jawed, staring. Every time I run by her, I'm saying, "Take the kid. Take the kid." We're going round and round in a circle and all these people are watching.

This bitch pulls her top down, grabs both breasts and starts spraying me with Gypsy mother's milk. I was amazed. It sprays a long ways. She was getting me with both barrels. There was this old baldheaded man sitting in there and he got hit right on top of the head. It went running right down the tip of his nose. I was laughing almost as much as everybody else.

I finally hand-off the baby to the nurse. I grab this

gal, get hold of her arms and pull up the top of her dress. I rush her back into the wagon.

The second one tried to do the same thing, but I was a little bit quicker. The people in there were just roaring with laughter.

For years all the guys claimed I was under the curse of the Gypsy mother's milk. They kidded me about filing charges: Aggravated assault with a breast. I've never had it happen again. But I was in that one instance attacked with a breast.

*

You get dispatched on a prowler run and you'll meet strange people out there who are calling the police at three and four o'clock in the morning. When you get there, it might just be a cat in the trashcan, but they'll invite you in for a cup of coffee. They're lonely. They want somebody to talk to.

I went to this house one day on a disturbance with another officer. A woman came to the door and said, "Come in, officers. Will you sit down?" We sat down and she says, "He's been bothering me."

"Who?"

"Him," she says, and she points over to the couch. There's nobody there. I look at my partner and I'm biting my lip to keep from laughing. Then I start talking to the lady and the next thing you know I'm talking to the guy who isn't there to make her happy. I'm giving him hell for giving her hell, so I can get the hell out of there in the first place. I ask her what his name is and then I start talking to him. She says, "See what them officers is trying to say?" In her mind there's somebody sitting there. Maybe there was . . . but I didn't see him.

*

The captain got a call two or three times from this lady who said she wanted somebody to come by and listen to what she had to say and do. He said she acted kind of strange over the phone. He wouldn't send a car because he didn't really think that it was an emergency. But after about the fourth or fifth day of her calling him up, he decided he would send me and my partner around there.

We stepped up on the doorstep and asked her if we could help her in any way. She said, "Come on in." We went into the living room and she turned around and told us, "I just want ya'll to sit down and listen to me play the piano. It won't take long."

She could play that piano like Devil Wood at the Grand Ol' Opry. She would ask us, "Do you have any favorites?" She knew a bunch of songs. We thought at first that she was just putting us on. But come to find out that she was kind of a music nut, so to speak. She could really play the piano, but she couldn't carry on a decent conversation. Every other day she would call and someone would just go over and listen to her play for fifteen minutes. That's all she wanted. But if you didn't go, she would call the police station continuously.

*

There was a call from a woman who said there was a man living next door to her who was really cutting up. The sergeant said he'd take care of it, but he didn't send no one. After getting a call every day for three or four days, finally he sent myself and my partner round there. We were supposed to get there by four o'clock because the man usually come in about 4:30 from work. When we got there, she invited us in to her living room and she says, "Here comes that man now. He's going in his house. He'll be in his room in just a minute and I'm telling you he carries on something terrible." The houses in this area was built in such a way that there was only about enough room between them to walk through. From her kitchen window you could see into his bathroom window, which was only about 2 feet square.

Sure enough, in a minute he come into his bathroom, and he was singing at the top of his voice. He pulled off his shirt. You could see him from about his breast up. He was making a racket and moving around. She says, "Look at him. Just look at that."

"Lady, we don't see nothing," I said.

She reaches over under her table and pulls out a little stool about 24 inches high. "Well, stand up on this and look down in there," she says, "and then you'll see what I'm talking about."

Naturally, we both took turns standing up on the stool. By this time, the man across the way was naked as a jay bird, getting ready to get into the tub. She climbed up there after we were through and took a good long look and said, "Ain't that disgraceful? What can be done about that?"

"Lady, the best thing I could advise you to do," my partner said, "is to cut the legs off your stool." We left it at that.

*

One time we got a call to the back door of a black lady's house. She had been threatened with rape and robbery. She told us about this white person who had come up on her back porch and knocked on the door. When she answered it and asked him what can she do, he dropped his pants and told her that he wanted to, "come in and get some of that stuff." Then he told her that he was going to rob her, too.

"My screen door is locked," she told him, "so you can't get in. I'm going to go call the police." When she said that, he run down the street with his pants in his hand.

"What did he look like," I asked her.

"Well, he was a white fellow about twenty-five years old. Muscular built."

"Can you describe any other features about him," my partner said.

"Yes," she said, and she got a knife, the blade of which looked to be about 8 inches long. "He had one about that long."

We started riding around the area that Sunday morning. Two or three people come out. They knew we were looking for something and one of them said to me, "Are you looking for a white person without no clothes on? There he is right underneath that house over there."

He was still undressed, hadn't even put his pants back on. We put him in jail.

When we went to court that Monday morning, the judge asked the lady, "Could you identify the man?"

"Yes, your honor," she said. She had brought her knife along and she pulled it out. "His was about this long." Everybody in the court just hollered, too. They bound him over for criminal court and he got six months on the county farm for indecent exposure and prowling.

*

Women alone, it's really kind of sad. Women left by death or divorce. The safest guy in the world is a cop—at least from their perception. Sometimes they're wrong.

So many precincts get calls in the middle of the night: "Burglar on my roof," "Somebody on my fire escape." The cops go over and the woman checks the cop out. She'll make a move on you, just because she's done that in the past and it's worked. Or a cop has come and flirted with her and she's never picked up on it. The cop never called her back, but there's other cops out there. So she calls the precinct and says, "Send a car over here."

*

I love working with Latins, because they love to flirt and I love to flirt. You don't have to take it any further than that. It's just this wonderful male/female game. You want to take it a step further, you can—if they let you. Most times, it's just simple flirting. You can get away with it in uniform.

I remember having dinner in a place in Spanish Harlem by myself. I had walked in in uniform, sat down and taken my coat off and I was getting my food. At the table opposite me there was a husband and wife and child. The husband and child had their backs to me. The wife was facing me and she was really cute, a really pretty lady.

I looked at her and she was like smiling at me whenever he was looking away. One time I look, she runs her tongue across her upper lip. I thought, "Uh-oh."

He went to the men's room and I made a hand gesture like, "What do you want?" She wrote something on a piece of paper and gave it to the kid who ran over. It was her address.

When they got up and left, I followed them. You're a cop. You can walk wherever you want. So I'm walking on one side of the street and she's walking on the other with this guy. They got to a corner and they shook hands and he left. In fact, he wasn't her husband, just a guy who took her out for a date. You could see that he was confused.

Then she walked into her building and I just walked in behind her. I said, "Did you want to see me?"

"Do you like Spanish coffee?"

"Yeah."

"Come on in and take your coat off."

I had a situation one night where I never saw the woman, what she looked like. I knew that she was good-looking. I saw her get out of a cab. It was dark and she was black or Hispanic—I'm not even sure. She walked past me. She stopped and looked at me. Then she walked on by and went into the building. And I went into the building. I went up to her apartment and just knocked on the door. I heard the peep hole open.

"Did you call the police?" I asked. I just heard a giggle. She pulled me inside and shut the door. I did not say three words to her. Walked into the bedroom, she was in there giggling. I undressed her and took her to bed, fucked her. It was nice. I got dressed and left.

I was on school crossing. You stand on the corner and all the mothers go past with their kids in the morning. I have a hundred women come past with a hundred kids. Out of that hundred, three are looking for an afternoon with some guy. They're divorced or separated. Maybe they're married, they see that cop and they're thinking the same thing you are. American women are shy, but a lot of them—if they like you—they'll come after you.

I had a woman walk past me for a week straight. There was a smile for me every day. Finally the last day, she walked past me and said—they always said the same thing—"You like Spanish coffee?"

"I love it." And into the Project.

*

I pulled up on a parked car one night and it turned out to be a guy and a girl necking. While I was talking to them the girl came on to me. The guy said, "Oh, we were just leaving. We're going to go eat."

"No," the girl says, "I've already eaten."

Knowing full well what she was talking about, I said to this guy, "You mean to tell me that you're the kind of man that would let this young lady eat, and you haven't eaten yet?"

The guy is sitting there between us and she said, "Oh, if he'd had anything to eat, the whole inside of this car would be torn up."

"Well, my car is right over there," I said. "You can tear up the inside of that car anytime you like." The guy is fuming since I'm standing there coming on to his girlfriend. I ended up getting her phone number.

*

One time they sent us on a call to pick up a Navy man who was AWOL. The man was only AWOL from the Navy for about three months, but they wanted him for grand larceny of some materials that they considered about halfway secret that he had stolen. The sergeant contacted his wife and she wanted him to come clean and straighten up. She said, "Don't send them in until about two or three o'clock in the morning. He stays here until about five o'clock in the morning and then he goes somewhere, but I don't know where."

I'd been sick with a cold for two or three days and on this particular night I could hardly talk above a whisper really. My partner told me, "You go to the front door and I'll go to the back. If he's there and he tries to give you any trouble, just shoot your pistol, since you can't holler. I'll yell and be to you in a minute."

"Okay," I whispered, "I'll get word to you some way or I'll ask his wife to holler if I need help."

Right about two-thirty I went up on the porch and my partner went to the back side. I knocked on the door three or four times and finally the lady come to the door. She was in her nightclothes and she stood there inside the screen. I told her who I was and I said, in my whisper, "Is your husband home?"

She opened the screen door and looked both ways up and down the street and said, in a whisper, "No, come on in."

*

A woman had stabbed her husband with a kitchen knife. There was blood all over the floor. He was really cut. So we stuck him in the wagon and shot him down to the hospital. But he was DOA.

We called the sergeant down to the hospital, which was the procedure at that time. He said, "Go back and lock her up."

We went back to the house and told her, "You're going to have to come with us."

"Why?" she said.

"Your husband died."

"What?"

"Your husband is dead and you're under arrest."

"That motherfucker. I stabbed him before and he never died."

At the time it didn't really register. But we got back to the station and I'm sitting there almost pissing my pants laughing. It just came out of her so natural. She was pissed off that he had died.

*

I took a big machete away from this lady who was going to chop this guy's head off. They had some severe alcoholic problems. I took off my gun and sat there and tried to convince her that she should give me the knife, and that I understood why she wanted to kill this guy, because I had had a husband who was a bastard. My partner stood there with his gun in his pocket cocked. If she would have swung, he would have shot her. But that was necessary I had to win this lady's confidence.

I get very depressed about that kind of incident. I could relate to what she was saying, because my first husband used to kick my ass. He used me for a carpet and a punching bag. I really cared about this guy. I still have a love for him, because he was the true love of my life.

I understood what it is like to be a battered woman. When I was in that situation, I knew I would call the police and sometimes it took them hours to come, because we were the family on the block that they had to go to every Friday and Saturday night. Sometimes they never showed up at all.

I would be hysterical and crying because my husband had beat me up. The police would come in and he would sit there and laugh and say, "Look at her, she's acting like a fool. She's acting like a little kid, crying and stuff." The police officers would look at me and here I am half deranged, looking for help and they would say, "Why don't you grow up, lady?" Then my husband would hit me again after they left. So I got to the point where I didn't call them. So I guess I have a lot of compassion for women who are victims of domestic violence.

On the other hand, I had to learn that because I am an ex-battered woman, I had to put that fact into the correct perspective, so when I went to somebody's house I couldn't involve my personal feelings and what's happening in the house. It's a tough thing to do. It's very difficult to say, "Look it, I can't get involved, but there are some resources for you if you want to get the help you need." You almost never resolve anything.

*

I have a guy that I still have nightmares about. We had gotten a call that a man was trying to kill himself. Those are always really scary to me. If somebody is robbing a store they're pretty much open game if they come running out with a gun. But if you go to a suicide call and he comes out with a gun, what are you going to do, kill him? He has no respect for his own life, so what does he care about me?

He was in the bathroom of the master bedroom. We got in and there's weights and barbells all over the place with the really big round weights on the end of the bar. Already we had some indication of what the guy is going to be like. The other obvious feature of the decor was knives everywhere—buck knives, souvenir bayonets and stuff. She says, "My husband is in there and he's already cut his wrists. There was blood on the floor."

So we decided to go in there and save him. We asked her did he have any knives or guns in there with him. She says, "He's got a straight razor." I'd rather be shot than have somebody come after me with a straight razor. He's got the door locked and we're talking through the door. He won't come out or unlock the door.

We managed to get him to open it a little bit. He goes to slam it back and I stick my flashlight in the door so he can't shut it all the way. We're both leaning against the door and he's leaning the other way. We're still talking to him, "Aw, come on out, Jack. Come on out." We give each other the high sign—at the count of three, we're going to shove the door through, go in there and grab him. "One, two . . ." We're both leaning against it with everything we got. "Three!"

The guy throws open the door. He's got a screwdriver and he comes out with it raised over his head and he tried to stab me in the face. As I flew past him into the bathroom, I put my hand up and he got me in the arm.

Then he went after the other policeman and knocked him into a chair. He's got the guy off balance over the chair and is coming down with the screwdriver. I'm grabbing him, trying to hold him, but he was all muscled up. There was nothing I could do. He comes down and stabbed the other policeman in the chest. This officer gave out a death moan. Really it just hit his breast bone and gave him a little scratch on his chest.

The guy kept fighting us. Another policeman got there by that time and we were able to get him handcuffed. His wrists weren't that bad. It was one of those fake suicides: "Hey, look at this. I tried to kill myself."

"Don't hurt him! Don't hurt him!" the wife is screaming. "You don't have to kill him."

We took him to the station. We ended up booking him on a bunch of charges including attempted murder.

When we started going to court it all came out. What killed me was his wife said we hadn't been invited in since we didn't have a warrant. The story changed to something that didn't include suicide. The police it seems just showed up and forced their way into this guy's house and tried to drag him out of the john for no reason. He was trying to defend himself and all he had was a screwdriver.

For a couple of nights I had a nightmare and the other officer said he had nightmares, too. When he came out with the screwdriver I had in my mind that it was a straight razor anyway. I thought I was cut. In my dream he kept coming through the door and he was jumping on me and we were fighting.

*

What scares me is the mentally disturbed, the people that lose it. They are so powerful. They will hurt you that quick and they'll scare you quicker. That's what I don't like. I don't like it when I'm scared. I know I'm in trouble then.

I was off duty and driving down the street towards my house. I see this couple—a guy and a pregnant woman—I thought were fooling around. He tried to grab her and she jumped. This truck had to swerve to miss her. I said to my wife, "Kidding around, I guess."

Then I looked in the rearview mirror and he had this pregnant woman by the wrists and was forcing her down to her knees in the road. Oh, shit, here I got my case of beer in the car and I'm planning to go home, have a barbecue, drink beer and have a nice day off. Okay, I back up.

I have a radio in my personal car. It's come in handy quite often. I called the station, told them I was stopping and I'd be out of the car. I get out of the car thinking this will be no big problem. "Hey, what's going on?"

I say. The guy gave me one of those looks and I said to myself, "Shit, I've got a squirrel."

"Ho-ah her-ah aargh," he says.

"He's hurting me! He's hurting me!" she's yelling. "He's deaf and he can't talk and—my God!—he's killing me!"

So here we go. I step in between them somewhat, trying to get him to let go of her. He looks at me and starts gurgling. He's deaf and dumb and he's not all that big. I got one hand off and got it behind him. About that time, he grabbed me by the wrist. When he wrapped his fingers around me I knew I was in trouble. That son of a gun nearly crushed my bones. I said, "God, what have I done?" I was in a bad spot now. He had me. He let loose of her and that was for sure. He had me now. Now it's my turn to be forced down to my knees in the middle of the road.

I grabbed his other arm and we looked like we were doing the old Chinese handshake. I reached behind him and tripped him up. Shit, he hit the ground and jumped right back up like he was spring loaded. What am I going to do with this squirrel? He's still got my wrist. He ain't let go of that yet, even for the few seconds he was down. My hand by this time is getting nice and white. It hurt.

I tripped him up again and got my wrist free. Halleluja! Now I was thinking about running back to the car, getting in and leaving. But I was pretty obligated at that point.

We're wrestling around. This son of a gun is getting ready to get back up and I'm not sure what I'm going to do. He does get back up. I've got him by the arms and all I'm trying to do is hold him off. He's on me like stink on shit. I yelled to my wife in the car, "Get on the radio and tell them to send somebody."

"What do I say?"

"Just tell them to send help. I don't care what you say. Keep it simple."

I saw this figure running up the road. I was hoping it was a friend. I got the guy tripped up again. This time I got him down and I got one arm partially twisted behind him. By God, it was a friend from the sheriff's department. He was inside a house on the block visiting his dad. His little daughter was outside and saw this going on. I'd never seen her before in my life. She went inside and said, "Daddy, I think there's a policeman fighting down the street." I wanted to kiss that little kid, because I was so glad to see her daddy coming up the road.

Jim grabs his other hand and we get the guy rolled over facedown. Jim is heavier than I am—probably weighs 250. He comes right down on this guy's neck with his knee. This guy is eating asphalt now and doing the shuffle. He has begun to bleed a little bit from a few spots on his face which may have had something to do with the 250 pound weight on his head. But this guy starts arching his back and lifting his head up anyway. I've got my knee in the small of his back with my weight on him. I've got his arm up behind him near his shoulderblades, holding it with both my hands and he's starting to straighten it out.

"God damn, whatever we do, don't let this son of a bitch loose. If he stands up again we're in trouble." He was totally gone berserk now. You ever see Chuck Norris in that movie with the guy he couldn't kill? That's what I thought I had.

I had cuffs with me in the car and I had brought them with me. I hit at his wrist and missed and put a hole in his hand. Then I hit again and it locked around his wrist. Jim has got the other arm but the guy is straining to get free. Jim can hardly hold it.

About this time, I see another figure hauling ass up

on my left. It is hollering, "What the fuck are you doing? That's my brother! Leave him alone!"

"Don't move," I said. "If you can calm him down, do it, so he doesn't hurt himself any more."

The deaf guy looked pretty atrocious now. He was really starting to get some asphalt burns. The brother gets down in his brother's face and he says, "Uncuff him." Bullshit. There's no way I'm taking the cuffs off this guy. We haven't even finished cuffing the other arm yet. He tried to talk to him and the deaf guy slacked off instantly. We popped the other cuff on the other wrist. We had both hands securely behind him now and we were HAPPY.

Now the brother starts getting upset. "You better let him go!"

"I think you better just get out of this general area," I said. Other units showed up now and escorted the brother away. We got the deaf guy up and over to the car. In he goes, quite violently, headfirst all the way to the other side of the car. He bounced around all the windows for a while, then went apeshit in the car, kicking, screaming, trying to push the cage out.

His brother went over and got into the front seat. This is a bad scene, because I could just see the brother driving off in the car. This female deputy goes over to him and says, "Get out of my car."

"Wait a minute," the guy says, real short.

Another officer heard this and he zeroed right in on the guy, grabs him by the arm and jerks him out of the car like a cork out of a bottle. He gets thrown right into this female officer and they go head over heels. She's pissed, so she's got him bent over the hood of her car and gets him cuffed. He's under arrest, too. Now the deaf guy's wife—the woman he was attacking in the first place—is going berserk. Her water is breaking.

"Rescue, somebody call Rescue." Rescue came and took her off.

*

It gets down to one thing. What kind of physical shape you're in at the time the incident takes place. How good you are essentially. Everyone's afraid and you respond as if you had no training. That's the interesting thing. You see somebody, all of a sudden, in a fighting situation, the training goes out the window. The guy fights if he knows how to fight. If he don't know how to fight, he's in trouble and he pulls his gun. "Enough of this shit, I'm not Joe Louis."

First of all, the fact that you're a policeman gives you a step up in almost every situation. Rarely, unless the guy is a total crazy, will he come at you first. If the guy's a total crazy, you're in trouble. A guy will use his mouth and get into a lot of screaming. In general, it's the cop who hits first. You say, "Nah, cops react, they don't act first." Not if they've been on the street for a while and they know how to handle the situation.

You get into a family fight, nose to nose with somebody. You know that you're going to try to remove this guy from his apartment because his old lady wants him out. Man, he don't want to leave. He don't want to leave for a lot of reasons, not the least of which is that, he gets out the door, she'll be fucking the guy who he's fighting with her about now.

All the focus is on this guy and he's going to show you and the bitch. The worse thing that can happen to him is that he's going to get beat up—and that will be her fault.

You go through stages. The first one, you just finished having coffee and talking about the crabgrass and stuff. Now you're in the apartment and there's this tremendous amount of tension. People get killed in this kind of tension all the time. But you're still thinking about the crabgrass and where you're going to have dinner, so you're not really ready. You grab the guy by the arms and say, "Come on, let's get out of here." The guy whaps you and you're in the middle of a big fight. You're getting your ass kicked.

So you learn. Stage two: "The next time I go in there and I look at the guy and I see that this guy is going to have to go, I'm going to take him out quick. I'm going to show him that it's a no-win situation and that he's going to get his ass kicked."

The guys who are afraid continue with the ass kicking for their whole careers. The guys who aren't afraid move on to stage three and just exert themselves, establish their authority and the fighting ends.

*

They sent me on a call once out on the west side of town. They said, "There's a lady with two kids out there in the rain. The neighbors across the street have called." So I pulled up and there, standing outside the picket fence, is this lady with no cover and two kids. I asked what was the matter. She said her husband had chased her out of the house with a shotgun. "He's in there now," she says.

Just by long chance, I happened to know the man. It's raining like hell. I opened the gate, walked up on the porch and knocked on the door. When he opened the door I was looking down the muzzle of a double-barreled shotgun. He looked over the sights and he said, "Mr. Louis, what in the hell are you doing here? Damn, I'm glad to see you."

"Well, now come on, Earl, put your gun down," I says. "You know that you're doing the wrong thing."

"Mr. Louis, would you take it for me. I know I'm going to get in trouble if you don't keep it."

"Listen, man," I says, "tell me real quick. What's

the trouble?" He had been drinking and he'd stopped by some bar on the way home and had lost his money in a crap game. He'd come home and his wife was nagging him about it and it just made him so damn mad that he didn't know what to do. So I asked him, "Earl, would you do me a favor?"

"Mr. Louis, I'll do anything you want me to do."

"Okay, I'll tell you what. You come on and go with me. I'll let you stay at a cheap place downtown for the night. Then tomorrow, you come to the police station and I'll release your gun to you. Then you can come home and everything will be all right as far as we're concerned."

"Would you do that for me?" he said.

"Sure," I said. I walked him right by his wife. I said, "Don't you have something to say to your wife?"

"Mr. Louis has told me that I was wrong," he said, "and all I know is that I'm sorry. I'll talk to you later. Please go back into the house."

I went back up on the porch and told her what I was going to do. She said, "He'll probably be all right tomorrow."

Two or three days later, I rode by there and he was out in the yard playing ball with the little boy. Everything was just fine.

I was never one to think that just because I had a badge and gun that I was little Jesus like some police officers do. But I don't believe that just anybody could be a police officer. You have to have above all an abundant amount of compassion for your fellow man. Also, you should have the ability to put yourself in the suspect's or the victim's position, just momentarily. "If I was in his position, what would I want done with me?"

*

I go to this family fight. This black broad wants to kill her husband with a butcher knife. She wants to cut his balls off. She comes home and finds him in bed with the neighbor.

But, that's not what got her mad. He's down eating the neighbor's pussy when she walks in. That's what got her mad, because he never ate her pussy. All she was doing was screaming, "He never ate my pussy. I'm going to cut his balls off." She's ready to kill this guy, and he's turning white. So we took the knife away from her and he pressed charges for assault.

*

It was about three o'clock in the morning. We get there. You have to see these apartments. This one was very spartan, very small. It looked like Ralph Cramden's apartment, except with dirt. A black-and-white TV with a bent aerial. A beat-up refrigerator.

It was two old people and they weren't married. They were shacking up together, which was cute. They had a falling-out this evening.

This guy had glasses like the bottoms of Coke bottles. He couldn't go from here to the wall without tripping. She is insisting on having him out of the apartment. It's three o'clock in the morning and there's sharks out there on the avenue would eat this guy alive.

"He beats me," she says. She pulls up her dress and you see a lot more than you'd ever want to see. She shows me the bruises. Whether this guy did it or not, I don't know.

I went out in the hall and I asked the guy, "What is the problem?"

"Well, we had an argument."

"Would you like to stay here? Why don't you tell her you're sorry?"

"Oh, I'd tell her, but she won't believe me."

I went back into her and I said, "You know, he was just telling me how much he loved you." She wanted to believe it. "If you just call him in here, I have a feeling that he'll say he's sorry. And if you're any kind of woman, like I think you are, you'll forgive him."

I go out and I say to him, "Okay, Bob." He goes up the stairs. He's standing up there on the landing like a little kid about six years old, kicking one foot on the floor. He says, "I'm sorry."

All of a sudden you see her arms just go out of the door and grab him and pull him back inside. That was really nice at three o'clock in the morning.

Of course, I had another one where a black woman threw a whole sectional couch down the stairs at her boyfriend. I wasn't going to tell him, "Tell her you're sorry." She would have taken him apart.

*

You go to a domestic fight and the guy is beating his old lady up. Her teeth are busted out and her eyes are all swollen. You ask her, "Do you want to file charges?"

"No, I love him."

"How many times has he done this to you?"

"Ten or twelve."

"Do you want to file charges?"

"No, I love him."

You can't do nothing for these people. There's nothing in the world you can do. A month or so later you go back and he's blown her away. If she could say it, she'd say, "No, I love him." But she can't. She's dead.

*

You work a four to twelve. Say out of the thirty jobs you've gotten on the shift, eight of them involve a spouse, male or female, telling the other spouse a palpable lie as to their whereabouts or as to who that was that didn't talk on the phone or whatever. On a given night you've got eight instances in an eight-hour period where somebody has said they were out bowling with their friends when in fact they were screwing around.

You go home and your wife isn't home. Ten minutes later she comes in the door. "Where the hell were you?"

"Oh, I was out with my girlfriends." And she probably was, but you've heard that lie eight times tonight. It engenders an emotional paranoia.

*

This idiot who drove off the pier is such a loser. He's got two, maybe three living brain cells left and that's it. He's been out of state prison for three months. He's been arrested four times in six weeks for drunk driving. He comes up out of the water and he's standing there spitting saltwater at us. You don't even have to go up and ask him his name. He's a local legend. Every cop on the street knows him. Everybody's arrested him at least once.

And after all this, he wants to fight. There's four of us there. I'm the smallest of the four. The lieutenant that was there is our weaponless defense instructor, the guy that knows more ways to make you hurt than the Marquis de Sade. Of the two other guys, one outweighs me by probably 30 pounds and the other one has four inches on me.

This nut is yelling at them, "Come on, let's fight! You'll never take me alive, coppers!" All this bullshit. Unfortunately, he turned his back on me, so I choked him out. We went down to the ground and it was a very, very short fight.

The pier has been there for 128 years. The only other time anyone else has ever gone off that pier is one Halloween in 1896. They grabbed a horse-driven carriage and ran it off the pier. All these years and nobody's driven off again. It's a half-mile long. Now that this guy made the front page, we're probably going to have a car a night going off the end of the pier.

*

We go out at midnight, we sit down and have a cup of coffee and wait for the events of the evening. So we were there and a call comes in from another sector of a robbery in a gas station. They put out a description of the two robbers and said that they had cut the gas station attendant's throat. The other car on duty for that area responded. The robbers were gone so we didn't have any reason to rush over there.

About fifteen minutes later we ambled down that way. The victim is still in the station. He didn't close up—a gutsy little guy. He was a drummer in a band and this was his second job. I talked to him, "What happened?"

"The dirty bastards, I wouldn't give them the money till they cut my throat." They didn't really cut his throat. They just kind of sliced it, but he's got a big bandage on and he's all full of blood on his shirt and he's still going to work. He didn't mind the money they took from the owner, but he says, "The dirty bastards took my TV." He had a small portable TV. He's mad and he's cursing them.

"All right," I says, "give me a description of the television." We go out to look around. Right around the corner from the gas station—I'm talking about less than a block—who's walking down the street but a guy carrying a portable TV. I turned to my partner and said, "Frank, do you believe it? Look."

"Yeah, there's the big guy and there's the other guy. They fit the description. And there's the TV."

I shut the lights off and I says, "Let's follow them." They never saw us. They're walking down the block like nothing is happening. They start up the steps of a house and I say, "Come on, let's take them before they get in the house." So we run up. The guys are on the top step. We pull the guns. "All right, freeze." The big guy takes out a knife. He's not thinking of attacking us. He wants to dump it. The TV is the same make that the victim told us. We get the guys and the TV and we take them back to the gas station attendant. "Is this the guys?"

"Those sons of bitches," he yells. He grabs a tire iron and he starts hitting the top of the patrol car. He's wanting to hit these guys in the head. "That's them, that's them." We took them in.

We asked them, "Where the hell were you for that half-hour between the robbery and when we caught up to you?" They had hid in an empty house on the corner. "When we saw the police cars left, we figured it was okay to come out." By us dallying and getting there later, we were doing the right thing.

*

I'm sitting in the radio car. This young guy who was my partner that day is in the deli getting us a couple of sandwiches for lunch. A woman comes down from the real estate office screaming, "Help, help, I've been robbed! He ran up the next street." Which was behind me. The kid starts running up the street. I ask her, "What's he look like?"

"Guy had a black T-shirt on," she says, "and big."

I made a U-turn and went shooting up the street. My partner is running up the block. I yell to him, "Keep chasing him. I'll get ahead of him and we'll box him." But by the time I got around, he had cut down a side street and was away from us. So I pass up my partner and I have to get him by myself with the car.

I'm driving the car and the guy is running on my right. The windows of the car are open because it's summer. I had my gun pointing out the passenger window and I'm going, "Stop or I'm going to blow you away."

He turns and looks right at me and says, "Kill me! Shoot! I'm no fucking good! Kill me!" But he stops running. I stop the car right in the middle of the avenue and I get out. He's a big son of a gun. I tell him to turn around. "Fuck you. Shoot! Shoot!" He had no weapon. I don't want to shoot no guy like that. He's still shouting, "Shoot, shoot! Kill me! I'm no fucking good!"

"Turn around," I tell him. I turn him around. He was wringing wet from the run and he was slippery. Now on TV it looks easy, but you need your hands to handcuff a guy, especially when you're holding a gun and he's not standing still. "Stop moving, you." I'm trying to get the cuffs on him. I hit him once with the gun and that didn't even faze him one bit. Finally a citizen helped me get the cuffs on him. My partner caught up with us and we took him in.

It turns out the guy is out of jail a week and he just couldn't live on the outside, actually. He was a bad, bad loser. That's why he said to kill him. That was weird. I had a bead on him and he looked me right in the eye and said, "Kill me." I knew right away I couldn't do it. If he'd said something different, like "I'm going to kill you," then maybe I could shoot him. They put him in the nut house. He was mental.

*

We got a call one day, a jumper. So we go to the building and the floor and I ask this old fellow in there, "Where is he?"

"He's out the window." I put my head out the window and I said, "There's nobody out there. What, are you crazy?"

"Yeah, he's there. He's hanging."

"What do you mean, he's hanging?"

"He's hanging from the fire escape. Look." I go back out the window. I see the two hands that I didn't see before. He's hanging free. I say, "Hey, stupid. Get your ass up here." And I walked away, right? A couple of minutes later he comes back in through the window. I said, "That's psychology and it worked." That was cute.

*

We got sent to a rape at four o'clock one morning. Nice-looking girl. She's in bed. She wakes up and there's a guy standing over her. He puts a pillow case over her head and rapes her.

"But there's something strange about it," she says. Her big German shepherd is there and he doesn't bark or growl. Normally the dog would go crazy if somebody came into the house. She said she scratched the guy.

We go over next door to see if the neighbor had seen or heard anything unusual and the guy comes to the door. He's got his clothes on at four o'clock in the morning, he's all nervous and he's got a big scratch down his face. We called the detectives. It was him. He just wanted to get a piece of ass, so he raped her. That's why the dog didn't bark, because he knew the guy. They made him on fingerprints, because she never got a good look at him.

*

I guess she was thirteen or fourteen years old. She was despondent and was not making much sense on the phone, but she needed help. I went over there.

She's crying. Her mother had left them—her, her father and her brother—two years ago. This is what she's telling me. But it's not making any sense, totally incoherent, in a state of shock. Her little brother is rocking in a chair next to her. I never found out how old he was—I would assume he was three or four. He's just rocking. She's not really telling me anything.

I call for backup, because I wanted somebody to watch the kids while I looked around. What happened was the father made them come in and watch him kill himself. He put a shotgun in his mouth and pulled the trigger. The whole wall was covered with the gray matter of his brain where he blew the whole left side of his head apart.

A few days later after they had a chance to calm down, a detective talked to the girl again and found out that the father was a real disciplinarian. He made them sit down there. He went through the whole thing and explained to them why he was killing himself: because he couldn't live without their mother and she was going to get married again and he couldn't handle that. Then he made them watch while he blew his brains apart.

The traumatic experience that was on these kids' faces made me want to cry with them. But I realized that there was nothing I could do. That shook me up as much as anything in police work—that total feeling of helplessness. There's no training for it. As much as he may have been sick in his own mind, they loved him and they couldn't understand it. I can't make it all right. They were placed in a foster care home and I never followed up on what happened to them, probably because I didn't want to know. I felt helpless and like I didn't do a good job.

*

We got an anonymous phone call that this man was abusing his kids. There were three children in the family. One of them was not abused at all by the father, but one was beaten and we couldn't locate the third.

We knew that there had to be a problem. This man at times appeared to be rational and then at other times irrational. We checked a few places the child might be and that came up negative. We got a search warrant so we could continue the investigation and we went in and searched the home.

I don't know for what reason, but I decided to look into the refrigerator. The frig is fine. I open up the freezer and there is the child, all butchered, arms and legs, and wrapped like a frozen chicken or a piece of beef. He had dismembered them and labeled them and put them in the freezer.

You try to explain this to someone and they just shake their head, and I just shake my head, in disbelief. Even now I cringe when I think about it. But that's an extreme case of what people will really do. Demented, sick. You look at that and you want to go home and hug your five-year-old. My God, how lucky you are to have a relationship with your own kids. How could that person be that insane to do something like that?

*

I had a kid just recently die on me. I got the call: "It looks like a guy's hurt in his car." I come up and it's a white kid from New Jersey and he's clutching his chest. He's still alive, but I can see that they got him right in the heart. The kid says to me—these are his last words at eighteen—"He stuck me, but he didn't get my dope, man." He's holding the dope with all the fucking blood there and he died. Life, right? How precious that shit is, man. So they kill for that.

*

A small farm. A suicide. This man had hung himself. He'd done some elaborate planning. He picked a branch in a tree that I'd say was 25 feet off the ground. Made a noose. Kept his two children home out of school so they could witness this. Climbed up and kicked the ladder away.

When I got there, the two kids were in a catatonic state. I got them inside and got someone to take care of them. Our ID guy comes and takes pictures. Then I got to climb up in the tree and cut this guy down and try to carry him down the ladder. The guy weighed about 210. I got him over my shoulder and cut down. It was an old wooden ladder. A rung broke and I fell all the way down on my ass. His body goes flying to the right. I almost break my back and leg. He almost killed me. Killed by a guy who killed himself.

*

We used to take the emergency runs. We were like an ambulance. But it got to where we were just a meat wagon. The fire department took over the emergency runs and all we did was haul drunks to jail and dead bodies to the morgue.

I could not stand dead bodies. If I had to do it I did it, but I just held my breath, went to the morgue and got it over with. They got us a new morgue out there. After it opened they told us, "Man, you can't smell nothing. They got this plastic duct system that sucks all the fumes out." Shit, it's just as bad out there as it was at the other place. You never forget the smell.

I've seen bodies with maggots crawling in and out of them. We hauled a guy out of the river who'd been in there, they said, seven days. Turtles had been chewing on him and he was green. He smelled. We stopped and got cigars. Neither one of us smoked, we just wanted to get rid of the smell on the way to the morgue.

I've hauled little babies. They died at the hospital and you have to take them to the morgue. They give you a little bundle about so big and you just lay it in the backseat of your car. Take it up to the morgue. That's kind of tough to do. I tried not to get too involved. I'd take them up there, but I didn't want to see them or anything. Especially little infants.

*

This one night we get a call to Haight Street. We were right around the corner as God would have it. Child has stopped breathing. Two things you really look for in this job—an injured kid or a cop in trouble. My partner is five-foot-five and five-foot wide. He wasn't fat, he was just broad. For some reason I was driving the wagon that night. Normally he drove and I was the observer. He had ten kids. He really reacted to kid calls.

Now this son of a bitch jumps out of the wagon, runs into the apartment and picks up this little boy baby. The baby was blue, practically gone. Somehow or another he got out of the apartment with the baby and the mother right behind him. Jumps in the back of the wagon.

This is not the kind of wagons that you see today. This was an old-fashioned wagon where once you were in, you were locked in, but there was a sliding door between the cab and the back of the wagon, so I could hear what was going on. He was trying to give the baby mouth to mouth, but this was before that sort of thing was really widely known. I got on the radio and called the Children's Hospital. "We're on our way with a baby that's stopped breathing."

The dispatcher came on and said, "Yes, we've notified them. They'll be waiting for you."

It took me maybe a minute and a half or two minutes to get there—we weren't far away at all. I jump out of the wagon, open the back door. As soon as I open the door, Bobby was on his way. He runs through the emergency room door, through the waiting room. He trips over somebody in the God damn emergency room with the baby in his arms. He falls on the fucking baby. Ping! Something comes out of the fucking baby's mouth, hit the fucking radiator and the baby was fine. This guy had to be 240 pounds. He was big. Whatever had been lodged in its throat just went shooting across the emergency room. The doctor says, "What's the problem? There's nothing wrong with this baby."

*

A car loaded down with a Cuban family came off the expressway and the brakes failed. The guy veered off into a vacant field by the creek. He made a wide circle trying to slow down, but the circle was too wide. The car went off into the creek and flipped upside down. He got everybody out except one infant child about fourteen months old.

The call went out and we were the first ones there. Only a portion of the car is protruding out of the water. So I stripped off my gunbelt and my shoes, jumped in and got up underneath the car. I got the baby out and we managed to revive it. The baby lived for twenty-four hours. It died later on, but we did save the child's life, even if it didn't live. At least we did something. I got several plaques over that.

*

You don't realize the impact you have on people. An old woman and her husband were broken down on the highway. I stopped, put out flares, got the tow truck and the guy to fix the car. I stayed there from the minute I found them. I put them in my car because it was so cold out. I didn't think anything more of it.

She sent this two-page letter of thanks to the captain. You'd think I'd walked on water. I really didn't think I did anything great. Here's old people that aren't treated that well in our society anyway. I just took the time to be nice to them. After I read the letter I really felt good. You can make a difference.

*

I remember an accident. It was a bad one, but it wasn't like people were injured all over the place. The car that got hit was flipped over. A woman got out, but she was dazed when I got there. Then she started coming to and she started screaming for her baby. I said, "Oh shit, now there's a baby inside that car."

I go crawling inside the car, here's this little kid, about six months old, a little girl. She probably bounced around in that car like a rubber ball, because they're so flexible. She's sitting there. She's not crying and nobody ever thought to go look for her.

When you pull the child out, you feel, "Oh, I can't believe this, that I did this." You're scared shitless to go and look, because you don't want to see that kid's head crushed and have to tell the mother. But then you come out with the kid. You're able to tell everybody something good. They're all clapping on the side. The ending was nice and those kind of things make you feel happy about doing the work.

*

There was an accident. This little six-year-old kid was in the middle of the street with a broken leg. All these people were gathered around him, looking down. You could tell by the scared look on his face that they were freaking him out. So I just laid down on the road beside him and cradled him in my arms. I told him to ignore those stupid people, look at me and we'd just talk. And we did until the ambulance got there.

I've had people die in my arms. It's easy to be hard-core, to be the macho man. But it's also nice if somebody is dying to say a little prayer for them. They might not be religious or maybe they didn't have a chance to say one for themselves. When I'm in a position that I'm with somebody and I know they're checking out, I try to say a little prayer to help them along their way. I don't care whether he's a criminal or an innocent bystander. Everybody should have a prayer. If that's the only thing you can give them, at least you've done something for them. It may be the least you can do, but you should at least do that.

I've seen a lot of death since I been a policeman. I've walked in blood flowing over my shoes from a mass murder. You've got to joke about it and you've got to forget about it. Also you got to remember that that could be you lying down there someday. You'd want somebody to help you.

I do not relish the thought of dying in the gutter someplace, having some wino standing over me going, "Jesus, what's the matter, fellow?"

*

I had a sixty-four-year-old woman who was raped by a male black. She had been seeing her doctor for years. The nurse knows her for years. She was raped on a Thursday. She wouldn't go to him until that following Monday. They knew something was wrong with her because she was drinking like you wouldn't believe. She was hysterical, emotional, but she wouldn't tell them what was wrong.

They called me to the scene. I talked to this lady for an hour and a half and she confided everything to me. I think it was very important to her that I was a female. But she said, "Don't tell the doctor. Don't tell the nurse. No one. No one."

I talked to her and talked to her. "I need your daughter's phone number," I told her. "If anything should happen to you, God forbid, I need to know how to contact the next of kin."

"Don't tell my daughter. Please, don't tell my daughter."

"I won't tell her. You got my word on it." I helped her through it and no one ever knew. Knife point right to her throat. Beat her unmercifully. She wouldn't talk to anybody. The guy who did it knew that.

I take the lady finally to the hospital. She walks in and the nurse says to her, "Oh, you were raped on Thursday and now you decided to report it, sweetie."

I went over to that nurse and I said, "Listen, you, okay? Be a little more professional. You're supposed to be a nurse. When people are sick, mentally or physically, you're supposed to help them. She doesn't need you to break her chops. She just went through an ordeal."

Every time I was going to leave the room, the woman was hysterical. I couldn't leave. Finally I explained to her, "Listen, dear, I have to go back out on patrol. I can't spend the rest of my career with you. You're going to be fine. I made sure you were fine. You're safe now. You'll be okay." Finally I left. She was hysterical crying when I was leaving. Later, I helped her get in the psychiatric center so she'd have someone to talk to about the whole thing.

That lady to this day still calls this precinct and asks for me, just to say hello, how are you. As long as I feel that I could touch one little life, I feel good about the job.

CHAPTER 3

Crimebusters

HOMICIDE, RAPE, burglary, robbery, narcotics, vice. Each detective division within the police department specializes in handling a certain type of crime. A cop with detective rank gets to shed his uniform and all the paramilitary posing that goes with it. Freed from the drudgery of patrol, detectives do the investigations, the stakeouts and the undercover work. Depending on his job and his personal inclination, a detective may wear a three-piece suit like a stockbroker or faded jeans and sneakers like Serpico.

The other specialized divisions common in most urban areas are bomb squads, hostage negotiators and special weapons and tactics teams (SWAT). These are the elite groups of highly trained individuals who get involved in the cliff-hanging stunts and emotionally charged confrontations that television "eyewitness" news teams love to cover.

The detective is the police officer most often depicted in novels and television programs. All the elements for a good story seem to be there: drama, mystery, danger, action.

But contrary to their popular image, detectives are not masters of deduction foiling the plots of incredibly clever criminals by piecing tiny elements of evidence and circumstance into an arcane but logical sequence. Neither are they pigheaded stooges, bungling all the cases that the private eyes will have to solve.

The world of the detective does not glitter. Drug busts are rarely made in million-dollar penthouses. There are very few diplomats operating houses of prostitution and slave trading posts from the back doors of exquisitely decorated embassies. Heiresses who bump off their favorite designer for a one-of-a-kind party dress are scarce these days.

The aftermath of crime is sordid, tragic, ugly. There may be bodies and coagulated blood, the smells of death and decomposition. There are bound to be pain and terror. The sounds are the sobs of the violated and the frenzied cries for justice from families of the victims. To one side are frightened children with hollow eyes. This is where a detective works.

At the scene of the crime, a detective oversees the collection of physical evidence and the preservation of the surroundings. A photographic record is often made. A thorough search must be conducted. This sometimes includes bodies to be searched. Fingers curled in rigor mortis must be pried open. Pockets are emptied and their contents are catalogued.

If he is fortunate enough to arrive soon after the crime has been committed, the detective will try to interview the victim or other witnesses to the crime. He must sort through the confusion of hysteria, panic and fear for the hard facts that might help him.

The detective may order the scene to be dusted for fingerprints, but this messy procedure is often performed merely to reassure the victim or relatives that everything that can be done is being done. All that black powder and the inch by inch scrutiny with a magnifying glass is what the public expects of a detective. If he should make that one-in-a-thousand find—an unsmudged, latent print that does not belong to the victim, a member of the victim's family or one of the patrol officers who answered the original call—it won't do the detective much good unless he already has a good idea of whom it belongs to. That an unidentified print can be compared to all the prints on file somewhere in Washington, D.C., and then positively identified is a myth. The unidentified print must be accompanied by a short list of the names of people whose prints it is to be compared with. And if the criminal has not been arrested on a federal charge, his fingerprints probably won't be in the central FBI file in any case.

"Cops don't solve crimes. I'm not Sherlock Holmes. I can only think of one or two instances in my career when piecing together physical evidence caught a criminal. It convicts them, yeah. But if we find out who did something, it's usually because somebody saw it happen and he drops a dime on the perp." In other words, a witness or informer calls the police and tells them what happened.

Most detectives have informants. These fall into two major categories—those he can threaten and those he can buy. The parolees and small-time local criminals that he can put pressure on for information will often tell him anything that comes into their heads just to get away from him. Those he can buy are often just as unreliable, and the five or ten dollars he pays them most often comes out of his own pocket.

A detective's major tool is his feet. His feet carry him on the endless journey of canvassing neighborhoods for witnesses. From door to door, upstairs and down, he knocks and identifies himself and asks his questions over and over again, hoping to come across the recluse insomniac who just happened to be gazing out the window at 4 A.M. when the crime took place. His feet are also handy in the battle against the bureaucratic red tape in his own department as he walks from section to section searching for information, standing in line filling out his request form for access, filling out the request form for request forms.

When not engaged in some other activity, the detective, like the officer on patrol, is writing reports. The system requires that he put everything in writing, with the hope that these reports will serve him as ready reference material when he is preparing his testimony against a criminal brought to trial. In the meantime, his mounds of paper protect him from his superiors' accusations of indolence and the public's outcry of malfeasance.

The most effective detectives combine a dedicated tenacity in the face of this endless red tape with alertness in the presence of mind-numbing repetition—and no little amount of luck. When they are able to bring a criminal to justice, the heroism in their effort goes beyond the outlandish plots of television dramas. If a suspect is actually tried and convicted it seems little less than a miracle.

Those other specialists—bomb technicians, hostage negotiators and SWAT Team members—are never called in except as a last resort. They expect the worst and for the most part the worst is exactly what they see.

Risking life and limb, they try to prevent deliberate acts of terror or perverted pleasure or they clean up after irrational bursts of hatred, anger or desperation. They do this job directly in the public eye. Because of their high visibility, every detail of planning and execution must be perfect. On those few occasions when everything goes right, they are heroes for a day. If anything goes wrong or can be interpreted that way, they are scapegoats for the press, the politicians and the public.

It's little wonder that the detective himself thinks his world is a good deal less glamorous than the public thinks it is.

I DID A four to one—four in the afternoon till one o'clock in the morning. Eight o'clock that same morning, I go back in to the desk. "Hey, you have a homicide," they say.

"When did it happen?"

"Happened at five past one last night."

"What you got?"

"We found a guy at Twelfth and Avenue A. Don't know who he is. No identification. He was shot in the stomach and died on the operating table. We got no witnesses."

So what do I got? I got nothing. If I caught it right from the get-go, there'd still be people out there in the street. Next day, you're out there at eight o'clock in the morning, everybody's gone.

We don't know who this guy is, so I go to the hospital and ask, "Was anybody up to see this guy?" You'll have some young rookies or inexperienced guys that might have let some family up there to see the victim and didn't notify you. Or let them leave and didn't ask if they had names. But nobody came to see him.

So I still don't know who the guy is, much less why he was killed. Was it a robbery? Was it a drug deal?

So we go to the scene and we talk to some people. There's an after-hours joint right around the corner, so maybe he went in there. We go in. People are looking at us. We go into the back room. What do the people think? They think you're getting paid off, of course. Everybody's saying, "Look at the cops in here. But they're not closing the place up. They must be on the pad." I don't want to close this place up. There's a potential witness in here to a murder. You are all my friends now.

Talking to one of the guys that ran the club and he says, "Yeah, I heard this guy was shot. His name was Clive."

"What do you know about it?"

"He sells cheba down on Ninth and Avenue A."

"Yet he's killed up here."

"Aw, I heard he ran up from there." Now we got a direction. Maybe he wasn't killed here. Maybe he was shot downtown.

The owner drops a name of a guy on us that carries a .22 and Clive was supposedly shot with a small-caliber gun. When I hear the name, it didn't click with me. I go to a couple of guys I know in the neighborhood and knock on their doors and say, "This is what I got. What can you get for me?" Send them on their little missions. Problem is, if I was the FBI, I could lay a C-note on one of these guys and he'd work for me the rest of his life. I can't give him nothing but five or ten bucks out of my pocket. I got to make my own mortgage.

Then I get a call and I'm talking to one of my stoolies. He says, "You know that guy with the .22 you're looking for? You just grabbed him last year." Then it clicked, "Yeah, I know him." I found him, went to his apart‑ment and started talking to him. He turned me on to a couple of other guys who might be connected. It's like a patchwork. You get some information here, then you jump over there.

I couldn't just send those two guys out and then wait for them to come back with the information, because I'd still be sitting there. I grabbed somebody off the street that deals there, dragged him in the car, brought him to the office. I told him I was going to make his life miserable and ruin his business forever and all of these horrendous things I was going to do to him unless he came up with some information for me.

"But I wasn't there," he says.

"Yeah, but you know, because you're out there all the time."

"No, I didn't see it go down. I heard from this guy Jimmy that was there."

The information is coming in from all around now. I get a phone call. "Hey, the guy, Jimmy, that was on the block when it went down is there now." Gave me a description of Jimmy. It's funny, a guy can give you any description—"He's wearing pink sneakers and a red shirt and a red hat with a feather in it"—you go down and there's twelve guys there look like that. It just seems to be that way.

Finally, I go up to Jimmy and—swoosh!—snatch him off the street. He don't know what he's going in for. Bring him in and tell him all this crap. He's not very cooperative. After talking to him for a while, he says, "You got it wrong. I wasn't there, but I know somebody who was there." Which turned out to be the truth as much as I sat there and said, "Aw, you're full of shit."

"The guy was leaning out the window," Jimmy says. "When I got there everything was finished, but this guy was leaning out the window and he was telling me, 'Yeah, a guy just got shot over a girlfriend.' He told me the whole story."

"What's this guy look like?" And he gave me the description. "Will you tell me which window he was leaning out of?" We took him down there on the QT and he pointed out the window.

So the next move is that we do a canvass of all the buildings in that area and see if any witnesses show up. That day in the tenements, it was so hot, it was almost like water in the hallways it was so thick.

We went to this one building there. It had only one apartment on each floor with real short hallways. Hot as hell. I'm knocking on the first floor. Man comes to the door with two Chihuahuas—yap-yap-yap-yap-yap. Go to the second floor—one Chihuahua. Third floor—another Chihuahua. My partner says, "Hey, instead of cockroaches, they got Chihuahuas in this building."

I'm up on the top floor. I knock on the door and this lady answers. I says, "Where's your Chihuahua?"

The lady looks at me. "What are you talking about?" she says.

"You got to have a Chihuahua to live in this building. It's in your lease."

We go up one tenement and if the door was unlocked, we'd go across the roof and down through the next one. Just me and one other guy. We did four buildings. I'm coming down near my potential witness. Figuring from the windows, he's in the apartment just below me. So we knock on this door. "We're the police. We'd like to speak to you. Did you hear anything the other night about one A.M.?" Finally I ask, "Who lives below you?"

"Oh, that's my brother-in-law."

"What's his name?" He gives me the name.

"He mentioned that he heard a shot," this guy says. "They're going to Pennsylvania today. They probably left already."

So I go down below and knock on the door. I always pull a weird act with people in the streets anyway. I always come in with my left hand and do a little circus act, so they don't know what the hell's going on. The guy comes to the door and I say, "How come you're not in Pennsylvania? Aren't you running late?" He looks at me totally confused. I tell him who I am and everything and then I says, "You know what I'm here for, right?" And he told me the whole story.

He was in the street and saw the whole thing go down. Legitimate guy. He worked. His wife was there and we're playing with the baby. Before I left, I got his work number, his telephone number there at home, where his mother lived, date of birth, everything. In case he suddenly no longer existed at that address, I could hopefully still track him down.

Anyway, I found out that the guy who did it lived over a barbershop a few blocks away. What happened was, Clive was selling smoke. He was trying to sell smoke to this particular girl. The girl wasn't going along with it, so he said, "To hell with it, I'll take your chains." So he ripped off her jewelry.

Turns out that she runs a drug operation—the heavy stuff—on Eleventh Street and Avenue C. They have a lot of girls working for them now. She went back and told her little Al Capone—I don't know if it's her relative or her boyfriend—"Ah, this guy ripped off my gold chains." She then went back to the scene with this guy to point out the smoke salesman.

That area, it's like Mexico. Ever been to Tiajuana or Juarez? "Hey, you want this?" "You want to buy that?" You can buy anything down there. Little Al Capone says he wants to see Clive. The smoke salesman on the street says, "Hey, I got the same stuff Clive's got."

"No, Clive gives me a better play than you."

"I'll give you the same play."

"No, I want to see Clive, man, you know."

When he saw Clive, he just lit him up and walked away. The next day the broad comes back and brags about it on that same damn corner. She went into where they have a few little video games and started bull-shitting, "I told that guy who ripped me off of my chains that I wasn't going to chase no dead man."

I have a legitimate woman in there that heard her say those things, so now I got two legitimate witnesses.

I got two other guys who were there and saw the thing, but they're petrified to testify, because they're drug dealers. These guys are punks that sell smoke. They'll gorilla you, maybe, but they're not tough guys. Let's face it, this girl comes right back to the situation where they're selling drugs and starts selling wolf tickets and they don't do nothing about it. These guys are punks. But she's coming from a group of heavy hitters. They've been involved in a couple of other homicides I had over there.

On the QT my people are going to find out her little Al Capone's name and bring it to me. The next thing you do is a photo array. I show my witnesses six photos and hope they pick out this guy. Once they pick the guy out, maybe they'll pick out the girl from photos.

I'll do a back history on these people, get as much information on them as I can, and then just snap them up.

I would like to snap the girl up first, hoping that she's going to puke up her guts. Or if not have them both in at the same time and play them off.

"You know she told me about the gold chains."

"That bitch."

Just give them so much information. Sometimes it works, sometimes it doesn't. That's the interesting part. When you interrogate somebody, it's all an act. You go in and say something off the wall to like relax them. Or maybe you just leave them in there for a couple of hours. Then you come in and say, "Hi, how you doing?" Walk out. Come back later, you say, "Can you stand over here for a minute?" You take them over to the mirrored window. "Now turn around and look this way. Okay, go sit down." Mind games. It's all mind games.

Years ago a cop probably could have beat the bejesus out of them until he got a confession. You can't any more. The laws are so ridiculous as far as the protection of the suspect. For example, I bring you in. I think you murdered somebody. I advise you of your rights with the Miranda warnings. It's like telling you, "Don't tell me nothing, man. Don't talk to me. What are you, crazy? I'm your brother and I'm telling you, don't talk to me. I'm trying to put you in jail, you dope."

I tell you this. Now I got to get you to talk to me. If you say one simple thing to me—"I want my attorney"—that is the end of everything. Now I got to take you and put you back in the cage.

An hour later, you get pangs of conscience, "Hey, can I talk to you for a minute? I want to tell you everything. I want to confess."

You can't even confess to me now. Unless a lawyer comes and agrees. And then if the lawyer agrees, some judge is going to say that the lawyer wasn't competent and throw out the case.

So you play these games with them. I advise them of their rights. After I do that, I don't go into the interrogation right away. I'll ask them something stupid to get their mind off what I just told them. Something really dumb, depending on the person. "Did you see that fight last night? Leonard really nailed him, didn't he?"

*

I've spent thousands of hours sitting and waiting. Sometimes based on a tip, but more often than not based on a probability. That's bullshit. That's like playing the big number in the lottery. The bosses say, "They been taking off Colonel Sanders all over the city. The chances are that this one will be hit." So you set up for two weeks and you sit and wait and wait and wait and wait and wait.

To pass the time, we look at women a lot if we're in the right neighborhood. We look at the women and make remarks. Not very gentlemanly remarks, but no one is listening. We score them. If they could hear us, they wouldn't appreciate it. But what else is there to do? You can't read a book.

Usually, one of us is going through some kind of marital problems. We'll hash that over for a few hours. We will try to think up every which way the robbery could go down. Try to plan for every contingency. How to cover all the bases.

You don't know what you're looking for. You don't know what kind of car they're driving. You just know how they're going to take it down when they do go in. Hopefully, you can see inside the store with your binoculars—if you're not sleeping.

It's just so boring, it will drive you crazy. You're sitting there with your partner and you start to get into an argument, for no reason. You been on this thing for two weeks. It is not glamorous. There's nothing glamorous about the job until the shit goes down and then it's not glamorous either.

The biggest fear that I have is not about getting killed. It's taking this guy off without hurting anybody else and not letting him get away. Mostly not hurting anybody else. But it happens so fast that you almost miss it every time. Once you collect yourself and figure out that it is—in fact—going down, it's almost over. Your decision to shoot or not to shoot is like a split second. There are so many things that can happen in the meantime.

This is what scares me the most: What's going to happen this time? Will it go all right or am I going to hit some innocent person? Am I going to make the wrong decision? Or will I make the decision to shoot when it's not appropriate, when the guy really doesn't have a gun? That's almost happened a half-dozen times. The hammer's been coming back and the guy doesn't have a gun. He's got something in his hand, but he doesn't have a gun. That absolutely scares me to death.

We did a seven-week stakeout in a Kentucky Fried Chicken joint. We were wearing the red shirts and red bow ties and we're packing the chicken in boxes. We got so good at it that the manager wanted to pay us while we were in the store. He didn't know what to do with his employees, because we were really efficient. We never caught anybody. We'd be sitting in this place with a little radio and one of us would have an earphone on. They'd go and knock off the one a few blocks away. Frustration.

Another time, a few days before Christmas, Alcohol, Tobacco and Firearms called our robbery squad. They had an informant who said that a supermarket was going to get held up. Two or three blacks were going to do it and they had gotten hold of a machine gun. That raised eyebrows. We worked it for the first night with ATF. They were sitting in their car in the parking lot and we were sitting in ours. Of course, nothing happened, which is the way it usually is.

The weekend rolled along. They went on their weekend—that's how much store they put in their informant. But we stayed on it. In a car, we had to sit so far off we had to use binoculars to see. So we went and borrowed this old van from narcotics. Now we can be up on the lot, right by the front door. There was a glass front all across the supermarket, so we had quite a view.

I was flat on my back bitching. It was closing time and the manager had shut off the automatic opener on the pneumatic door that goes into the store. We were just about to pack up our shotguns and put them back in their cases. My partner is sitting at the wheel and he looks out this little side window and says, "Hey, buddy, this guy sitting in a car right here just tucked a gun in his belt."

"Fuck you, asshole," I said. I didn't believe him. But I got up, since he did have a little bit of urgency in his voice. This guy gets out of his car and walks towards the store. He pulls open the door and all of a sudden you see the security guard's hands go up inside.

Meanwhile, in the car which had been sitting right beside us, there was a second guy. He rolls the car right up in front, opens the door and jumps out with what looks like a fucking Thompson. Have you ever seen one of those with the canister? Jesus Christ. It turns out that it is not an authentic Thompson, but it was a damn good representative. The same configuration—semi-automatic, a 40-round clip with .45-caliber ammunition which can go right through them dinky vests they give us. Suddenly, you see sixteen people, all their heads disappear. He's put them all down on the floor.

It's my son's second Christmas and I'm thinking about him. And I do not want to get out of this van. I'm really upset by that Thompson. I didn't like that. I said, "Somebody's going to get hurt out here. I don't think there is any way to avoid it." I got my shotgun and I chambered a round. There's not cars anywhere to hide behind and we can't hide behind the van in the position that it's in. So we're just kind of standing out there in the middle of the fucking parking lot.

Right before these guys are coming back out, a whole car load of people rolls up in an old Chevy, apparently to pick up an employee, one of the cashiers. I wave and shout, "Get the fuck out of here!" They're looking at us with that dumb look that people give you when you shout at them. We're standing there with shotguns and wearing our baseball caps and screaming at them. Finally the guy puts it in drive and gets out of the way.

No sooner did they get out of the way than these guys are coming out the door. The guy with the Thompson is in the lead, he comes out the door and he's looking right dead at us. One of us yelled, "Freeze, motherfucker!"

He's got the gun cradled like he's Machinegun Kelly. He thinks that he's the baddest thing that ever hit the road. He's strutting. He all of a sudden saw us and he brought it up. I waxed him. I said to myself, "Fuck it. If he gets a burst off, we're all going to get it." Right behind us there is an entire apartment complex and a four-lane main drive.

I went, Boom! He took off running like a jackrabbit. Now, I've got a shotgun full of 00 buck which is the equivalent of nine .32-caliber slugs all at once and he took off running. We're all following him in our sights and thank God it's all bricks down through there. You can see the powder coming off the brick wall as the shots hit behind him one after the other. He's going 90 miles an hour. Finally, he goes down.

The second guy has a gun in each hand. He's got the security guard's gun and his own gun. He's got the cash drawer balanced on his forearms in front of him. He caught one of the 00 bucks right in the spine and went down immediately. The other guy had taken all the rest in the heart from the first shot and still made that run. The autopsy showed it. It's scary. You been watching cop shows all your life and you think when you shoot these people, they're supposed to fall down. They don't do it.

The one guy died. The other guy lived and he's in the penitentiary. He's filed a $7 million lawsuit against us as well as a homicide sergeant that put some nasty things about him in the newspapers. He's suing us for violation of his civil rights.

I want the city to go to federal court and say, "Dismiss this. It's a frivolous lawsuit." They won't do it. So we're just sitting around with it hanging over our heads.

I didn't feel bad about any of that. I had an appointment with the police shrink two days after it happened because my wife and I were going through some serious marital difficulties. I walked in his office and he said, "Well, well. Haven't we been busy? I've been reading about you in the papers again. How do you feel?"

"I'm a little upset, Doc, because I don't feel bad at all."

"That's okay," he said. "From what I read in the paper you don't need to feel bad at all." And I didn't. I was just glad to be home on Christmas Day.

A female news commentator on the local news while covering the story said, "They gunned him down without letting him fire a single shot." They had pictures of the rescue squad working this guy over. Then they had a picture of them putting the white sheet over him. There it is.

*

We had a robbery. Three people are coming out into the parking lot of a restaurant in a real nice area and they're held up by a black male and a white male. They saw a female driver of the getaway car. They describe the getaway car and they had written down the license plate number. We run the vehicle registration on the car and it comes back to an address not too far away. We put out the description of the car and the suspects that the victims had given us.

So they staked out the address that the car came from. The people who were staking the place out were undercover, junkie-looking plainclothes officers. Sure enough, here comes the car. The officers come up and yell at the people to freeze. The people dive to the floor of the car. The officers think they are going for guns. One of the officers smashes out the window of the car. They get them out at gunpoint.

They call us on the radio that they've got our crooks in custody. So we took the victims and we drive to the area. We're going into this real nice residential area. I'm thinking, "Wow, this doesn't look right."

We get there and the victims say, "That's the car. That's the car." They've got the two people there who are saying, "We live here." The suspects are a middle-class couple. The guy is an attorney. His wife is a school-teacher. These are not your typical robbery suspects.

The victims say, "She was the driver of the getaway car." So we take the man and woman down to the station. I talk to the man. He is a prominent local lawyer. His story is that they had dinner at the same restaurant as the victims. They came out, got into their car, went to one other place and came home. When they arrive at their driveway, all these people are pointing guns at them and he said, "We didn't think they were cops. We thought we were being held up."

We piece it together. When the victims were held up, the robbers ran around and away from them. The first car that just seconds later came by the victims, in their minds, these were the crooks. The robbers had run right by these other people in the dark as they were getting into their car. The victims were scared. It's scary when somebody sticks a gun in your face. So we've got three people saying, "We were robbed." And they were. "These are the people who robbed us."

The two people are saying, "Hey, we didn't rob anybody or do anything."

Here we are. We've done everything right. We responded. We got the victims. We broadcast everything they told us. The officers got the information and they stake out the house. They see the people. Those men were working under the assumption that these were armed robbers. The people go down to the floor, so the cops break out the window of the car. Handcuff the two of them.

So here's this mess and as the police officer you've got to unravel it. You realize that there was a mistake made by the victims—an honest mistake, because they really believed what they said. It wasn't a lie or malicious. Basically what we did was unarrested the people. Technically it's a form. We talked to them at length to explain what had happened because they felt like they were being terrorized for no reason. Nothing is quite what it seems. They'll probably sue.

*

The kid went missing Tuesday. I'd taken off Monday, Tuesday and Wednesday. Thursday morning when I came back to work, I said, "Is that kid still missing? I read something about it in the paper."

"Yeah," the guy I work for says. "I want you to go up to the golf course behind the kid's house and lead the civilian search party. Check the golf course very thoroughly. There's going to be some Civil Air Patrol kids there."

I get out there at nine o'clock in the morning, me and my search parties. I send them out to look over the first hole, seventh hole, the ninth hole and out they go. They come back about two hours later to the staging area. Didn't find anything.

"What are you going to do now?" says this deputy there.

"We're going to get something to eat and see what's up next."

"Okay," he says, "but they're getting a little hinky downtown. You better bring the search parties back after they eat and look over the golf course again."

"Hey, I just did that. And they did it the day before and the day before that."

"But this is the spot the kid was last seen, that's where he's missing from."

Okay. But this time when I go back, I grab a golf cart. I go out onto the golf course myself and just try to familiarize myself with how the kid got onto the golf course from the housing area where he lives. I get out of the golf cart and walk up the path toward the housing area. I see two older women standing outside and I ask them, "Can you tell me where the missing boy lives?"

They said yes they could. They were his aunts. I made sure they'd checked out his house real good, under the beds and things. Then I told them, "I've been off for the last few days and I just came on this morning. I just want to familiarize myself with the location and how the boy would enter the golf course."

One of the aunts says to me, "You go right down by Gerald's house."

"Who's Gerald?"

"He's the boy Jimmy had an argument with the other day."

"About what?" It seems that Gerald had accused Jimmy of stealing his pocket knife. "Oh, did you tell the other officers about this?" She said no. So I was going down toward the house and she says, "There goes Gerald."

I was calling him. I says, "Gerald!" He stopped. I looked at him and I said, "Weren't you in one of the search parties this morning at the golf course?"

"Yeah," he says.

"What are you doing now?"

"I came home," he said, "to change my shoes. My feet got soaking wet this morning."

"Yeah, mine, too. They're still soaking. Did you know Jimmy?"

"Yes, sir, I did."

"Did you have an argument with him?"

"Yeah, Billy told me that he stole my pocket knife."

"Oh, yeah? What'd you do?"

"Well, I got upset."

"How about Jimmy? Was Jimmy upset?"

"Yeah," he says, "Jimmy was upset, too."

"So what happened then?"

"I invited him to my house to play my Atari."

"What happened then?"

"Well, I took a shower."

"You what? At three o'clock in the afternoon?"

"Yeah, well," he says, "when I sweat, I take showers."

"Would you mind coming out and checking the woods with me? Just you and I?"

"Oh, yeah, sure."

A thirteen-year-old kid playing with a five- or six-year-old kid, I knew something was wrong here. So I started talking to him and come to find out this kid is almost a genius, loves computers, does very well in school, but emotionally couldn't get along with his peers, so he plays with little kids.

I got on the radio and I called this other sergeant that works with me and I said, "Get over here, I think I got something."

"What do you got?"

"I'm not sure. I just feel like I got something."

I go out in the woods with this kid. I asked him if he ever came out into the woods with Jimmy. He showed me all their clubs and forts in the trees and rocks and stuff like that. I figure the little son of a bitch has got the boy stashed out here someplace. You know, they were out playing in the woods. The little boy fell. This one panicked and he buried him.

He's talking to me and I've got this feeling that this kid is close to insane. I say to him, "Wouldn't it be nice if we found Jimmy in one of these clubs. Maybe he hurt himself and we could help him. At the worst, if he got killed, we could take care of his body and make sure he got a proper burial."

"That would be nice," he said, "but I hope we don't find him."

"Why?"

"Because I don't like blood."

Oh, Jesus, it's getting better. I get called on the radio, "Do you still have that kid there? Well, come on back." When I got him back, the sergeant says, "We got a phone call. Somebody saw this boy hit Jimmy."

"Shit," I said, "what are we going to do?"

"We'll search his house."

"But his mother's not home."

"How do you know?"

"He told me."

"Well, we'll wait." Just then the mother pulls up.

This sergeant went up to ask her if they could go in. I went back to the staging area to tell my boss what was going on.

"You stay here. I'll go down to the house," he tells me. Ah, shit. All day in the fucking woods and now I miss the most important part.

Sure as shit, my boss and the sergeant go into the house with the mother and the kid and they start searching the house. They go up to the kid's bedroom. The sergeant is in the bedroom all alone and he sees a plastic bag up on the top shelf of the closet, so he grabs it. But it's . . . cold. He takes it off the shelf and opens it up and there's all the fucking kid's clothes, his sneakers and socks, his underwear and a vest he was wearing. "Holy shit," he says to himself, "he's buried him in the backyard."

But he goes ahead and looks in the closet. The closet is filled half way up the wall, but in an orderly fashion. The sergeant is kind of a ferret. He just doesn't stop on the surface. He starts digging and digging. All of a sudden he gets to this plastic bag. He puts his hand on the plastic bag and it gives. "Jesus Christ, he's in the fucking bag. He's in the fucking bag!" My boss couldn't believe it. So they slit open the bag and sure enough the kid is in the bag. They grabbed Gerald and got him the fuck out of there.

I come back down from the command post. I couldn't stay up there any fucking longer. The medical examiner shows up and pulls the kid out of the bag. The sergeant just kept telling me, "He was in the fucking bag." He had trouble dealing with it. I wasn't there for the actual discovery, so I could handle it a little better.

I felt good that I'd been instrumental in finding the body. Had that kid got the bag out to the dumpster, we would have never broken that case. The only reason he didn't put the kid into the dumpster right away was that it was too full to get the trash bag in. It was a tragedy, but at least I helped put an ending on it and that satisfied me.

*

This guy lived in an apartment that looked like a submarine. There was just like a trail through all this shit to a clearing over here and a bed you wouldn't let a dog sleep in. He strangled this girl that he used to hang around with.

First, we go to the apartment and the guy said the girl OD'd. She's in the bed in the back room with all this shit. Lividity is all set in. Lividity is all the blood in your body, because of gravity, will settle in you and make all the down side look like a bruise, like you were beat to hell on that side of you. You could die of a heart attack, say, and if you were laying on your face, your whole face would look like you was bludgeoned. You can lose blood from your mouth and your nose. It'll break and go on the floor, so it looks like you were assaulted instead of died of natural causes. If you get shot and you die right away, you don't bleed. What pumps it out is your heart. If your heart stops right away, all the blood is left inside you. Anyway, lividity had set in and you couldn't really tell if she was assaulted or whatever. We've actually had a medical examiner come look at a body and say it looks like an overdose when in reality the guy took a round in the face. Now if he can miss it, we could miss it.

The guy claims that she OD'd. When anybody dies in the precinct, we got to respond. OD is considered natural causes in this precinct. She was sent up to the morgue and they did an autopsy on her. They found out that a bone was broken in the neck that would only result from strangulation. That's what they told us: She was strangled.

All right, we go back. Charlie is the guy's name.

"Come on, Charlie, want to talk to us?" We bring Charlie back to the station house.

The guy I work with, it was his case. This guy is good, but he's like electric. There's a bulge in his eye. Wow! When he comes into a room, it like lights up. He's like "Brrrrrrr!"

Charlie is talking to the Electric Man and he's keeping up with the story, "Oh, she overdosed. Blah-blah-blah-blah." Electric Man finally goes, "DON'T HAND ME THAT!" He like explodes in the office, you know?

The problem with that is that Charlie is the only person that we have. That tactic could either work or it's not going to work. You explode and the guy might say, "Whoa, I ain't saying nothing, man, because now you're not believing me."

Electric Man exploded all over the room. There was no recovery. Now Charlie is like, "What? What happened? We were friends before." This guy is like shrapnel all over the room and Charlie is really upset. "Now, I don't know if I want to talk to you guys any more. I mean, if you're not going to be friendly and nice I just don't think I want to talk to you at all." But he's babbling on. Charlie's been shooting speed so long, Electric Man just blew a fuse in his head. "Arrgh. You're not believing this story now? I thought this story was so good. You were buying this only *two seconds ago.* Now you're calling me a liar."

Electric Man leaves the room. I go back into Charlie and he's talking to his left, talking to his right, talking to the ceiling, talking to the floor. Talking about everything that comes into his head, all over the highway. "I don't know what he's yelling at me for. I didn't do nothing to him. How come he don't like me any more?" All this unnecessary shit.

"Let's get back to *her,*" I say. I grabbed his face, one cheek in each hand. We're nose to nose across the table and I say, "Now, talk to me." It's like talking to a little kid, a two-year-old. But I seemed to have his attention.

Finally, he says, "Look, to tell you the truth, she didn't OD. She hung herself. That's right. She hung herself. We had an argument and all this stuff and I went to another part of the apartment. When I came back in the room she was hanging by the *neck*. By a *rope*. In the doorway."

I just kept saying, "Go on. Go on, Charlie." He's going through this whole thing. I says, "All right, if that's the truth, there's nothing wrong with that. We go back to the apartment and you can show us the rope and show us where she hung herself. Everything will be okay."

So we go back into this pile of refuse, just garbage, and he's rumbling through it. Digging and digging. He's probably saying to himself, "There's got to be some rope here somewhere." He keeps going through the trash and he finally comes up with some rope. "Hey, here's the rope."

"Oh, good. Bring it over here. Where did you say she hung herself?" The Electric Man gets up there on a chair where the rope would hang. There's dust an inch deep all the way across. You don't have to be Mr. Moto to tell this is bullshit. But he's saying, "Okay, yeah, yeah." We have the guys from the crime lab come down and they're taking photos. This goes on and on.

Finally we go back to the medical examiner himself and speak to him, "How could this have resulted, from a rope?"

"No, that was the result of thumbs, had to be," the M.E. says. That little shit. Charlie's lying again. We bring him back. "Charlie, Charlie, she didn't die from a rope."

"What do you mean?" he says.

The case is still in court. Charlie didn't confess. How he could have beat the whole case was simple. They used the apartment as a shooting gallery. People paid to go in there and shoot up. He could have said, "Yeah, she was there and she shot up and went into the bed. Then I left and went and shot pool someplace. When I came back, the door was open and there she was. I thought she'd OD'd." Then what do we do? We got nothing.

But Charlie couldn't think of that stuff. He thought, "I think I'll hang her from the ceiling. I *saw* her hanging from the ceiling." The guy is unfortunately stupid. But, hey, he did find a rope.

*

Every now and then in the decoy section, you want a woman victim, so we have to dress up one of the guys. He is drafted to be the woman. The guys outsmarted me at first. They started growing mustaches. Before long, they all had one, so I had to draw the line. Somebody has got to cut their mustache off.

I can see Jimmy Rain right now. He was dressed up as a little old lady down on Main Street one night. The thing about teenage kids, fifteen or sixteen years old, is when they grab the money, they run. The guy they steal from can be passed out cold, but they're going to run when they get it from him. The older ones get the money and then walk on off and you don't normally have to chase them.

Here's Jimmy Rain dressed up like a little old lady with a purse. These two young guys grabbed his purse and took off running down Main Street. I can see him right now with that dress up over his knees just barreling down the middle of the street with traffic stopping in both directions.

Later on that same night, we were down in the park where we'd had some complaints. Jimmy had his dress on and he's walking through. We had him bugged with a radio. He was telling us what he could see as he went along. "I'm about in the middle of the park and there's one old drunk vagrant just bullying the hell out of another one, beating on him for no reason at all," he says. Jimmy, dressed up like this little old lady, walks up to this drunk and just backhands him right onto his backside and says, "Behave yourself." Then just walked right on off.

*

I had been working with my informant, George, for a long time. And I started to trust him. At Christmastime I did a little something for George. His old lady got sick and had to have an operation, I took care of her moneywise. I got very cozy with them. George didn't get as cozy as I did. I was a fool and I trusted him.

George comes up to me and he says, "Listen, man, I got a buy and it's an ounce buy."

"Well," I say, "that's okay, not bad, better than a couple of cheap-o bags. Cool."

George knew me well. He says, "The only thing is, man, we got to cop it in the crib."

"No way, you're out of your fucking gourd. I'm not going in no fucking sleaze bag apartment to cop a lousy ounce. You might as well just put a tag on my toe and ship me to the morgue. That's a setup. Bad news."

Now I should have started to suspect something. Hey, George don't like to work and all of a sudden he's hammering me into this deal. He says, "Well, man, I know it's only an ounce and you don't dig the apartment, but the truth is he won't deal any other way. And if you bust this cat, oddly enough, he's a direct link from ounces right to keys. You can turn him." I was greedy so I went against my better judgment. I said, "Sure, we'll bust him. Why not?" You cannot make mistakes like that in police work, particularly in the narcotics trade.

I put a wire on. The device allows me to broadcast, but I can't hear anything from them; therefore I'm never really sure that the fucker's working. We've tested it, but mechanical things are so unreliable, usually when you need them the most. My backup team is a bunch of jerks and they're half a block away in a van. The idea is, if they hear that it's going down bad or if they don't hear anything at all, they will come busting in after me because the safety of the officer is supposed to be foremost in their minds. They were a couple of assholes who could have cared shit less about me.

I go into the stupid buy and the shit starts right from the get-go. We start up the stairs and George tells me it's the fourth floor; then he changes it to the fifth. As we're arguing and walking up, he keeps getting in back of me and lagging. I'm grabbing him and pushing him in front of me. The fuck don't want to go up. It was only about two floors up and we got to a landing and some fucking guy comes out with a .45. It was a setup. The fucking guy, George, set me up. I couldn't believe it.

For some shitass reason I had this little .25 automatic hidden down in this like jockstrap. All I remember is trying to get into my fucking pants and he was shooting. That was a very bad situation that seems to be going by very slowly, when in fact it all happened within a matter of seconds. Come to find out he took seven at me. There were holes in the walls and in the floor next to me. It stopped because I was unloaded and he was dead. I had no more and everything stopped. Then I heard sirens and my fucking partners hadn't even gotten there. The uniforms responded.

I didn't want to kill that guy. I did want to kill George. While I was on the floor I didn't think, "I could die." I thought, "George, you motherfucker, you set me up." But the fucker got out.

*

At the beginning, I thought it was great. I was chosen secretively out of this organization to be one of the guys who was going to work this undercover job. I thought that was fantastic.

I leave the station in the middle of the night. A call came from headquarters saying, "A sergeant is to stay on the desk and everybody else is to be out for whatever reason. Mitchell is going to leave the station and he's not going to sign out."

I just left. My uniform is there, I'm gone. A couple of days later a personnel memo came down, saying I had resigned from the state police. I'm no longer a member. A follow-up order went right into the commander's safe and the attorney general's safe saying that the first memo was not true, that I'd gone for an undercover job.

So now there was the whole question about where did I go? Why did I resign, and all that stuff? It was kind of funny, like being at your own funeral. People that I thought were my friends start bad-mouthing me. Prior to going undercover, I took two weeks vacation and went to Florida. So the rumor said that when I was in Florida, I got in trouble. I stabbed a broad or slapped her around. Because my old man had been on the job and was a lieutenant, they covered it up, but they told me to resign. Now, can you imagine who the fuck made this story up? Where did it come from? Unbelievable.

An undercover guy pretty much does what he wants; nobody bosses you around. The first six months, I thought it was glamorous. I grew a beard, I wore shitty clothes, I didn't look like a cop. I didn't even look like the people I'm working with. I'm working with the Mob. It took me six months to realize what was going on. Nobody was walking around with long hair and a beard. They got three-piece suits and fancy shirts, silk ties.

We're making cases, but it's starting to get long—a year and a half. Several times I think that they're going to wind it up and then they change their minds. They say, "Let's go a little bit longer." The target date keeps getting extended. I didn't know there was an end.

We're doing some deals with some pretty high-level organized crime figures in the state and around the country. For instance, I would fly to Florida and have lunch with them. Pretty big-time guys, the kiss on the cheek and the whole bit.

In undercover work you come from this world of black and white into a world of "We don't give a fuck and whatever happens, happens." You're living like that and it's crazy. I never carried a gun when I was undercover. You only carried a gun when you wanted to do business with it. That's a very disrespectful thing to do, carry a weapon into a meeting. Among criminals, they have their own code of ethics. If you and I are going to sit down and do a deal of stolen merchandise or dope and we're just in the talking stages of it, why do I need to have a gun at the table? I am either a cop or extremely paranoid about my own survival or I'm out to do something to you. Then nobody will deal with me and how am I going to make my money? So that's the reason why you don't carry that weapon.

I'm wearing this recorder between my legs. I know they'd kill you in a minute. There's nothing on me that says that I'm a cop. I'm there by myself. My nerves are really up. I'm starting to get to where I can't keep a meal down. I would eat with them and I'd be all right there with them. But when I would leave, twenty minutes later, I would be throwing my guts up on the side of the road. I started to feel these chest pains. I really felt like I was having a heart attack. I would have diarrhea on a daily basis.

I go to this doctor that I'd known since I was a kid. That seemed safe. He checks me out on an EKG. He says, "I don't really see anything wrong with you. A little overweight, maybe. Are you under a lot of stress?"

I started spilling my guts, because I had to talk to

somebody. I'm really acting stupid. He writes this thing down on a piece of paper from his prescription pad that due to excessive stress it might be necessary for Officer Mitchell to change his position in the state police.

Now I got this little piece of paper. Like a little kid, I go to my sergeant on the undercover gig the next day and say, "I went to the doc and he wrote this down for you." I figure this is it. I have a note from the doctor saying I'm under stress, too much stress. They'll have to let me out of this job.

He laughs. I say, "What are you laughing about?"

"We got a million dollars wrapped up in this. You're not physically hurt. You're going through stress. You'll be all right. You can handle it." That's the mentality of cops: You can handle anything. Don't worry about it, kid, you can handle it. I was devastated.

But finally when he gave me a real ending date, it got all right. There's a goal line. It will be over soon. Then I was fine again.

The big day arrives. We go to the National Guard Armory that day at four o'clock in the morning. We're going to lock up like twenty-eight mob figures in the state, then it was going to expand from there, once the investigation went to the grand jury. There's one hundred FBI agents, two hundred uniform troopers there when I walk in. Law enforcement up the ass. I think this is going to be the greatest day of my life. After two and a half years, I'm finally coming back, the prodigal son.

I'm one of the main figures in the investigation, so I'm standing there next to all these people. We're supposed to get ready for this big press conference on the big raid. I don't have anything in common with them. They're the people I say yes sir and no sir to, that I have a military-like relationship that goes on between us, but it's no more than that. They don't come from my world and I don't belong in theirs. I wasn't able to sit with the troopers either. Nobody that looked like

me was with the troopers. Those guys are turning, looking at me, pointing, but nobody is waving.

They start bringing in the defendants. They've picked
them up and arrested them at their house. The armory
is going to be the processing site. I was supposed to
interview some of them. It would be a real shock value
with me interviewing them. Maybe they would turn over
quicker.

I go downstairs and they're ready to fingerprint them.
The troopers standing around, they think it's great. I
thought it was going to be great, too. But I felt like the
biggest cocksucker in the world. What a fucking bum.

I'm coming in, wearing a three-piece suit. My hands
were behind my back. One of the guys says, "What did
they pinch you for?"

"I'm with them," I said.

"You cocksucker," he says, and then he spit. They
were just looking at me. I couldn't even look these guys
in the eyes. Here's guys I hung out with, guys I broke
bread with. I really came to like some of them. And
they liked me, trusted me.

One guy comes up to me and says, "How could you
do this, Ben? You're my friend. How could you do
this?" He was sixty some years old. He was like anybody's grandfather, a nice guy, but he dealt in stolen
securities. That's what we locked him up for. He put a
heavy guilt trip on me. I couldn't look at him. I had to
put my head down.

I'm not in the troopers' group any longer and the
friends that I've had for the past two and a half years
I've just delivered into the enemy's hands. So now even
the bad guys have told me I'm no good. I felt like a
piece of shit. I felt bad and I had problems for a while.
I never verbalized it, but I would have problems in my
mind, being a stool pigeon.

Undercover is a very strange way to do police work,
because you identify with them, the bad guys. It's a

strange feeling to be trusted by somebody and then betray them. I knew this one guy whose kid was retarded. A lot of the money he was using for special schools for his kid. I know it was stolen money. But I also knew he wasn't going out whoring it. He was a family guy. How he put the bread on the table was by stealing. He was paying a lot of money out for his retarded son to be educated enough to just feed himself.

I've thought of those people on Christmas morning when I wake up. I thought, "Those kids' fathers aren't home because of me. I got that guy in trouble."

On the other end of the coin, I've got to say, "Hey, you're a cop. That's what you were told to do and that is what your assignment was. Maybe through conventional means of police work, we would have never gotten these people. And anyway, what they did was wrong." Boy, it can get gray out there.

It's difficult because you've come too close to the defendant. It's a lot nicer not knowing anything about their personal life. It doesn't make a difference on the criminal act that they did. But when you don't know their personal life, you just go in, put the bracelets on them and you take them away. It's very neatly defined. The job's over. They're the bad guys and we're the good guys. In undercover work it is not neatly defined, because personalities come into it. Just because a guy's a criminal doesn't mean you can't like him and that he doesn't have the same interest as you do. They have company softball teams and wives and girlfriends. They drink beer and go fishing.

They live in a very treacherous world. Everybody says, "They're so tough, these criminals in the mob." I don't see anything tough about shooting a guy in the back of the head. I don't see anything tough about setting a guy up in the middle of the night when he comes out of his house and four guys open up on him.

That's tough? No. That's a difference in morality, if you're able to do that and live with yourself.

A tough guy to me is a guy that says, "Ben, I don't like you, I never liked you and I'm going to take you out in the parking lot now and clean your clock." And he does it. That's a tough guy. What's so tough about saying, "We're going to dinner tonight." Somebody picks you up. Now you're sitting in the front seat and the guy pulls the trigger from the backseat.

*

Vice is a strange part of the job. It's basically a lot of people doing what they want to do. But you have to draw the line somewhere and it's not really my job to draw the line. Somebody is going to draw the line for me and then I go out and try to keep everybody in line. I hate to think that's my job in life, to go around telling guys to cover their buns and girls that they can't get their T-shirts wet and show their boobs and that you can't go out and get a friendly handjob now and then. But the line has to be drawn somewhere.

I hold the distinction of being the only cop around here to bust a male stripper. On Tuesdays and Fridays, they have exotic male dancers at this one club. Only women can get in and the men have to stay out at the front bar. The guys strip down and they neck with the girls, etc.

We have a city ordinance and there's a state law that says, if you're in a place that serves alcohol, you can't show any portion of the buttocks. You can't show pubic hair. If you are going to show that or a woman's breast—some places it's below the nipple, some places it's the entire areola—then you have to have an elevated stage and there has to be eighteen inches between the customers and the dancers at all times.

This place didn't have any of that shit. They had a bunch of really rowdy male dancers. These guys would get started and they'd roll their bikini underwear and stuff it up the cheeks of their buns. We kept telling them you can't do that, you can't do that. I got a female officer and some of the girls from work and told them, "I'll pay your way in and pay for your drinks. Just go in, use a camera and take pictures for me. They don't mind if you take pictures. Come out and let me know and we'll go in and raid the joint." We did that—twice. They decided that was too expensive. It cost the owner a hundred and the dancers fifty each.

This place was big on Friday and Saturday nights, but on the week nights, you couldn't pay people to go in there. Next they brought in mud wrestling. I go to the door, supposedly undercover, but I've known the bouncer for years now. He says, "Hey, Sam, what's happening?"

"I want to come in to see the show tonight."

"Well, shit, you don't have to pay."

"No, I really have to."

"Aw, shit, come on in, sit down and have a beer on me." He sent the barmaid over with a beer. I'm sitting there with my partner drinking free beer. There's also two off-duty cops in there. I'm there officially, but they're there to see the mud wrestling.

The show starts. The music is going and the announcer starts warming up the crowd. This chick comes bombing out. She has on this little tiny bikini, doesn't even make an attempt to cover her buns. One of the doormen goes running over to the MC. The MC puts the mike over his shoulder to talk to this guy. In doing so, he basically sticks it right in the guy's mouth. So it blares out over the PA system, "The fucking vice cops are here. Get that bitch out of here or put something on her." I'm cracking up. It's a real high-class undercover operation.

Then the fight starts. I'm standing on a chair watching the show and beneath me is my partner, a brand new rookie. The guy next to him turned around and said something to him. I don't know what it was. I can't hear or make myself heard over the noise in the place. The rookie has no idea what it was anyway. The next time the guy turns around, he hits the rookie. I can see the bouncer and the doorman heading this way. I know what they're going to do. I have seen them in action before. They are going to trash both of these guys. So I jump down, grab the rookie and run him out the back door. I tell the bouncer that I'm going to arrest this guy and take him in.

They got rid of the mud wrestling on their own. It caused too many problems. Guys start watching the girls fight and then they want to fight.

Working massage parlors is a crack-up. I knew absolutely nothing about it. I never got involved with this stuff before I got on the job. I've been here since I got out of high school. I go into this massage parlor where we had made a case before. The broad won't do anything. It's obvious that it's a whorehouse, but the first time in they don't trust you.

I lived about a mile from there. About a week later, I went home and changed into a sweat suit and I ran from home to the massage parlor. I walked in all sweaty. "I just got done working out and this is going to feel great," I said. They started laughing at me. I got undressed and laid down on the bed. She massaged my shoulders for five minutes and then rolls me over and grabs on. She's going to give me a handjob. I'm embarrassed, and there's some basic physiological responses that you can't stop. Let's face it, the woman is a professional.

You can't consummate the act, because then you are a willing participant. You lose your case. In this state it is illegal to solicit for the act of prostitution or engage in the act of prostitution. What the D.A. wants to see is the solicitation. If you can get them to offer it and then somehow get out from under it, so to speak, that's what you want to do.

So I'm laying there and she gets me turned on and she grabs ahold and I push her off and say, "No, no. I can't. I can't. My wife, my wife." She only speaks broken English. After about ten minutes of being in the place you start talking just like them. We're having this intelligent conversation. She pushes me back down on the bed and says, "No, no, no. Everything all right."

I push her off again. "No, I can't, I can't. My wife, my wife."

"No, is okay," and she pushes me down again. So I knock her away and walk over and start getting dressed. She reaches over and grabs me again and pulls me back over. I finally fight this bitch off and get dressed up in the sweat suit—which is kind of hard in this shape. I go outside to get my partner and my badge so we can come back in and arrest them. But I found out that it is entirely ludicrous to stand there with a raging hard-on and try to convince somebody that "I'm really serious and you're under arrest."

From that point on, I figured out that capitalism is the way out. I go in and my story is that I'd really like to do this, but I don't expect it for free. I can't bring up money and I can't bring up sex first. Once I get her to bring up both of those then I can do whatever I want. You have to get her to talk and talk and talk and talk. Get her to bring up both of those, then you say, "That sounds neat. I'll be back tomorrow night or next week. How much money do I need to bring and what am I going to get?" I've gotten chicks to give me the whole menu, run it all down.

Then we go for a warrant. All the girls who are massage techs have to register with the city. We take their pictures and everything. So I have a copy of all their registration cards and pictures. If they are not one of the ones I recognize that works there, then we set up outside late at night just before closing. We wait for them to get in their car to leave and have an officer make a traffic stop on them to find out who they are. We process the whole thing through and get a warrant for their arrest, which may take a week or so. An officer goes in and serves them. They don't go to court for another week. By the time they see the report, my name is on it, but they have no idea who their customer was at nine-thirty on Monday two weeks ago. Never had to go to court. Got a lot of convictions.

It worked really slick, until the last one I worked. The department was doing a survey during this big siege to shut them all down. I'd already made sergeant, but they brought me back, just for old time's sake. At this point they said, "Don't worry about making a case. Don't spend an hour playing all the word games. All we want is a rough idea of which places are dirty and which ones are clean. The ones that are dirty, we'll go back through and hit them hard." So I don't have to worry about letting them bring up sex, I can just start talking about it right away.

The way you can tell whether or not it's a dirty spot is this: You're always laying on your stomach and you're naked. They rub down your back. Then they come back up with their middle finger right between your ass cheeks. I guarantee you—I don't care who you are—they hit that two or three times and you are at full attention. You spend very little time on your stomach. They roll you over on your back and make no attempt to cover your crotch. They rub your shoulders a little bit, then move right down and get to it.

The Oriental parlors, the handjob is just part of the massage. You paid for a full body massage and they're going to massage your full body. So this broad does this right away. I mean, she has me rolled over real quick. I said, "I feel really embarrassed here, when you're dressed."

145

"Oh, okay," she says, and she takes off her blouse. That was easy. I'll see what else I can go for. She starts to put a little baby oil on her hand and indicates to me what she's going to do. I say, "Why don't you use your mouth?"

"You mean French?"

"Yeah, yeah. My wife never does it and I always wondered what it was like."

"Oh, no. This is your first time. I can't do it on your first time. You come back again."

"Oh, God. That's terrible. My wife never does it and everybody says it's so neat."

"Okay," she says.

"Okay?" I said. Now I got to find a way to stop it, because you can't go through with this whole thing. I might have to testify to this later. Everything is a total shock. I am not prepared for this at all. I've never had the slightest desire in my life to pull a woman's head off that part of my anatomy. So I go through this same thing as the very first time, "Ah, I'm too embarrassed. No, I can't . . . really." I felt like an idiot. What a stupid job.

I went home and I'm changing my clothes and talking to my wife and I tell her, "I think this is the funniest thing I've ever done. Honey, you're not going to believe this," I told her.

"You did what?" was all I got. And those were the last words I heard for four days. Man, it was cold in that house.

The good thing about working vice is that when you do get caught up and you have some time, you can spend city money doing this shit. You get to go in and get drunk for free. They have a wet T-shirt contest at this country and western bar. It's always been fairly mellow. I said to this guy I've worked with in the past, "Hey, I've got to go down to Wet T-shirt Night and see what those broads are doing. If they start flashing their crotch, we'll write some tickets. You can't be doing that shit."

We get in there at ten, but it turns out that the show doesn't start till midnight. Well, what can we do? We got to sit there and drink. This guy is telling me, "Any broad in here flashes her tits, we're going to hook her up right there on the dance floor and we're taking her to jail."

"Yeah, okay," I say.

Twelve-thirty, the show finally starts. This guy is drunk on his ass, standing on a table, yelling, "Take it off, bitch! Let's see some tit!" I had to carry him out to the car and drive him back home. All the way home, he's hitting the dashboard and saying, "God, I want to see more tit."

*

We got a report from a confidential informant that one of these little Jiffy Marts was going to be held up on a Sunday morning. So we staked the place out. It was built in such a way that it faced the hard road, but on either end and in the back of it was wooded area. The nearest business or house was maybe 300 or 400 yards away. There was no back door to this building, so the only way to come out was through the front door. The lady inside didn't even know that we were staking it out. I was directly across the street in plainclothes and I had a walkie-talkie and was supposed to alert the others if something happened so they could close in.

About five minutes after nine, I saw this black fellow park his car about 50 feet away from the building and raise the hood to make motorists think that he was broke down. He came walking up kind of stiff-legged and I could see with binoculars that he had what looked like a rifle or shotgun in his pants leg.

We waited till he got in good and I could see the lady putting the money in a bag. Then he pushed her into the cooler in the back. I was telling all these other fellows what was happening on the radio. We were set to move.

About that time a car pulled up right behind this fellow's car and a man got out. He had his hand inside his shirt. He goes easing up to the Jiffy Mart. Inside, the first robber puts the shotgun back in his pants, got the bag of money situated real good under his arm and he was walking to the front of the store. The other fellow had gotten onto the concrete within two or three feet of the door. That's where they met. The second gunman pulled out his pistol and put it into the first robber's face and backed him into the store. The first man dropped the bag of money and got put in the cooler with the woman clerk.

When Number Two comes back up front to pick up the money, he was told not to move or he will be blowed to bits, because there was three of us there with the drop on him. He dropped his pistol and his money. We put handcuffs on him. Then we go to the cooler. Number One comes out and we put handcuffs on him and grab his gun out of his britches leg. The girl is, of course, really upset and scared. We call her husband and get her taken care of.

In the meantime, we tell the two robbers their rights and that we're going to put them in jail for armed robbery and grand larceny and a couple of other things. The first one turned to us and said with a straight face, "I'd like to prefer charges, too."

"For what?"

"Against that man who come in and held me up."

*

It started out one evening when one of the patrol units got a call that somebody had shot a gun in the street. When the car pulls up to the residence, he's greeted by a pistol shot that blew his windshield right out. When he saw the guy in the window, the officer fired a shot as he retreated behind a tree and got across the street. He called for reinforcements. The guy shot several more shots out the window.

The original complaint came from the woman across the street who said the guy who lived over there was shooting a gun and her child was outside. She didn't know what he was shooting at, but she felt it was a dangerous situation.

They activated the SWAT Team and we responded. We surrounded the house, withdrawing the patrol officers and putting our people in. We cordon off the area and called in the negotiator. We only shoot somebody as a last resort. We try to talk to them and get them out.

We never could talk to this guy. He wouldn't answer the phone. We actually took more chances than we should have. If I had it to do over again, I wouldn't take so many chances. But we were trying to save his life. We got our negotiator right up to the window one time and he was talking to him. But the guy was really crazy. He'd gone off the deep end. The only response we ever got from him was, "I know that ya'll are going to get me. But I'm going to take one of you with me." About that time—Kapow!—another shot would come out the window.

He had a shotgun and a pistol and a deer rifle and he'd take turns shooting these firearms. This is pretty flat country. If you shoot out a window, you can hit somebody 500 yards down the street.

Before dark it didn't get any better, although we kept talking to him. His wife was out of town. His son was graduating from some military base and the reason the father didn't go was that they wouldn't let him take his pistol on the base. This guy was very, very gone.

The news media picked up on it. I looked down the street and I could see people standing on rooftops in the next block and people on top of cars. Television had a picture with a telephoto lens and it was being broadcast live on TV. My wife is home watching all of this at about five o'clock in the evening. The reporters are telling everybody where it was and how to get there. It got like a circus.

Finally the decision was made. "Let's gas him out. It's getting dark. Get him out. Put a stop to it."

We have procedures for doing this. You put the gas in the back areas of the house and drive him out the front door, rather than put the gas in the door and chase him back into the far corner of the house where he'll just hole up if he can.

Our command post was in the trunk of my car, next door with the neighboring house in between us and him. I had a blackboard there and we're standing there in a huddle drawing pictures of where we're going to put the gas in and all. The gas man was standing right beside me with a 55 mm tear gas gun with the barrel resting on his shoulder pointing up in the air. The gun is probably fourteen inches from my head. A whispered conversation was going on between the gas man and another SWAT team member which I wasn't privy to at that time. The gas man was new on the gun and had not used that particular one before. He wasn't sure if it was double action or single action. "Is this single action or double action?"

"No," the other guy says, "you just pull the trig . . ."

Boom! That damn thing went off just inches away from my head. The only thing I couldn't figure out at that moment was how that madman got out of the house and shot me without anybody seeing him and stopping him. Then I looked up in the air and I could still see the tear gas projectile spiraling away up into the air. These things are fairly incendiary, too. I thought, "Oh, my God. This thing is going to land on a rooftop and burn the house down and the chief and the undersheriff are going to wonder what's happening."

Then again, luck is on your side sometimes. Remember about the crowd at the end of the block? This projectile landed right in front of them, so help me God, and they dispersed beautifully, clearing the area.

The sad part of it was that we had to gas the guy out and, when he came out, he wanted to go away in a blaze of glory. We had to shoot him. We couldn't let him leave the property still firing. I was one of the triggermen who shot the guy. Everybody's sitting at home in front of the TV eating dinner and watching this. My wife is watching all this on television.

The next day, the news media went out and canvassed the neighborhood for statements. Naturally, the guy's already dead and the neighbors ain't going to say, "Yeah, that son of a gun, they should have shot him." They said, "Well, you know, he was a pretty good guy really. I didn't know him." Then the news media tears us up.

We went back with a follow-up investigation in the neighborhood also. The woman from across the street who called us in the first place was quoted in the newspapers talking about what a good guy this fellow was. One of our investigators asked her, "Ma'am, did you look at your car out there. There's a bullet hole in the fender. Do you recall where your little girl was on her tricycle when this whole thing started?" It appeared that those first few shots he fired, he was shooting at the little girl, because the bullet holes were right about where the tricycle was. But they didn't put that in the newspaper. So you're damned if you do and damned if you don't. You can't win.

*

We get a lot of pipe bombs here, a lot of bombs with timing devices. Seventy-five percent of them go off and 25 percent we have to disarm. We get five hundred or six hundred suspicious packages every year. It takes its toll on you. You don't know it's not real until you work on it. I enjoy doing a job that nobody else would even think of doing.

It hit me once when I was new on the job. I had my tool kit and me and my partner and the dog are walking into this building. Everybody around us is running in all directions to get out of it. It gives you a strange feeling. What the hell are we doing?

You never know what you're going to get. I worked on thirteen sticks of dynamite in a lunch box as one of my first jobs. Another time me and my partner were on a suspicious package in an office building. We had this thing on a desk and we're working on it. We had the dog on it and the dog didn't react to it. My partner and I are cutting the package. It takes a while. It was cardboard all wrapped in tape. Finally, we get through and about that time my partner says, "Holy shit, what'd the dog do?" He thought the dog either shit or passed gas. I started laughing and I'm still cutting off a piece of the box and then I realize that the smell we're getting is coming from this package. I opened up this aluminum foil. Inside it was human shit that had literally melted from the heat. We call them the shit bomb. We get thirty or forty a year.

I had an unusual one. It was a lovers' dispute. This Armenian guy—he was a real wack-o—he had a girl-friend and she broke off the courtship with him. But he didn't want to hear nothing about that. He's from the other side over there and he's macho. He threatened to kill her, several times. He talked to her this one day and said she would be dead by that night. Then he delivers a package to her door. He's seen entering the building and leaving the package in front of the girl's doorway to her apartment.

Everyone's panicking now. She's inside. Her mother's inside. So we come down and they tell us this story.

We X-rayed it and we couldn't see nothing. I put the bomb suit on. It's a real tight area. There's bad lighting in this old apartment building. I got a flashlight and I'm cutting into the bottom of this box. You always cut into a package where it would be least expected to be opened, because it might be booby trapped where they think you're most likely to go into it. I cut it at a low corner and I'm looking into this thing. I can see something in there. But I can't tell what it is. I'm cutting the hole a little bigger and a little bigger. I got the light shining in there. I recognize this thing, but somehow I just don't know what I'm looking at. It's got me puzzled. I know what it is in the back of my head. The damn thing is looking at me, but I cannot for the life of me fathom it.

It's a fucking tongue I was looking at. A fucking tongue sticking out between teeth. The guy had a goat's head in there. I suddenly realize that it's a fucking tongue. A fucking goat's head.

*

I responded one day to a rooftop. There was a man standing up there getting ready to throw a baby down into the streets because he loved this baby so much and felt so inadequate himself. He thought the baby would be better off dead—classic homicide/suicide.

"Wait a minute," I said. "Maybe there's other ways. What other options do we have for this baby? Sure, if the baby is dead, you're right, it will not be under the influence of the people that you think are so bad." We're not going to argue his value judgment. That's going to get us no place. "Are there other ways to provide for the well-being of this baby?"

You try to figure out what's going on. Okay, this guy is not a total psychotic who just wants to kill a kid. He's not doing this out of some other hidden motivations. He has a real concern for the child. It is basically a family squabble. He thinks the mother and grandmother are not raising the child correctly, that the child would be better off dead than under their control. It is really what you see. This guy was doing just exactly what he wanted to do because of why he said he wanted to do it. Sometimes that can make it more difficult. So you say, "Maybe there's some way we can help."

An easy thing would be to tell him, "You're right. Screw your wife and mother-in-law. You get the baby. You take custody." It would be a very tempting thing to say. "Okay, you got it. He's yours."

But to tell him that he can have custody is a falsehood. I know it is and he knows it is. Therefore, it's not a credible solution. If you're trying to take control of the situation and solve the problem, you have to be credible and believable.

"Okay, I'll tell you what. How about if we ask the family court to look at the situation here, to review the problem and let them make a decision? Courts can make this kind of decision. Cops can't."

"Okay," he says, "that sounds good. Okay, good."

So it seemed like we had broken it right there. "Give me the child."

"No."

"What's the matter?"

"How do I know that you'll follow through?"

"I just told you. You got my promise. You got my word. We'll shake hands on it."

"Cops have been known to lie."

"I guess so." On the one hand you want to hit him. On the other hand you want to hug him. "Well, what will it take to convince you? I'm saying this in front of witnesses, both police witnesses and civilian witnesses." There's no privacy on a rooftop, especially when other rooftops are right nearby and people are gawking out their windows. You can't clear the world from the scene. If he had a gun, we could clear people and they'd be more willing to move. But when his weapon is the baby that he's going to kill, it's very difficult to clear every fire escape. It's no threat to them.

"It will have to be in writing," he says. Here's a man standing on a rooftop ready to toss this baby. But he really cares about the baby, so you got to look into that. So I get a piece of paper and I write. I hand it to him and he says, "That's no good. It has to be notarized."

Now when you tell this later, it sounds almost like a comedy act. How could you take this serious? But the picture is you're up on a rooftop eight stories above the ground. There's a man with an infant. He is distraught. He is occasionally crying. The baby is just lying there in his arms. They could just as soon fall as throw and jump. If he sobs and staggers once, he could step off backwards.

I totally forgot that, at the time, because of some other work I was doing for the department, I was a notary. So my backup negotiator reminded me. He said, "Hey, dummy, you're a notary."

That's right. I got a card in my pocket that says I'm a notary public. I show him my notary card. It was just too smooth and too pat for him. It was all true. Everything we'd done so far was true. But he went back to his, "Nah, cops lie." We were just too adept at what we were doing. If you ask me to be a rabbi, I'll whip out a yarmulke. You ask me to be whatever and I'm going to whip it out on you. This gets back to credibility.

We established in his mind the perception that this was not the only way it had to go. We established in his mind the support that the courts and the social agencies could provide. But we just couldn't get him over that last hurdle of how it was going to happen, the mechanics of how we were going to help him in a believable way.

So now we're back to square one. I get nervous again. "Well, you tell me," I said. "You tell me what we have

155

to do. It's your problem. It's not my problem. I can turn around and leave. You help me. It's your problem and therefore it has to be your solution." You say that to people without using those words. "What can we do that'll convince you? If it falls within the framework of what we are allowed to do, both legally and within the organization, we'll see if we can do it."

"The only person who can draw up papers like that," he says, "is a lawyer." He's really testing me, because if I whip out a card that says I'm a lawyer, he'll know I'm not on the level.

Could we have done that? Could we have produced some cop dressed in a nice three-piece suit with a briefcase who says, "I'm a lawyer." Sure, we could have. But why do it when you don't have to.

So what do you do? You turn to the backup negotiator and you say, "Go get me a lawyer. I don't care where you get him, just go get me a lawyer."

We send cops out into the neighborhood. There is a law office nearby. They walk in, "Mr. Lawyer, can you prove you're a lawyer? Can you bring some papers or something with you to prove that you are who you are?" We tell him what's going on. He takes his diploma down off the wall. We bring him to the rooftop. He draws up a request for a hearing at the family court for the custody of the child. I have to give that guy a lot of credit. He helped to save that kid's life.

As soon as the guy surrendered the child in exchange for the document, we then jump the guy, which the bystanders on the surrounding rooftops were very upset about. We were asked later on, "Hey, you know, he gave you the kid. What'd you jump him for?"

We jumped him so he wouldn't kill himself. For the entire three or four hours that we were talking to him, he exhibited great manifestations of suicide. Stated suicide, which is one manifestation, regardless of what people say—"Ah, if they talk about it, they're not going to do it." Bullshit, if they're talking about it, it's because they're thinking about it. They just haven't made up their mind yet. And he went through all the classic justifications in his mind. He surrendered his valuables. The most valuable thing he surrendered, of course, was the child. But he'd also taken out his wallet and gave it to somebody, saying, "Here, I don't need this any more." So we had all the clues we look for. We prevented him from thinking about jumping any more. We just didn't give him the chance.

Another time, after work, on the bridge I go over on my way home, there was a traffic jam. I'm annoyed at that. I see a car from another agency with its light flashing, so I figure, "They got a breakdown. I'll try to make my way around it." Everybody is slowing down and looking. It wasn't a breakdown. The guy parked and he was out climbing this bridge to jump. So I felt a responsibility to stop. It's something I supposedly know something about.

I get on the radio and call for Emergency Services, call for people to block off the bridge and get some safety equipment and some lifelines and all that.

I start talking to the guy. He was distraught over a personal relationship. His girlfriend, she didn't love him any more. Stuff that you hear time and time again that doesn't make good TV shows and movies. This was a nice-looking young kid thinking of jumping off the bridge because of a broken romance.

A lot of them realize at a point in time, "These cops are right. I shouldn't do what I'm doing." But they have the tiger by the tail. They don't know how to let go. They can't look like total losers. It's heavily losing face.

This young man's concern was with being arrested. He's up there and he's serious. He's going to go. I believe these people when they say they're going to go unless there is a way we can stop them from going. You don't have a threat to other innocent people unless he lands on somebody which is unlikely in this case. But you have the threat to the people who have to go after him. I'm going to talk to him from the roadway, but cops have to go up with lifelines and try to get this guy back in. So there is a safety factor for them and we try to minimize their danger.

His concern finally became, "I don't want to be arrested."

"Okay, we're not going to arrest you."

"Are you sure you're not going to arrest me?"

"I promise you, I'm not going to arrest you."

"How do I know that you're telling me the truth?" It's a replay, right?

"You want it in writing?"

"You'll give me something in writing that says I won't be arrested?"

"I certainly will." I got a piece of paper out of the car and I wrote, "We will not arrest So-and-So on this date for trying to jump off the bridge." I signed it and handed it to him. He walks in.

What did we do with the man? We took him into custody for psychiatric evaluation, which we are required to do by law. It's not against the law to sit on a bridge and try to kill yourself. People will turn around and say to me, "Yeah, but you know, you cheated. You hedged." Of course, I hedged. Did I tell a lie? I didn't tell a lie. He was not arrested and he wouldn't have been arrested for that anyway. I didn't tell him, "Yeah, okay, you come on down and you walk your way and we'll go ours." That wouldn't solve the problem. What I've got to do is come up with a temporary solution for a long-term problem. The problems we encounter in policing, somebody else starts and somebody else has to ultimately finish. We get the little pieces in between.

*

One of the mental out-patients walked into the hospital off the street and demanded some type of drugs from a male nurse, who wouldn't give them to him. So the patient pulled a revolver and stuck it to the male nurse's head. They were in the psychiatric ward, which is right next to the Intensive Care Unit. There is a kind of lounge area right in the center with glass walls all around. A hall runs down both sides to rooms surrounding this lounge. There are a lot of patients on this ward.

He's sitting right in the middle with a gun on the nurse demanding these drugs. Somebody alerted the police. When the patrol got there, they alerted the SWAT Team.

We didn't want him to know we were there until we had gotten set up. The tightest cordon we could get on him included about twenty-five other patients in nearby rooms. The first thing I did was send a group around to Intensive Care and told them to barricade that area. Under no circumstances were they to let him through there. "Get tables, anything you can use for a barricade and then we're going to set a barricade up in each hall. We will gradually tighten the barricade. As we close in we will evacuate as we go" was what I told them.

Before we could really get going on this and get our people deployed, somebody came on the radio and said, "The hostage is walking out." One of the patients got disturbed, came out of his room and started walking down the hall. The suspect was talking to a doctor on the phone. When the male nurse saw the patient, he instinctively got up, took the patient by the arm and walked him back into his room. They said to me on the radio, "The nurse wants to go back in. Should we let him?"

"No, hold him right there." I went down there and asked the nurse where the suspect was in the room. He said, "He's sitting in the middle of the lounge talking to a doctor on the phone, but he's still got his gun."

"Does he know that you're gone?"

"I don't know for sure, but I don't think he does."

What bothered me was, if that patient got up and walked into the lounge, what was to stop any other patient from doing the same thing. This is a nut ward. "Hey, what are you doing with the gun?" This guy is going to shoot him.

What would you do right then? What decision would you make?

I decided to go in there right then. I came right up to the doorway about fifteen feet away from him. I knew his name, so I said, "Mickey, drop the gun." He never said a word. He just looked at me. "Mickey, we don't want to hurt you, buddy. Drop the gun."

I did this three or four times. He stopped talking on the phone. I'm looking right at him and he's looking right at me. Then he starts raising the gun real slow.

One of the guys beside me had a shotgun and I'm waiting to hear the shotgun go off. I didn't want to be the triggerman. I was the leader of the SWAT Team and I'd been the triggerman on the last shooting, so I was waiting for him to shoot. But then I realized that of the three I was the ranking officer. A sergeant was there and a patrolman. One of them was waiting on the other and both of them are waiting on me. There was enough hesitation that none of them did anything.

So now I'm looking right down the barrel of his gun. What would you do then?

I had a fifteen-shot 9 mm. I could have fired fifteen times at him if I wanted to. I fired one shot as I ducked behind the door. The last thing I saw as I was squeezing the shot off was the gun go flying out of his hand and he was sprawling into a chair. So I didn't shoot any more.

If I was trigger happy, I'd have fired more than one shot because that thing will fire just as fast as you can pull the trigger. He would have been full of holes. But I saw that he had been neutralized and that was it.

I found out one thing that was very, very important for anybody in police work in supervision. You need to have a good rapport with the news media. You need to talk to them. You got to tell the news media something. They got a boss and they don't want to go back to him and say, "I didn't get anything." They want to print something. You better get with them, because if you don't tell them anything, they're still going to print something. Nine times out of ten, it's not going to be what you want. The public information officer at the scene didn't give them an adequate enough statement, as far as they were concerned. I didn't tell them nothing. I just got in the car and left. Things were secured.

According to one of the more liberal writers, it came out that the dead man was a good old boy and we overreacted. At that time we had changed administrations and the director had a different philosophy than I did. His philosophy was that I should have held off, that I forced the suspect into a position where I had to shoot him. They asked me. I told them after thinking about it and critiquing it, if I had it to do over again, I'd have to go about it the same way.

The word was that they didn't want me to be labeled a killer, that I acted a bit hastily. They took me off the SWAT Team that I had helped to establish for this department in the first place. What was bad about it was I got the word in the hall from another officer. I'd been on vacation. When I got back, I got the rumor that I'd been transferred. That was the first time I ever cried on duty, the day they told me that.

*

A young girl was sleeping in an apartment with her girlfriends. They had recently graduated from college and moved to this area. She was six foot tall and looked just like Susan Anton, blond hair, good-looking, twenty-three years old. About four-thirty in the morning she was awakened by someone standing over her in the bedroom. This black guy put a knife to her throat, made her blow him, then he raped her and got out of the apartment. She left the apartment with her girlfriends when she got away and they went to the fire station. The firemen took her to the hospital.

A report of the incident goes out and about two hours later an officer stops this black guy walking down the street in the area who fits the description she gave us. My partner goes and gets the guy. He's saying, "Shit, man, the only reason you're stopping me is because I'm black."

I come in about 7 A.M. My partner tells me about all this and says, "I've got a guy who fits the description upstairs."

"Where's the victim?" I ask. She's in a room there and like most rape victims she is very upset and confused. I get two black cops who work with me and I get them and the suspect together. I bring her into an adjacent room and ask her if any of these men look like the man who attacked her. "It looks like him," she says. Not good enough. "It is him," she says. Because of the fact that she was hesitant, that means that I have to be careful.

We go back to her apartment to do an on-scene investigation. It's a basement apartment and you can see where the window had been systematically removed. We could see how he came through the window, jumped down into the living room and went into the bedroom. But we couldn't find anything to hook the bastard. There was no weapon recovery. We couldn't find any prints. We dusted the glass and there was nothing there. I looked at the windowsill and it's made of white tile. I had the officer dust the tile and he came up with a heel print, a sneaker pattern with some notches that made it recognizable. We lifted the print and I took it back to the station.

I went down to the room where they were holding the guy and I said, "Lift up your foot."

"What?"

"Lift up your fucking foot and let me have a look at it." He did and it looked like the print matched perfectly. I said, "I got you, you motherfucker."

"You ain't got me."

"I got you!"

Now the girl's mother comes from the city a few hundred miles away where the family is from. Here's a girl who has just been raped at knife point and she's telling her mother how nice we've been to her. We've had a lot of work to take care of so we've been with her the whole day in the apartment.

Then we finally got a search warrant for his apartment and found the chisel that he used to scrape out the putty around the glass. We found clothes with putty on them. When I take the sneakers off him down at the fucking courthouse, there's a big glob of fucking putty on the bottom of them.

So he's arraigned at three-thirty that afternoon. The judge says $10,000 bail, which is $250 cash. Two hundred and fifty fucking dollars cash bail for a rapist. I'm ready to go out of my fucking mind. I says, "Thank you, your honor. Please, excuse me, now I have to go tell this girl and her mother that the guy is going to be out on the street before we can finish the investigation."

I go back to my boss and I say, "Hey, we got to do something. We got to keep that cocksucker off the street."

"There's only one thing to do," he says. "Get the girl down to the D.A.'s office, tell him what the story is and get him into the grand jury."

I call up the girl. Needless to say, her mother has taken her back home. So I call down there and I talk to her father and I tell him, "We got to indict the son of a bitch to keep him off the street."

"I'll handle it," he tells me. The next morning, the three of them get into the car and drive all the way back up here. We bring her right into court. She gets in front of the grand jury and it finally happens. She finally lets go in the grand jury room. It's the first time she's told the whole story and she's very upset, to say the least. Bam! We got our indictment.

We go to his house and he's not there. Two days later a call comes through with the report of a break-in. This guy that we're looking for has seen where we broke into the house with the warrant to search and he's called in a burglary. This is the first time he's been back there since he got out of jail. One of my guys remembers the case and the address. As soon as the call comes in, he shoots down there and asks this guy, "Are you Joseph Reynolds?"

"Yeah, how did you know?"

"You're under arrest." Bang! The guy knocks the cop on his ass and takes off. But the cop that backs him up on the call is twenty-four years old, six-two and can run like a fucking deer. He got him.

So I take them out to lunch, the mother, the father and the daughter, the district attorney and myself. Great vibes. Everybody feels better. Then the case goes into the files until we go to superior court a few months down the line.

I had a couple of very depressing cases to work on in the meantime. I came into the station one Friday night at midnight, all tired and hungry. I just wanted to get the fuck out of there. The sergeant tells me, "There's someone here to see you. They been waiting for a couple of hours."

"Jesus Christ," I say. "All right, I'm going into the john and I'll be out in a minute."

I come out and there's the girl and a couple of her friends. She's got something in her hands. "What's this?"

"I moved back into town and I'm living over on such-and-such a street. These are some of my friends," she says. "I made this cake for you just to say thank you." That was the best cake I ever ate in my life.

CHAPTER 4

Deadly Force

A PISTOL is an amazing piece of machinery. Its compact simplicity is ingenious and frightening. The standard issue .38 caliber revolver with a 4-inch barrel, which is used by most police agencies in America, weighs about two pounds. That is about twice the weight of the book in your hands. The weight and solidity of a gun seem surprising; they don't seem to correspond to the size.

The mechanics of a revolver are very elementary—a lever, a spring and a hammer. It takes eight to twelve pounds of pressure to pull the trigger, roughly equivalent to putting a finger in the handle of a gallon jug of milk and lifting it off the refrigerator shelf. That energy is stored in a spring as the hammer is forced back. Then the hammer reaches the cocked position and is released. The hammer strikes the shell casing, detonating a small amount of primer inside the shell, which in turn ignites the smokeless powder. This powder burns so fast that the result is an explosion. The expanding gas from this explosion forces the lead 158-grain projectile out the end of the barrel at somewhere between 750 and 900 feet per second. Spiral grooves along the inside of the barrel give the bullet the spin that keeps it going in the direction the gun is aimed.

The noise a gun makes when it is fired is quite distinctive. The tinny speakers on an average television set just don't do justice to it. Moviemakers often amplify and synthesize the sound for psychological effect, making it resemble a small nuclear blast. It is not loud exactly, although the concussion from five or six rounds fired in a row at arm's length will make your ears ring. Late at night in a big city, some people mistake the far-off backfire of a truck or the report of a firecracker playfully tossed from the roof of a building for the sound of a gunshot. If his nerves are worn, a cop might make that mistake, too. But usually he recognizes the sharp, crisp sound of gunfire. The word "crack" comes to mind with plenty of "kuh" at both ends.

In TV and motion pictures, the bullet is often portrayed as a very discreet piece of metal. When it strikes a bad guy, it produces a round, red polka dot approximately the diameter of a pencil. There is usually very little blood and never an exit wound. Good guys are regularly shot in the arm, shoulder or leg and are up and around in no time.

For all this prim propriety, when it kills, the TV bullet is incredibly efficient. One shot—two at the most—and the bad guy drops like a rock, face-first onto the tarmac. Three shots can launch him on a long arcing trajectory through windows and doors and off balconies.

The reality is both more and less than the Hollywood illusion. Bullets aren't sharp. They don't drill neat holes in flesh. Bullets rip and tear. When they hit bone, lead slugs don't produce neat fractures. Bones are burst and splintered. No longer able to support body weight, the jagged end of a broken bone is sometimes jabbed up and out through the skin as gravity pulls the flesh down. Flattened into an irregular shape by the impact, but unspent, the bullet tumbles off and away through the body, often bursting out with a fist-sized ball of meat at an odd angle and a remarkable distance from where it entered.

Considering the small size and corresponding surface area of a bullet, it is extremely rare that someone's body is simply "grazed"—a bullet coming close enough to plow a shallow furrow in the skin but not close enough to penetrate. The extremities—the hands, feet, arms and legs—do not contain vital organs, but they are packed with bundles of blood vessels, muscles and nerves. A wound in any of these areas almost certainly will result in a permanent loss of strength, mobility and/or feeling.

For all this destructiveness, a single pistol shot usually won't stop a human being unless it is especially well placed. There is really no such thing as instant death from a gunshot wound. Inertia and momentum can carry an attacker to his target through a hail of gunfire. A body pumped up with adrenaline will keep coming for a second or two even after the heart stops. Two seconds is plenty of time for an assailant to lurch a few steps and stab, to fall and take someone with him, to pull the trigger of his own gun. If the heart does not stop right away, that organ can pump most of the blood the body contains through the wound and out onto the ground in a matter of minutes.

The person who fires a weapon on television always does it with calm deliberation. He is a very good marksman. In fact, he usually takes the correct firing stance and actually aims his weapon, even at close range. He is never panting so hard after a hundred-yard sprint that he can't even level the sights. He is never so pumped up with anger and fear that his whole being vibrates. He would never jump behind some cover, stick his gun out and blindly fire off a few rounds in the general vicinity of his target.

But in fact most police shootings happen fast at very

close range, amid surprise and confusion. All an officer usually has time to do is pull his gun quickly from his holster, shove it toward the torso of his assailant and pull the trigger. If he's lucky, the machine does its job, and he has chosen the right time and person to employ it on.

The TV policeman doesn't seem to be bothered by extinguishing a human life. The more sensitively portrayed cops reflect on their actions following the commercials. Killing doesn't usually give them nightmares. It doesn't make them constantly nauseous for a month. It doesn't ruin their sex lives or drive them to alcoholism.

After the smoke clears, the TV cop is rewarded, not second-guessed, investigated and sued. It's no wonder he so often solves crime with his gun.

The average police officer never fires his weapon in twenty years on duty. Some of them rarely draw their weapons except at the firing range—if they practice at all. But it's there all the time, hanging from a hip or riding in a Velcro ankle holster, in the nightstand beside the bed or—all too often—under the pillow.

The gun is an ego booster. Cops don't want to hear the words "gun" and "penis" in the same sentence. But there is still the cop who will make a display of putting on and taking off his sports coat as he gets in and out of his car, flashing anybody who cares to look a glimpse of that big leather codpiece snuggled under his armpit.

That .38 service revolver is a police officer's final authority. He has the responsibility to take life, if it becomes necessary to protect the public or to protect himself. Because he does carry that gun and that responsibility, he also becomes a target. His gun is a constant reminder of his ultimate power and his worst fears.

"It's a dangerous job, but sometimes the fear becomes paramount. It takes over some police officers.

It's all they think about when they go out into the street. So they need psychological buffers against that. They carry two guns, carry extra ammunition. What do you need all that for? If a guy pulls a gun on you, you're not going to fire 40 rounds at the guy. You got a gun. You pull it out and shoot. That's it. You're only going to shoot one gun at a time. But it's a psychological thing.

"You talk to a guy, 'Hey, I hear you got to fly uptown to work a tough neighborhood.'

" 'Yeah,' he says. 'But I got it covered.' He pulls up his pants leg and there's another ankle holster with another .38 under there. 'I got my Barretta in my pocket.'

"Is this going to help him? No. But he needs that."

The gun can become a crutch and then an enemy. At best, the pistol an officer is required to carry—in most departments—off duty as well as on becomes an inescapable burden.

"I get tired of carrying a gun around twenty-four hours a day. The kids probably think it's great to carry it around. I think it sucks. You got to watch out where you go. You're limited to what kind of clothing you can wear. It puts a lot of restrictions on your freedom of movement. You have to be cautious, if you take it off, where you leave it, what's happening. It's a pain in the balls.

"People accidentally see it, say in a shopping center, my philosophy is, 'Well, they'll instantly think I'm a cop.' That's not so any more. They call a cop.

"I was in a department store at Christmastime shopping for my kid and my wife. I just had a sweatshirt on. I was wearing jeans and sneakers. I had my gun on. I had a lot of stuff in my arms and I was looking through it. The salesgirl called security. I turn around and I got three security guards all over me. Once I identified myself it was all worked out. But, fuck, I can't even go Christmas shopping without somebody blowing the whistle on me because they think I'm going to rip them off. I don't blame them exactly. But Jesus, you get embarrassed yourself. Everybody's looking, 'Hey, what the hell is this guy getting shook down for?' "

Rather than trigger happy, many cops are hesitant to use their weapons. Firing that pistol puts an officer in a no-win situation. If he handles a shooting incorrectly, makes the wrong decisions, his whole career will be in jeopardy. He could easily end up on the unemployment line, or worse, in prison. If, by care and good fortune, he shoots the right person at the right time for the right reasons, he still may suffer. He will be subjected to an investigation conducted as though he committed a criminal act. In all probability, he will be suspended from active duty and stuck at a desk job shuffling papers until the investigation is concluded. He is more likely to be excoriated by the media than praised. If he is involved in more than one such incident, he may be considered a troublemaker and be passed over for promotion. If the criminal survives, he may sue the officer for civil rights violations.

The point so often overlooked in the discussion of deadly force is the damage done to the humanity of the man or woman who is obliged to do the shooting. Everyone knows that a police officer's conscience clobbers him if he kills or injures an innocent bystander, but what about when he shoots the bad guy? For all the Dirty Harry bravado bandied about in the bars, every cop I talked to who had been involved in a shooting felt some guilt or regret for having been the agent for the death or injury of another human being.

"All the guys are patting you on the back and congratulating you. Making jokes about the poor fucker. Taking bets about when he's going to die over in ICU. I never told anybody, but I didn't feel good, I didn't feel proud. I was glad it was him and not me; otherwise all I felt was empty. It still makes me swallow hard to think about it."

I WAS WORKING in a neighborhood best described as a ghetto. It was drug-infested, it had whores and that's why we were there. We're standing in front of this fleabag transient hotel. We're all spit-shined and ready for action. Up comes this black guy and he's bleeding like a stuck pig. Something had been severed and he is pulsing blood out. He comes right up into my face, squirting onto my uniform. My first reaction was, "Back off. You're bleeding all over me." I'd already seen blood before. The guy's cut and I'll get down to business, but don't bleed on me. I asked him what happened and he said, "My woman cut me." He was cut from ear to ear, but he's standing up. He told us where it happened, which room in the hotel. I told my partner, "Call an ambulance and get some help. I got the portable radio. I'll go up and check it out. No big deal, it's a woman up there." That was a mistake.

The hotel has got a raggedy-ass little elevator—two people and it's crowded, smells of piss, takes five minutes to go up the seven floors. I get off and it's a hallway that's maybe four feet wide and that's it. Like all those places, nobody's seen nothing, nobody's heard nothing. They may open the door a crack and see you're the Man and—Blam!—they slam it. You ain't getting no help from nobody. The elevator is also the only way out. There's no exit on my end of the hall.

The elevator door closes and it starts back down. Here comes another guy bleeding as bad as the first guy. Behind him is the biggest, blackest woman I've ever seen in my life and she has a very big fucking knife in her hand. She has death in her eyes and she is chasing this little twit down the hallway. She has not only cut him, she is going to dissect him now. He spots me and I am his protector.

There is no way out of this shit and there ain't no room to tussle. I didn't panic too much because I was too young and too dumb at that point in my career. I also figured that this cannon I held in my hand was my savior. That was stupid, too.

Now the little guy is behind me. She's coming and I got the gun on her. I yell for her to stop, but she's not hearing a thing I'm saying. She's looking through me to him. I let her get too close. Bullets don't always kill a person and in any case they don't kill them right away. A person in a rage will keep right on coming, driven by momentum alone. For all intents and purposes he may be dead but he's still got a lot of juice.

She was close enough for me to really see her eyes and I'm shitting. I really didn't want to shoot her. I don't know why, but I didn't really feel threatened. She didn't want to get me, so I didn't really want to hurt her. But I was still going to die because I was in her way. I should have shot her.

I was really afraid. I couldn't hold the gun still. It was also cocked which means it only takes a little squeeze to make it go off. I'm down in a crouch and I decided, This is it. I got to let it go. I said, "Lady, you're dead." She stopped immediately about six feet away from me. She talked to me in the softest, soothing tones for a big woman. She said, "Don't shoot. I'm laying the knife down now. Don't be nervous. Point the gun away. The knife is down on the floor. I don't want to hurt you. I wanted the motherfucker behind you, but I've put the knife down, Officer. I'll do what you want. Just point the gun down."

I thought to myself, "God, I'm so fucking nervous, I won't be able to uncock this thing without shooting a hole in my foot." By this time help is there and everything is under control. Turns out the three of them live together and they're winos. The two guys got her welfare check out of the mailbox while she was out, cashed it and drank up the money. She found out and she cut them. Now these two guys have both stopped bleeding and they're telling me they don't want to press charges. I've almost blown this woman away.

*

A fellow named Ronald O'Quinn and I were driving adjoining beats one night. We'd been parked next to one another talking for a good twenty minutes. He went one way and I went the other. Thirty seconds later, he called me on the radio. He said, "Come back up here." Right around the corner from where we'd been parked was an auto parts place, Handiman's Auto Parts. He said, "I hear impact noises around Handiman's. I'll take the back."

"Okay, I'll be there in a minute." When I got to the front of the place, I let him know I was there and I got out. There was a long tin divider fence between the front lot and the back lot. I could hear him and he could hear me, but we couldn't see each other unless we ran down to the end of this tin wall. It was one of those fences they put up to hide a junk yard. To the south of us in the direction that this tin wall ran was an apartment complex about 300 yards away. Just before you got to the apartment complex was a creek 30 feet across and 10 feet deep.

As I walked up on the front of the building, I heard the impact noises, too. We had been very quiet and the guy obviously didn't know we were there yet. I saw the top of his head through a window. I ordered him to stand up and put his hands in the air where I could see them. He was in the open shed part of the business. The door to the office had been pried open. He walked out of the shed and produced his hands so I could see nothing was in them. Even though I had my shotgun on him as soon as he cleared the shed, he ran.

"Motherfucker," I yelled. "Ronnie, he's running south." Ronald ran south parallel to me on the other side of the fence. It was obvious to me that the guy wasn't going to be overtaken by me. When I was right at the end of the tin wall and Ronald rounded the corner, we both dropped down at the same time. I unloaded my shotgun. Ronald unloaded his. I unloaded my revolver. Ronald unloaded his. I had two extra shotgun shells under my belt. I snatched them out, flipped him one and racked one. We both shot simultaneously and the guy hit the ground.

We saw a patrol car rounding the bend near where the guy went down. I knew who it was, so I ran back to my radio and said, "Carl, stop where you're at. He's in the field right across from you, laying face down. Just walk straight into the field about 150 yards parallel to the creek." He walked over and gave us the high sign that he had found the guy.

We were—God a'mighty—a hundred yards away from him, being conservative. We're trying to piece together the crime scene, because Carl's got the suspect on the ground. We don't need to go down there. The guy is shot . . . to us.

Our supervisor rolls up. He says, "Did ya'll shoot him?"

We look at each other. "Is he hit?"

"Come on now," he says. "Did you shoot? Did you fire your weapons?"

"Is he hit?"

"We're not playing any games here now. Did you shoot or not?"

"Yeah," I said. "We shot."

"How many times?"

"I don't know," I said. "He shot a couple and I shot a couple."

The lieutenant got there and Rescue came. Carl sent Rescue away, so Ronald said, "He must be shot." We walked down there and I said to Carl, "Where's the suspect?"

"Rescue carried him."

"Man, they were awfully fast," I said. "Was he shot?"

"No," Carl said. "The motherfucker had a heart attack." This is real humorous. We have a good snicker over this, that the guy's had a mild heart attack. He's on his way to the hospital and we have to follow him and put him under a police hold so that we can book him when he gets out. We go to the hospital and process the right paperwork. The guy's okay. No problem.

We're patting ourselves on the back for getting him. He's one of the real bad guys that's been doing a lot of break-ins in the area. We feel pretty good about ourselves when we get back into our cars. On the radio, the lieutenant calls us back to the scene. He says, "How many times did y'all shoot?"

Ronald smiled and I smiled. "We didn't even hit the guy."

"How many times did you guys shoot?"

"Well, I shot some and he shot some."

"You see that apartment complex over there? We got damage on twenty-three cars and two apartments. I'm just glad nobody was looking out the window."

"Holy shit, *you're* glad?"

*

I was responding to a call of a berserk male. As I pull onto this street, about ten houses down I see a commotion. The way it came over the radio it was bad. I figured, "Let me hold up a couple of minutes until my backup comes."

At the time we were driving those Plymouths that had big rectangular headlights in the front grill. You could spot them a mile away. I look in my rearview mirror and maybe a half a block behind me, I see these lights. I said, "That's got to be him." So I pull up to the house.

There's this maniac in front of his parents' house picking up garbage pails, throwing them at the neighbors. The guy was like an animal. I got out of the car, two people pass in a Plymouth which I had thought was my backup. Oh, shit. With this, the maniac sees me and goes running into the house. The neighbors have come over and they look at this and they hear the language he's using, so you've got to do something. You've got to get this guy off the street. They're afraid.

The father comes over to me and says, "He just got out of the mental health facility. He's not taking his medicine. He's just going off the wall."

"Has he ever hurt anybody?" I say.

"Yeah, he hurt me and he attacked the neighbor a few prior times."

I figured I'd go into the house and find out a little more information by talking to the father and wait for my backup. With this, the idiot comes running back out of the house with a hammer. He's coming at me. All the neighbors split. They leave me. Bullshit. I pull my gun, cock it and say, "You come one step closer, pal, and you're going to get it." He keeps coming. One step closer, one step closer. He was about eight feet from me. I had two pounds of pull on the trigger with it cocked and I was ready to let go.

The father comes running over to the son and gets the hammer away from him. Then the backups come. He starts running into the house. I start running after him, while everybody bails out of their cars.

As we're running, he's snarling. I mean, this guy was really off the wall. I take out my Mace. They tell you Mace doesn't work on berserk people. Well, it worked beautifully. I hit him square in the face with this stuff and he went crying like a baby. Then I put the cuffs on. Then we committed him.

That was the closest I ever came to shooting somebody. When you get all hyped up everything is like slow motion. I could see the guy just moving and moving. It's a matter of one little touch and his head's going to be splattered all over the place. I didn't want to shoot. He backed me into a corner. Luckily, the father stepped in and grabbed the hammer away from him. I go deer hunting. I know it's hard to kill something unless you hit them in the brain or sever the spinal cord.

*

One Sunday afternoon, I was dispatched to this family fight. When I got there I had a six-foot-five, upwards of 250- to 300-pound man—a giant—standing in the driveway of this house with his arms folded, with a real pissed-off look on his face. A guy gets out of the other side of a pickup truck and he's the same size, twenty-ish, obviously the man's son or little brother. I said, "What's the problem?"

"I didn't call you," he said.

"Okay. No problem." I walk up to the door and knock. A man answers the door which is as tall or taller than them and just as big. I am six feet tall—barely— and I am no bulky individual. I was intimidated. I know that they're pissed at each other. I assumed that they were relatives on first visual inspection and their similarity in size. "Did you call?"

"Yeah, I did," he said. "I ordered a cord of firewood from these guys. They came up here with a pickup truck and commenced to throw it across my fence. That pickup truck does not hold a cord of wood."

"You're right," I said. "That's not a cord of wood. I've bought firewood before myself. What's the problem?"

"The problem is, I told them when I got home and

179

they were just finishing up, that wasn't a cord of wood and I wasn't paying them what they wanted for that wood, because it is not a cord."

"Okay. Well, what is the problem?"

"The problem is they're threatening to kick my ass."

"Oh, okay." Now in the process these two gentlemen are loading firewood back on their truck. I walked within a reasonable distance of them and began talking to them. I inquired of them what the problem was. I told them that if they thought they had been cheated or misused that they had courses to follow through civil court.

He wasn't interested in anything I had to say. The first thing he said to me was, "I don't care about any of that. That motherfucker owes me money and I'm going to kick his ass. I'm going to kick his ass right now."

This man is coming out of his house now to meet this guy in the yard. I turned to him and I said, "Look, ya'll are too big for me to fight, pal. You called me. Don't jeopardize your own safety. Go back into the house while I handle this." He goes back up on the porch and stands.

There's other conversation between those two while I am trying to interject, to which the guy out here in the yard says, "Aw, fuck you. I'll kick your ass right now." He throws down two pieces of wood and starts toward him.

"No," I said, "you're not going to fight, not while I'm here. Because I'm not going to let you." The son is standing over there helping to load the wood. The father says, "I'll stomp your ass, too, boy."

"Let me explain something to you," I said. I was speaking in a conversational tone of voice, because you don't want to piss these guys off any more than they already are. "Let me explain something to you. You're not going to fight, because I'm going to get between you. If I get between you and I get hurt, since I cannot physically come close to matching you two, somebody is going to get killed. Now that's all that I can tell you about it. I'm not playing. This is nothing to play about."

"Yeah?" the daddy said. "I got something in the truck for you." So he walks out of the fence to where the truck is parked in the street. I glanced at the truck and inside there is a rifle in a rack behind the seat. The son is to my right. The fence is between me and the truck. I said, "Don't go near the truck. If you put your hands near that gun, I'll kill you." At that time I unsnapped my holster.

The son steps at me and says, "Don't you draw that gun. If you do, I'll bash your fucking head in." He's got a log in his hand. Now the daddy has not broke his stride. He is going for the truck. I step up close to the fence and the son is blindsided to me. If I'm looking at the father, I can't see what the son is doing. He has the full capability of hurling that log at me. This piece of lumber is a quarter of my weight. The father put his hands on the door of the truck, at which time I cocked my revolver and leveled it at the back of his head. It was only about a foot and a half from the back of his head since the truck was right on the other side of the fence.

"Look, you don't realize what you're forcing me to do. I can't see your son. All I know is, if somebody makes me jump, the back of your head is going to come off. I don't know what to tell you, friend, but you do what you have to do." Luckily, he stopped where he was at. But his hand is on the door. His son is standing approximately ten feet away from me in a batting position, behind me, with a log. My gun is cocked at the back of this man's head. The idiot on the porch is doing nothing. I am in a Catch 22 position. I can't take my gun off this guy to look at the son, because he's got access to a firearm.

Two black kids came down the street dribbling a basketball, just bebopping around. They kind of look over to see what's so interesting—like, "What the hell's going on?" I screamed at them, "Hey, I need your help!"

"What do you want?"

"My patrol car door is unlocked. Go over there, open the door, pick up the microphone and all you have to say is '31-16, signal 34.' "

"Thirty-one-sixteen, signal what?"

"Signal 34. Thirty-one-sixteen is my unit number and signal 34."

He picked up the microphone and he said, "Ah-huh, this is 31-16. Signal 34," and put it down. I hear the dispatcher saying, "Ten-nine, 10-9, repeat, repeat." I'm ignoring that. Everybody else out there has heard it. I hear sirens everywhere. When everybody slides up sideways, my heart came back up into my chest from my feet. I just knew either I was going to die or somebody else was or maybe both. That was one of the scariest situations in ten years of police work. That had my adrenaline jacked up.

*

I'd taken somebody to jail and went back out to my beat. There's a 7-11 out there on a corner in the middle of nowhere. I stopped in there not only to get coffee, but also to make sure they were still alive and hadn't been robbed. I pulled into the parking lot and there's two hemorrhoids standing inside. One of them is leaning over the counter into the center of the cash register and the other one is standing by the door with his arms crossed, looking out. Immediately I just knew. Alarm bells went off. Something is wrong.

I just eased into the parking lot. The guy standing by the door was the lookout. He saw me and told the guy by the counter, "Here's the police. Goodbye, every man for himself." Then he bailed out and took off across the parking lot. But Leroy, leaning over the counter, was not sure what he should do. He had the gun out when I first pulled up. When his buddy told him the police was here, he took his gun and slipped it back down in his belt, grabbed the money and stuffed it in his pocket.

This whole time I'm getting closer. I stepped out of the car. He started for the door. I got to hand it to the old guy behind the counter. He called, "Look out! He's got a gun." But it was too late for that hemorrhoid, because the adrenaline was pumping real strong. Before the counter man had the word "look" out of his mouth, I had a bead right between the sucker's eyes. He just stood there and up went his hands.

The next thing that ran through my mind was, "Damn, why didn't he try to shoot or something?"

I grabbed ahold of him and threw him on the car. While I was handcuffing him, I was concentrating hard on the other one. I know he's getting away. I handed my magnum to the old guy from in the store and I said, "If that son of a bitch moves, fill him full of holes." The old guy could hardly hold the damn gun up. That poor hemorrhoid just knew he was dead now.

I grabbed my shotgun, put the situation out on the radio all in one breath and hauled ass after the other one. I ran him down. He was about two blocks away, trying to get into his car. I put the shotgun on him and had him lay down. I didn't have my handcuffs, so I just waited with him for the backup to get there.

They finally got there and handcuffed him. I got back in my car and I sat down. That's when it all hit me. Naturally, the hands start going like crazy, shaking a mile a minute. I looked back at my shotgun and said to myself, "I better get that round out of the chamber." I racked it back and there wasn't a round in the chamber. I had never racked one in. That's the kind of thing that scares you more than anything else.

*

I'm sitting there in the White Castle parking lot and I'm looking at this gas station across the street. There's these two dudes standing by a telephone. One of the dudes is looking all around. I thought, "There's something hinky about this. They may be thinking about doing a robbery." So I just watch them for a little bit.

The one guy leaves and brings a car up. When I see this car, I say to myself, "That's the damn car we were looking for out west. It might be these guys they want for aggravated robbery."

So I called another car and told them to meet me over here at the White Castle. The other car shows up and I said, "I think the two dudes over there are wanted for robbery, but I'm not sure. Let's take them out. You take the front and I'll drive up behind them. That way we'll have them boxed." So we did.

I got there first, since I always like to get into things first, which this time was a mistake. I jumped out of my car, walked up there and took my badge out. At that point, I didn't know whether they were the guys or not, so I had no reason to pull my gun. I say, "Police officer. Can I see some identification?"

The one guy is still talking on the phone. The other one said, "Sure, officer." He reached into his pocket and pulls out his wallet. He's getting his driver's license out. The other guy shoves his hand under his coat into his pants. I said, "Hey bring your hands out where I can see them."

"Sure," he says and brings out a .25 automatic. I thought, "Aw, shit."

"Now you're going to die, pig."

"Well, there's two guys behind you," I said. "They're coming up on you."

"Sure, there are," he said. About that time he was into his trigger pull, but I had just a split second when he looked over his shoulder and his gun hand went down as the gun went off.

The other officers pulled their weapons. I dove over the hood of my car to get some cover. I was going for my gun and I hear these shots going off, maybe eight or nine shots. By the time I get my gun out and get back around the car, the shooting is over—a matter of two or three seconds. The guy is laying there dead. I go over and check him out. His partner is stretching for the heavens saying, "God, don't shoot me. Hey, man, I'm not even with this guy."

Then I felt this warm sensation and I said, "Shit!" I looked down and blood is coming out of my tennis shoe. I said, "Hey, Ed. I'm shot."

"What do you mean?"

"Look," I pointed to the ground. "I think I been shot in the foot."

"Go sit down," he says.

I went over and sat down. Then one of our police tow trucks showed up on the lot. I went over there and grabbed the radio and said, "Better get a couple of squads in here. There's an officer shot and there's a suspect 10-18," which means dead at the scene. All the cruisers started rolling in, one after another.

Some news station is just driving by so when the squad takes me and puts me in the ambulance, some female reporter comes up and says, "Officer, how do you feel?"

I looked up at her and said, "I think I've had better days. How do you think I feel? My foot hurts like a son of a bitch." She quick grabbed the mike away.

The guys took my tennis shoe that I was wearing that day and they had it bronzed. I have it at home on my wall with a big ass hole in the son of a bitch.

The guy who shot me is pushing up roses or probably

weeds. That was the last time I ever told somebody to take their hands out of their pants.

When I was going through training, we went out to the state police officers' academy. One of the things in my training was, you'd approach a guy and the guy would have his hands in his pocket. The trainer says, "How would you talk to this guy?"

"Take your hands out of your pockets," was my first reaction. He'd pull out a gun—and bang! bang! bang!— I'm dead.

So we start again. I walk up to the guy and say, "Could you take your hands out of your pockets?" Before I could get my gun out, he goes bang! bang! bang!, I'm dead. Well, shit.

So the next time, the guy's walking up to me, I go up behind him and take out my gun full of blanks and go Pow! Pow! Pow! in his back. The instructor looks at me like I'm crazy and says, "Why did you shoot him in the back?"

"Because I'm tired of this son of a bitch killing me. So I'm going to kill him to begin with. The hell with it. I know he's got a gun in his pocket."

It should have sunk in out there. What I did on the street and what gets police officers killed is, I took too much for granted. You think he'll come out with his hand empty. You give people the benefit of the doubt. In this case, I shouldn't have.

Since then when I see a guy with his hands in his pockets, I tell him to keep his hands in his pockets. I'll go up and grab them and make sure he doesn't come out with a gun.

*

The first thing they ask you after a shooting is, "What was your backstop?" This is a standard question. "What was your backstop in case you missed or in case the round went through the person?" My backstop was a four-lane heavily traveled street full of traffic and the major shopping mall parking lot adjacent to the building. That's what it was.

"Did he fire at you?" they ask. They love to ask that question. "How many shots did the suspect fire at you before you shot him?" Like you're supposed to give the guy a couple of freebies to make for a better sense of fair play. Bullshit.

The headline in the next day's paper was, "Buckshot Shooting Cop Critically Injures Youth in Robbery Try." I was the fucking bad guy. This guy got a raw deal, but he managed to survive this terrible assault by law enforcement.

He didn't die, so that made it easier. I had to go up into the hospital one time while he was there to talk to an officer who was guarding him in the hospital. He was fucked up and I felt bad. I didn't go around telling anybody that, but I did feel bad.

Believe it or not they rolled the guy into the courtroom in a wheelchair and he pled not guilty. I get up on the stand. This guy has got a wife and a baby that I didn't know about. They're sitting in the spectator seats of the courtroom. I had to testify that I was the one that shot him. I could see her looking at me. He's going bye-bye into prison in a wheelchair. We're going through all the formalities of the sentencing and the wife jumped up and started calling me a motherfucker. She almost got locked up for contempt. Unpleasant.

I almost felt, one time, like going up and saying that I was sorry that it happened that way and that he got fucked up so bad, but I never did. For one thing, I knew he wanted to kill me. I could tell when he got shot and he still went for that shotgun. I said, "Fuck it. He didn't care about nobody. He didn't care about that pharmacist or the girl. He didn't care about me, certainly."

When somebody gets a gun stuck in their face and they get put in the position of not knowing whether they're going to be alive in the next few minutes, those are the people that I feel sorry for. It works on you for a long, long time after that. All these little girls that work in the hamburger joints and carry-outs and stuff, you see them quitting every time there's a holdup. You know what they're going through.

*

A guy robbed a store. Two of us were dispatched. I really was going to wait on the blind side of the business for the backup, but the blind side I chose was also the robber's escape route. He came around the corner. When he saw me, he dropped the loot.

He ran behind a barbecue business on the opposing corner from me. I chased him in my car. As I got next to him, I realized, "Hey, I can just bump him and knock him down."

When I bumped him, the car slid a little bit and went too far. He hit the ground and I ran over his shoulder from about the midchest area to right next to his head. I hit the brakes. I thought, "Holy shit, I've killed this son of a bitch."

He gets up running, uninjured. I'm out of the car now. I snatched my shotgun out. He runs around the barbecue. I run around the barbecue. When I see the lead he's got on me when I get around the corner of the place, I figured, "Whoa, fuck this."

Boom! I shoot one time and he hits the ground. It turned out that one pellet had struck him in the head and knocked him out, along with his teeth and stuff when he hit the ground. He was not mortally wounded. It had flattened out and slid around the side of his jawbone and clipped his Eustachian tube and got his pharynx. He couldn't talk at all or hear out of one side of his head.

They connected him to several burglaries and robberies. Big loss amounts and they were really glad. But

I was real nervous because I knew that this guy had a tire print on him. He's wearing a white shirt with a tire print right up his damn back and over his shoulder. "Oh, God damn, man. Should I say something about this? Is he going to say something about this?"

Now the brass rolled out for the shooting, civilian clothes, uniforms, everything. It is crawling with everybody above a captain in the whole damn department. But nobody has said anything to me yet except the lieutenant gathering facts for his shooting diagram that he's required to fix.

The captain walks over. He's in civilian clothes. He says, "Is that where you shot him over there?"

"Yes sir."

"Did you see the teeth over there in the road?"

"No sir."

"Come on over and look." I went over there and there's two whole teeth laying in the road right where he hit the ground. "They're not even broken," he says. "They just came out. Do you want them?"

"Do I need them for evidence?"

"No."

"Well, then I don't want them."

"Good." His face lit up. "I'm going to have them covered in gold for a necklace."

"My God," I said. "You're what?"

"Yeah, I'm going to have them covered in gold for a necklace. Souvenirs."

Jesus Christ.

I go to the hospital to check on the guy. I walk down the hall there just as the lieutenant and another officer are going into the room. I hear as I'm approaching, "Is he bad?"

"No," the doctor says, "it's just superficial. He's got a lot of damage to his voice box and his ear. Otherwise he's all functional. He's not going to die."

"Good," the lieutenant says.

"By the way," the doctor says, "how'd he get the tire print up his back?" I made an about-face and split. In all the confusion no one ever, ever asked me how he got the tire print up his back. The guy never brought it up.

*

We had a silent alarm at the Sears & Roebuck store. When the officers got there and looked over the building, they found a plate glass window busted out. Some of the things in the display behind it were knocked over, too, where somebody went through. So the officers were searching the building. One of them took the escalator going down. Since it was night, they were turned off and it was like a staircase. As he got to the bottom of the escalator, he turned and in the glow from one of the emergency exit lights, he saw the silhouette of a large man standing there with a shotgun or a rifle cradled in his arms. He yelled halt, spun around with his flashlight and fired a round. He hit him right in the heart, a mannequin in a Sears & Roebuck sporting goods section, displaying shotguns and hunting equipment.

*

I've been shot at a lot more times than I've shot at somebody else. This one particular night, we were riding in a two-man car at the time. We received a call to an address on a street that we knew dead-ended in the woods at that hundred block. But you got to go to the call. We had been there on three different occasions, the last two days after dark, similar calls. Nothing there. Nothing happened. "Code Alpha. There's nothing here, HQ. We're leaving."

On this night we were both particularly nervous about going to this call for some reason. We were talking about it on the way. "I don't have a good feeling about going down there."

"No, me neither." So we took a little extra precaution. I opened my door and he opened his door and we coasted in with all the interior lights off down toward the dead end.

Somebody opened up with a small caliber weapon and fired several shots. We could see the flashes. We jumped out and returned fire. Just filled the woods up around that flash with bullets and reloaded.

After we did that, we thought, "What kind of a predicament did we put ourselves in? I'm not going to go walking into those damn woods now to look for blood or a body. But if we don't, if we walk away and let somebody die out there, we could be in trouble." We optioned for trouble and left.

We went back the next day before it got dark and never found anything.

If you tell that story, it seems like a really big event. But really, on my one-to-ten scale, that's four- or five-ish in my career. Doesn't rank high at all.

It's a split-second thing. It happened and you reacted. You didn't have time to give it any consideration. Except that you're pissed off that somebody has the gall to shoot at you. I thought about it later. There are people out there who would like to kill me just for the hell of it. Just because I'm in blue.

*

We got a call—man with a gun in a candy store. We get to the candy store and the owner says to me, "It's this kid, just ran around the corner. He's fifteen, he's wearing a blue jacket, a white shirt and dark pants. He pulled a gun on me. He had a fight with me earlier here and he came back and he pulled a gun on me. He just ran around the corner."

I jump in the car and drive around the corner. I see

this description going into a building that turns out to be a youth home. I never really got a good look at him. I just had an impression of the clothing. I jump out of the radio car and I run through the door of the youth home. The place is crowded with kids, but I can hear footsteps ahead of me, running down the hallway.

I'm running, chasing the kid. I'm always just a little bit behind him. He's always one turn beyond me in the hallway. Up some stairs. Down that hallway. Up some other stairs. Down another hallway. Always one turn ahead of me. Then the hallway dead-ends where some elevators are and I finally come up on him.

He turned around and he sticks a gun in my face and pulls the trigger. I watched the cylinder rotate. Nothing happened. I knocked the gun to the side. The kid doesn't even fight at this point. He's as stunned as I am that he pulled the trigger at point-blank range and I'm still standing there. I get his arms behind him. I cuff him. I get the gun and I stick it in my pants.

My first reaction wasn't to beat the hell out of him or to even touch him. My first reaction was, "Why the fuck am I still here? Why aren't I dead?"

By this time the kids in the youth center have followed the commotion and they're all around. We get the kid out and put him in the car and take him to the station house.

He's fifteen years old. As near as we can make out from the situation, this kid has been sticking up cab drivers. We get the gun in the house and I open it up. It's a .32 Smith & Wesson. The .32 uses a shorter cartridge than the regular .38 police special. But you can make a .38 bullet fit into the chamber if you cut the head off the bullet. He had two spent rounds of the correct ammunition, three full .38 rounds with the heads cut off and an empty chamber. The gun had landed on one of the spent rounds. If it had landed on any one of the three .38s, I would have gotten my brains splattered all over the hallway.

He was a juvenile offender. I didn't hit him. I processed him through to the juvenile detention center, went down to youth court with him and they let him go. The worst punishment he got was when his mother came into the precinct and she started slapping him around because he'd taken her gun. He'd taken her gun out of her drawer. She slapped the shit out of him. Tried to kill me, had been sticking up cab drivers and got nothing at all from the authorities.

*

I was at the Belaire Apartments, standing in the parking lot. Out of my jurisdiction, which is a terrible no-no. But it was only just out of my jurisdiction. I was talking to Jim Sloane and his daughter. He was the manager there and we were just shooting the breeze, you know. I was leaning up against the patrol car. I laid my walkie-talkie down, which is something I hardly ever do. I won't never do it any more, I'll tell you that right now.

As we're talking, I see this person walking out by the street. I didn't think anything about it. I looked again and he's coming right through the sprinkler system which is getting him wet, so then I started thinking something's going on here. I said, "Jim, you know this guy?"

"No, just some weird-o, I guess." He's still a good distance off, so we continued talking a few more seconds.

"What's he got in his hand?" Jim's daughter said. I looked again and the damn hairs started raising on the back of my neck.

"Something ain't right," I said to myself. Then to her I said, "Why don't you go into the house?" She did. As he got closer, I said, "Let me see your hands." He wouldn't put both of them where I could see them. I could see his left hand. Then I saw this brown thing on him which suddenly resolved into a holster.

He had his right hand down by his thigh. He had a gun in that hand. His hand swung too far forward one time and I saw for sure that it was a gun. I'd unsnapped my holster when I told him to show me his hands. I said, "Jim, get down behind a car." Jim had this big German shepherd—beautiful dog—which had been trained and everything, but which only attacks cats. So Jim and the dog got down behind a car. I shouted, "Let me see your hands!"

He's about thirty yards from me now and about this time he started coming up with the weapon and Boom! I got down and moved. Everything went so fast, I left the walkie-talkie on the car where I had laid it down, so I couldn't say, "Help, send help." I went down about four cars, looking for cover and trying not to get my head blown off. I got away from the patrol car just in case Jim decided to poke his head around the corner or something.

Boom! He fires another one at me. Shit, this guy is for real. I come up to see what he's doing and I see him stick his head up behind this station wagon. Ba-boom! I fired off two. Evidently, I didn't get him, he's still there. But he didn't hit the car I was behind. So they were in my direction, but he wasn't placing them well. I, on the other hand, killed two cars.

After he popped off his first two rounds I wasn't saying nothing. I wasn't giving myself totally away. But he said something strange. He said, "Police! You're surrounded. Give yourself up."

"Aw, shit," I thought, "I'm surrounded by these guys." Thinking all this crazy stuff.

"Throw your gun out," he said. If I'd been thinking, I could have thrown my extra gun out. When he came out to get it, I'd have blown his peter off or something.

There are just so many things going through your head right then.

The whole thing didn't last more than two minutes. I'm sitting there thinking, "What am I going to do?" I'd had guns pointed at me before, but I'd never been shot at. I can't even begin to tell the things that went through my head. "Jesus, why didn't I wear my vest? Who is this crazy son of a bitch? Why is he doing this? Jesus, they don't pay me enough for this shit." A million things. Plus you're trying to count bullets. You think about the investigation that's going to happen after this is all over. "God, they're going to kill me. I blew away that station wagon. What reason will I give for being all the way over here in the first place?"

Boom! I got another one coming at me. I come up again and fired off a round and went down another parked car. Maybe he'll still think I'm in my original place.

He had about the same idea, because when I'd made my move, he backed up to a dumpster. I came around the car thinking I've got him and there he is in a new spot. He's got me. But he didn't shoot.

I moved again and popped up to look for him. I didn't see him. What he'd done was just to step backwards into the black shadow that the dumpster cast. The next thing I know, he's back up at the street. He's booking. He's gone. I'm not going to shoot now.

Finally, I get to the radio. I was scared. I mean, I was *scared*. When I got on the radio I thought I was screaming, but everybody said afterwards that I was talking very softly and measured. In fact, they had to listen twice because they couldn't believe I was saying I got shot at. I identified myself and gave the signal for urgent traffic. "I been fired at. I returned fire and I believe I wounded him in the arm. Description follows."

I gave a total description of this guy. The only thing

I missed was the color of one of the thin stripes in his shirt. White male, approximately six feet tall, possible Latin-looking, dark hair with a mustache. I gave them the color of the pants, wearing a pullover type shirt— it was reddish-looking with a black stripe. And it was dark as a well digger's ass that night. 'Course there was light in the parking lot.

Then I reloaded my weapon and it's the waiting period. Is he going to come back after you, or is the help going to arrive first? All of a sudden I heard that beautiful noise—sirens and blowing engines. You feel good when you see all those guys coming. And they were coming out of the woodwork—off-duty deputies, anybody who had their scanner on. They were coming out in jockey shorts. They brought the dogs and the handler and the gunners. They were there and they were pissed.

They put another man with the dogs. I said, "No, I'm going with the dogs. It's my turn. I'm going to get him now." Once I got over being scared, I got mad because he'd scared me so bad. I'd never seen this guy. I didn't know this guy. As it turned out we had seen this guy before.

When he left the apartments, he went through a vacant area—sand and briers and everything else—walked over to the next housing development and knocked on a window. This older lady was at home talking with her daughter on the telephone. He tells her, "There was a shoot-out. I was helping the police. They've arrested the suspect, but they forgot about me and I need a ride to the hospital." He's standing there with a gun and his arm was bleeding. I did hit him.

She tells him okay, picks up the phone and tells her daughter, "Oh, there's a guy out here who's been shot helping the police arrest somebody, but they forgot him. So I'm going to take him to the hospital." She hangs up.

"What?" her daughter says. So the daughter calls the

sheriff's department immediately. She says that there is some guy over at her mom's house who's been shot and claims to be a law enforcement officer. They come on the radio with it right away. "There is a subject shot on Lake Road at such and such an address." This is right across from us. We know it's him. They converge on the house.

The lady had come out by then and was getting ready to get into the car. We almost had a bad situation, because an off-duty deputy who came up on one side of the house had almost the same description as the suspect. He's got the mustache, the Latin look, the automatic weapon, everything but the striped shirt. Another deputy came around the house from the other direction with a shotgun leveled down on this off-duty officer. He saved himself by yelling, "No, Dick, no. It's me, Mack. That's the guy over there."

The suspect is standing over to the side, holding the holster with the gun in it. They tell him the usual. "Drop it." The only reason he didn't get blown away was because of the lady standing there. They knew that if they blew him away with her standing there she'd probably talk. Instead, they went over and helped him to the ground and made sure his arm wasn't hurt too bad and got him to rearrange the grass a little bit. They called me when they had him in custody and requested that I come over for an ID.

I got over there, got out of the car. The first thing, the lieutenant walked up to me with four deputies and said, "You are not going to touch him. There are too many people watching. Do not do anything. Leave your gun in the car, too."

"I'm not going to do anything to him," I said. So he let me keep my gun.

"Okay, but don't even act like you're going to go for it, because I'll have one of these deputies grab you." I walked up there with them all around me. They didn't let me get too close—about twenty or thirty feet, which was equal to the distance we were shooting at each other from. I just glanced over and said, "That's him." There wasn't no doubt in my mind. I knew him. I knew that face.

"Can I walk up closer?" I asked. They let me. I kept going and they stopped me. I just wanted to choke that son of a bitch. I was so angry. I just turned around and left. Standing there was just boiling me over.

I went back to the other sight and got ready for the big investigation. The sergeants came round and then the lieutenants and the chief and the reporters. They were putting little circles on the ground where all his cartridges were. They found all the slugs. When he shot at me, his rounds hit right in front of me in the asphalt and dug in. The bullet I hit him with was only a flesh wound. The car that was right next to where I'd been firing from was killed. I think it was one of the first rounds I shot, because when I came up the first time I was just letting him know I was going to shoot back. I didn't stick my head up too far. I killed a station wagon, too. I didn't break any glass. Not the first window.

His name was Andrew Such-and-Such. He hadn't been out of the service too long, rank of captain. Had a prior mental record in the service. He did know how to use fire and concealment real well. He had training in it. He used the car, moved to the dumpster and used the shadow to get away.

Two weeks before this shooting this guy had been seen by quite a few officers. He'd been baiting cops. Kid had a Corvette. He drove into the municipal parking lot, caught a few eyes, including the chief. Then he went to the entrance, gunned it and screeched out of there and was gone.

About three days after that two of us had just finished a call and were parked window to window having a chit-chat. This red Corvette driving down the road passed us pretty slow. When he got about 100 yards away, he took off like a bat out of hell and was gone in a flash. We looked at each other and said, "Shit, we're not going to catch that stuff. Not in these cars."

He had started wearing camouflage fatigues to work and carrying his gun all the time. He beat the crap out of his brother right in their business office. When we went into his room later, he had set up a battlefield with toy soldiers. All the light bulbs in the room had been removed so none of the lamps would go on. The windows were covered for total darkness. He was supposed to have been on medication, but I think he'd stopped taking it.

That night when I was standing out there talking to Jim, it just so happened that he was living in the apartments just next door. He had just come home and when he saw me over there he must have decided, "Now's the time." He figured he could just walk up on me, which he almost did. I don't think he came at me personally. It was just the uniform.

You know what they done to him? Five years' probation. They declared him mentally incompetent. I don't think he was. I think he had a problem but he knew what he was doing.

"Do what you want with it," I said to the state's attorney. "Just don't bother me no more. Let me forget it." I've done real well with it. But I can still lie down and with my eyes wide open I can see that face. That crazed face.

*

We got a call to Houston and Market. There was a little confectionery there on the corner. There was supposed to be a breaking and entering in progress. I had a rookie with me that night. I stopped in front of the store with my lights out and told him to watch the front while I went around back. When I got around back, this guy was coming out of the window. I was so close that I thought he would never run. I told him to halt. He hit the ground going 90 miles an hour. He was fast and he was already into the dark. We had the law at that time that you could shoot at a fleeing felon, so I fired a shot at him. I missed him, but I kept running and was shooting at him. I'd just gotten the .457 Magnum and it had a different grip than my other gun. I ended up firing four shots at him. I was trying to hit him anywhere I could. The last shot went right through the bottom of his shoe and out his big toe. That knocked him down.

The paper wrote it up that the officer fired four warning shots, telling the criminal to stop. When he wouldn't stop, he shot him in the foot. I felt bad at the inquest. His mother came up to me and said, "I sure appreciate your not killing my son and shooting him in the foot instead."

*

I had a traffic stop and before I could do anything, this guy dove under the seat, reached down and started coming up. I almost killed him right there in the seat. He was getting a flashlight to go in the glove box for his wallet.

Maybe it would have come out officially in a courtroom that it was justified and acceptable. But I would have had to live with it.

I said to myself, "This is it, buddy. He's going to take you out." Nobody—I don't care how understanding you are—nobody is truly going to understand what my feelings were at that point. They are going to read, "COP MURDERS CITIZEN WITH FLASHLIGHT IN HAND." That's going to be the headline.

That's not the worst part of it. The worst part is how I would feel for the rest of my life.

We've had a couple of officers who have been casualties of a malicious press. They will never be right again. It goes with the territory, but it's the thing that scares me the most about the job. It's a split second decision that you've got to make and if it's wrong, shame on you.

*

This guy ran a light. We went to chase him and give him a ticket. He started running from us. I love a good high-speed chase. Nothing nicer. My partner was driving and I liked his driving style, so it was not a big deal.

He finally lost it with our help and he crashed into a building. We went through a skid sideways. The guy jumped out of the car and started running. The driver's side of our car is facing this guy's car so my partner started running after the guy off to the side. I stayed on the passenger side and put my gun on the roof of the car and just followed this guy with the sights. He hit a chain link fence and started to climb over it. He was almost to the top of the fence, his head was even with the top bar, and I heard a shot. My partner shot. I don't know why he shot, but it was the guy running from us that my partner shot at, and I was so used to relying on his judgment that it never even crossed my mind to think—I just pulled the trigger. I was aiming for the middle of the guy's back. I squeezed off my shot. I'm an expert marksman and that guy went down. I thought I'd put one right between his shoulders.

My partner runs over and kicks him. I said, "Pat, what are you kicking him for, man. For Christ's sake, the guy's got two bullet holes in him?"

"What do you mean, bullet holes in him?" Pat says, and he turned around to look at me.

"You shot him. I shot him. I hit him. I never known you to miss." We used to go to the range together and he was an expert shot since he was a paratrooper in the Army. I didn't figure he missed him. The guy had started to fall before my bullet got to him, so I figured the guy's got two shots in him. I'm looking for his gun. I figured that's why my partner shot—the guy had a gun and he didn't want him to get over the fence where he had cover to take a shot at us and put us in jeopardy.

"I didn't shoot him," Pat says.

"What do you mean, you didn't shoot him?"

"I fired in the air."

"Since when do we shoot in the air? You never fired in the air before. We never threw shots for no reason. What do you mean? I thought you shot at him for a reason. I hit him. I shot him in the back," I yelled at my partner. "The fucking guy's dead! I put a fucking bullet in his back!" I was 100 percent sure I hit this guy.

Now I'm scared. Now I don't have a reason. My partner didn't shoot at the guy. He'd done something that was out of character and it scared the fuck out of me. I started looking for the bullet wound on this guy. I'm turning him over and I can't find any blood or any bullet holes. I've got him on his stomach and I'm looking for an entry hole in the back of his jacket. Nothing. Then I feel him breathe. I realize the motherfucker is playing possum . . . and I kicked him. I gave him a kick in the head and said, "Get your ass up, you motherfucker." There's these big round eyes looking at us like "You fuckers are crazy motherfuckers." I says, "You're lucky you're not dead."

"Lucky," he said. "I felt that motherfucker pull on my nap." Meaning his Afro. When my partner shot, he let go of the fence and started dropping. I squeezed off my shot and the bullet went right through his hair, just missing him. He was playing fucking dead because he didn't want to be shot no more. He was going to lay there and do nothing. I thought I killed the guy for nothing. I was so mad at Pat. Ah, was I mad at Pat. "Why did you do that to me? You never done that before!" You get so used to each other that sometimes it can be bad.

*

The last shooting I was on was a comedy. It happened Friday, August 13. We were working plainclothes at the county fair. We're pissed. We're not even on the fairgrounds. We can't even look at the women, because we are assigned to the perimeter. It's in a pretty bad neighborhood and all these kids come and rip off the cars while the people are in the fair. We've got to sit out there and chase hubcap thieves and stop kids from ripping off CB radios. It's hotter than hell even at night and the dust is flying. It's a shit detail.

I've got a new partner. He's young and he's a hotdog. Somebody calls up the radio room and says, "They're going to knock off the Rax Roast Beef on the hilltop tonight." Click. No name or address, no particulars, no nothing. Just a one sentence phone call.

The dispatcher calls us. This technician tells me about this phone call she has received. It was probably about nine-thirty at night. I didn't know whether to go cover it or not. But it would be like an hour till closing, maximum. I said, "We better go up and cover it. It's only an hour. We can eat, too." We went rolling on up there and another guy riding by himself went out there with us.

We walked in the door of the restaurant. I went up to the manager and showed him my badge and told him, "We got this tip you were going to be held up tonight. We're going to be in the area until you close." He said that they did indeed close in an hour.

I ordered a cup of coffee. My partner ordered a carton of milk and some chocolate chip cookies. Like I said, he was young. The other guy gets there and he orders a cup of tea. But they don't have any tea made, so we're sitting at this table, waiting for his fucking tea. We're arguing about how to cover it, because we don't know what we're looking for. If a guy comes in slipping a note that says, "Give me all your money," and he's not showing a gun or anything, if you're sitting across the street with binoculars, you're going to miss the whole thing. They'll give him a Rax Roast Beef bag full of money and he'll walk away.

The door bursts open and two huge guys come in screaming profanities. They are dressed in dark blue hooded sweat shirts, dark blue ski masks, surgical gloves. They are carrying twin sawed-off 12-gauge shotguns. Here we sit.

One guy immediately vaults the counter. The second guy has the whole dining room covered. We've got elderly couples, we have two mommies and their little toddlers, and various other and sundry people.

I'm sitting there in a knit shirt with this Model 59 nine mm. It's a huge frame gun. Everybody thinks it's a .45. It is tucked in my belt. The knit shirt is over it, but there is this huge bulge. I have this police walkie-talkie. Thank God that instead of on the table it is on the seat beside me and it was off. It probably should have been on, but it was off. At least it didn't go, "Lincoln Mary Six, call the station."

I've never ever been this scared. These two were the most intimidating things I have ever seen in my life. They were dressed for the part.

The one guy in the dining area had a straight shot right down the aisle at our table. We are three adult males sitting together at a table, so he ain't looking at nobody else. Nobody else there is a threat to him.

We all are ordered on the floor: "Every motherfucker on the floor and start throwing out your wallets." With our police IDs in them, of course. There's nothing else to do. We throw our wallets out. I'm on the floor on my belly and I've gotten under my shirt and have my hand on this nine mm and I'm laying on top of it. I'm thinking to myself, "When he finds our IDs, he's going to start executing us. When he does I'm going to roll over and empty this gun into him. At least, he's going with us."

The other guy has the manager and all the employees on the floor in the back and he's cleaning out the safe. In the meantime, there's this mental who gets up from the table and goes and starts hassling this guy. He's just some old guy and he keeps at it and keeps at it. So the guy blew him up. He shot him. He didn't kill him, but he just about blew his leg off. He's crippled now. The old guy tried to pull his ski mask off. We'd seen him in there earlier and he was definitely a mental. He was nasty to the counter girl who was out there with a vacuum cleaner. He made her go and get a fresh bowl of lettuce for the salad bar. He was really shitty about it. I almost said something to him then, but I thought, "We're not here for that."

He's now slumped in the corner. I said to myself, "Enough is enough." I stood up and started blasting. I'm highly trained SWAT man. I can't miss. This guy sees us, runs across the dining room, into the vestibule and out of my sight. I got about three off at him as he ran across the room. I thought maybe he's ducked down in the vestibule there, reloading, so I pumped about three into the vestibule. My two side kicks went over to the far side of the dining room and they are shooting through the plate glass windows as the guy is running across the parking lot. He had gone straight out the door and they were busting glass all the way across the front of the building. This is a trip now. All these customers—fifteen or sixteen of them—are laying on the floor during all this. One of the toddlers is running around through this firefight.

When this happens you get tunnel vision. Your focus is limited to the particular thing that is going on. I cut out the asshole in the back room. He could have gotten out the back door and gotten away. He came back across the counter and unloaded on me twice with his 12-gauge pump gun. Blew out the glass immediately beside my head. I could feel the glass flying and knew I'd been hit. He blew up a chair on the other side of me. About that time, we all started focusing where we should have been focused and all started firing. He had eighteen entrance and exit wounds in his body. After he went down, he was still trying to get back up. Looked like he was doing push-ups to get back up. My gun was empty and that was it.

I jumped up and I started checking myself for holes. Literally. They say you can't feel a gunshot wound. I've heard that a hundred times. So I figured I had to look for it. We got the smoky haze and we got glass everywhere. There is blood everywhere.

The first thing that happened was one of the mommies jumps up and says, "My baby's been shot!" My heart sank to the bottom and I lost it. It's the only time I've lost my cool in thirteen years. I'm screaming into the walkie-talkie to get the rescue squad in there. I was totally, just totally . . . I don't think they could even read me on the radio. I totally lost it. I thought I'd finally gone and fucked up big time. And this little kid is going to buy it, is going to pay. To this day, that is the worst experience I ever had.

It turns out, she wasn't shot at all. She'd been blood-spattered from the mental getting shot.

There was a police chief from a small town that bordered on this precinct in line with his wife and son getting a roast beef sandwich when the whole thing went down. They had all got put on the floor. He jumps up and pulls out a gun and a badge now that it's over. He waves his fucking gun and says, "I'm a police officer."

"Well, so the fuck are we," I said. "Who'd you think we were, you dumb shit?"

"If you hurt my little boy," he starts screaming, "you're in trouble." His little boy had blood spattered all over his face. Everybody did by that time.

The guy who got out, dumped the shotgun in the river and ran home. Two more guys from our team went to his house and he was waiting. His name had been reported in a second anonymous phone call. He came to the door and said, "I give up." He was scared to death. He had holes in his clothing. It had been real close. He went to prison.

I didn't have any problems with that shooting as far as remorse goes. You think about the fact that this guy's got a mother and you wonder how she feels, but you don't feel sorry for them. He almost got me.

I wondered after that if I had any nerve left. You always wonder about your nerve. What are you going to do? Will you back down when the time comes the next time? Probably everybody goes through that. You don't talk about it. But you wonder how you're going to react. You hear stories about incidents where a policeman is faced with a similar situation and you wonder how you would have done it.

There's a lot of Monday morning quarterbacking going on. Policemen are not very kind to one another at all. I get involved in the shit and there's three hundred guys saying, "I would have done this and that. You shouldn't have done this and the other thing." Terrible. I stopped doing it myself a long time ago. But I used to do it. Now I say, "If you weren't there, then don't say nothing, because you don't know what it was like."

CHAPTER 5

Blood Brothers

THE MAJORITY of police officers socialize exclusively with other police officers. The first reason a cop will give is that his unconventional work schedule imposes constraints on his behavior. Rotating shifts, odd days off and unpredictable overtime puts him out of synchronization with other working people. The cop is finishing a ten-hour shift and dropping into a bar for a cold one when his peers in other professions are eating their breakfasts and heading for the office. His weekends one month are Wednesday and Thursday, next month, Monday and Tuesday. Once he has canceled a few dinner engagements on short notice, he explains, his civilian acquaintances drop him from their social register.

Every cop can tell a story of how his introduction at a party has suddenly put a damper on the fun of all the other revelers because they can see him only as a representative of moral authority. Or how some irate civilian has button-holed him in a social setting and proceeded to air all his grievances on the subjects of law and order, abuse of police power and local parking regulations.

Most cops will tell you they don't talk to civilians because only another cop can understand the pressures that shape a police officer's attitudes toward life and work and society. Consider this illustration of that point from a highway patrolman: "We found a guy in a 55-gallon drum. Somebody had put him in there. It was a professional hit. The body just turned to shit. Pictures were taken for evidence. Then we tip the barrel over and the body just pours out. This situation has 'Janitor in a Drum' written all over it.

"Great sense of humor, huh? You just can't say that kind of thing to a civilian. They want to barf on your shoes."

Gallows humor is a defense mechanism all people in stressful situations use to relieve tension and to defuse horror. If a person's job concerns primarily the ugly, brutal side of life, his shoptalk is bound to be somewhat ugly and brutal. Even if he is simply reciting the day's events as blandly as possible, his stories can be shocking to an audience unprepared for such graphic conversation.

This brings us closer to the core of the issue. "Nobody understands but another cop." Police officers work under hazardous, stressful conditions and this draws them together into a kind of brotherhood.

A cop's life can depend on whether or not his partner and other police officers—some of whom he doesn't even know—are willing to lay their lives on the line for him. As one officer put it, "It's a contact sport and if you don't watch my back for me, there's no one else I can count on. If you're not looking out for me, I'm going to get hurt." Mutual defense in the face of physical danger is as essential for cops as it is for troops in combat.

However, when the very real threat of harm is combined with the habitual suspiciousness police officers develop on the job, the result can be a kind of paranoia. Many cops begin to see themselves as under siege from all sides. They develop a classic "Us versus Them" mentality. The protection of the brotherhood is then stretched and overextended to cover "hurts"—both real and imagined—from any front.

The real reason most police officers socialize exclusively with other police officers is that they just don't trust the people they police—which is everybody who is not a cop. They know the public generally resents their authority and is fickle in its support of police policy and individual police officers. Older officers teach younger ones that it is best to avoid civilians. Civilians will only try to "hurt" the cop in the end, they say. That hurt may range from a personal insult to social ostracism to a formal complaint of abuse.

The "Us versus Them" attitude also applies within the ranks of the police themselves. Superior officers from sergeants on up are regarded by patrol officers as "Them." They are the brass, concerned only with their own careers, not with the welfare of the cop in the street. The adversary relationship between patrolmen and their bosses is much like worker/management conflicts in any business, but the existence of the brotherhood makes it more virulent. Any decision from upstairs is considered a potential "hurt" and so it must be guarded against. It is therefore very easy for a cop to lose his membership in the brotherhood simply by trying for a promotion. One of the most difficult transitions a new sergeant must weather is the suspicion with which he is now regarded by his former colleagues who are still on patrol.

The ultimate outcast from the brotherhood is the cop who works in the Internal Affairs Division (IAD) of the department, the people who police the police. That a fellow officer could stoop so low as to join in investigating and prosecuting corruption and abuses of police power, actively trying to "hurt" a member of the brotherhood, is simply unthinkable to many cops.

There is racism within the brotherhood. Recent federal charges of discriminatory hiring practices and the resulting effort to hire and promote minority officers has put a real strain on the bonds among black and white and Hispanic cops. But the unwritten law of the brotherhood does not allow discussion of racial tension with outsiders. Most police officers will claim that all cops are blue and race is not a problem, even though they just finished punching it out along color lines in the locker room.

On the other hand, almost every male officer will say that women do not belong on the job. The police officers' peer group *is* a brotherhood, and female officers are sometimes entirely excluded. The women usually try to tough it out without complaining—which would just alienate them further—but most of them have had a personal experience with sexual harassment or discrimination. There have even been reports of intentionally slow backup from male officers when a female officer is answering a potentially hazardous call.

For all their talk about staunch loyalty and a united front, police officers also know how ephemeral the bonds of police brotherhood can be on an individual basis. Let an officer come under investigation or indictment and he is ostracized from the brotherhood. Many of his brothers will desert him to avoid any possibility of guilt by association.

Most police officers are not surprised when they see their brothers' feet of clay. They know that the blue tribe of blood brothers is made of human beings who have fears, faults and prejudices like everyone else. Deep inside they understand that the brotherhood of policemen is part necessity, part neurosis and part myth.

* * *

YOU WORK the paddy wagon and you go to work at eleven o'clock. You get in the wagon and there's a dead body back there that they didn't bother to take to the morgue. They left it for you. All the paperwork is there, but they didn't tell you. You can't get them, because you are the one who does the relieving. They don't relieve you. They got you.

They'll spray tear gas on the microphone or put it in the heater ducts in the wintertime. You turn the heater on and that shit blows out. You sit there and cry all night.

Put live chickens in your locker. I've seen it happen. Dead things. They'll go out and scrape up some raccoon off the street and put it in the front seat of your car before you go on a run, or put it in your briefcase. They're crazy, crazy.

*

One time me and my partner were in a key shop getting some keys made. It was snowing pretty bad outside. One of the other officers on the beat told radio to hit our recall. When they do that, your beacons go on to let you know that you're wanted on the radio. So I said, "I'll go see what they want."

It was an ambush. I went out to the car and these two guys started pelting me with snowballs. When they let up, I got in the car and told them to back off a little bit. I hit the siren and waved at my partner to come on, like it was an emergency. He come running out and I locked the doors of the cruiser and these guys just beat the shit out of him with these snowballs.

"You're no partner, man," he yells. "You left me out here with the wolves."

*

When my partner and I would go in on a burglary, I'd unscrew some light bulbs out of the fixtures. My partner

213

would be going down to check out the basement in an abandoned house. He's creeping down the stairs real cautious. I'd take the light bulbs and throw them—Pop! Pop! Pop! That would scare the hell out of him. I'd laugh my ass off.

*

We're going on a domestic. At the apartment we were called to, there was no protection. Once you were in the hallway, the doorway was right in front at the top of the flight of stairs. My partner was going up the steps ahead of me. There was a hollow door off its hinges at the bottom of the steps. I took out my nightstick and hollered, "Watch out, Danny!" And I hit this damn door so hard it sounded like a shotgun. He fell halfway down the steps. That was the first time he really got pissed at me.

*

I was working with this real character. We were going by the freeway off-ramp on Bright Street and there was a family there that looked like they were broken down with their station wagon off to the side of the road. We pulled over to see if we could help them out. What happened was, they had some kittens in the back of the station wagon. While they were stopped at a light, the mother cat jumped out the back window and was in the tall grass.

So this asshole partner of mine says, "Well, that's tough."

"Come on," I said, "let's help them find the cat."

"I ain't helping look for no God damn cat."

"Well, you just wait here for me. I'm going to go and try to help them find their cat." It's kind of like a company sweep; we're going through the tall grass looking for the cat. I accidentally scared the cat. She ran out onto the freeway and got run over by the first car that came along.

This fucking partner of mine starts laughing. I'm real upset. I apologize to them. They don't know what they're going to do with this litter of kittens now. I had to load this partner of mine into the cruiser and get out of there before we had a complaint filed on us. The boy was crude.

*

Everything happens nights, even on the wagon. They sent us on a shooting. We got there and this guy is laying in the doorway of a restaurant. He had definitely been shot. In fact, he's probably dead, but we're not doctors so we can't say that.

We throw him on a stretcher. I was driving. I take off for the hospital, red light and sirens. My partner is back there bandaging this guy up, putting a hell of a bandage on him.

Get him to the hospital and rush him in there. Get him on the table and pull his shirt off. Unwrap my partner's bandaging job and wipe everything all off so they can see the wound. He's been shot in the back of the head. But all the blood had run down and collected on his chest. My partner was a first-aid instructor, too.

*

We were having a series of pizza deliverymen getting held up as they would make a delivery. It would be a phony delivery. They would go back to their car and there'd be two guys standing there with knives or clubs. They'd smack the deliveryman and take his money. It got to be a problem after it happened about eight or nine times, so we contacted all the pizza places in the immediate area and told them if they got a suspicious call to call us. We could become their deliverymen and try to catch these guys.

A pizza place calls us with a delivery that's about a block over from where their driver had been robbed before. So we get in the car and go over there. My partner is hiding in the back. I've got my apron on and my shirt undone, no tie. Deliveryman disguise, right? I've got my gun underneath my apron.

It's a dead-end street, a court with a little circle at the end. Driving down the street, I see these two guys standing there, so I just keep on going. I tell McGuire, my partner, "There's two guys standing there, but they're not doing nothing." I get out of the car and get the pizza out of the back. I tell McGuire, "I'm going up to the house. I don't know where the guys went to."

I get up to the house and the lady says, "Oh, we didn't order a pizza. This is the second time this has happened in a week."

"I'm sorry to have bothered you, ma'am." I go back to the car and open up the hatch and the two guys come walking up out of the bushes. I told McGuire, "Get ready. Here they come."

I put the pizza back in the oven and close the hatchback. They're coming around from the front of the car and I'm right in the back. So I kind of back up against the car where they can't get behind me. One of them gets on my left and one of them gets on my right. One guy has a club in his hand. The other guy has something shiny in his hand. I don't know what it is, but it's black. I said, "What's happening?"

"Give me all your money," one of the guys says. He's in a batter's position with this club.

"Okay," I said. I pulled my gun out from under my apron and I shot him—Boom! If you read the report, it says I announced that I was a police officer. But I wasn't going to get smacked in the head with a club. Piss on that. He was cocked and ready to nail me. So I shot him. He went down and the other guy took off running.

McGuire jumps out of the car and cranks one off at the guy running. The guy keeps running and McGuire takes off after him. So they're running up the street toward the opening away from the dead end.

Unbeknownst to us, there's another detective that has followed us out and is just kind of laying back to see what will happen. As McGuire is chasing this guy up the street, this other detective hears the shots and he thinks one of us are hurt. He comes roaring down the street in an unmarked police car. All he sees is a blur of someone running. He figures it's the bad guy and he's going to wipe him out. The only thing is, it's McGuire that he wiped out.

He knocked him forty feet in the air. McGuire went flying. He ended up in these people's patio flower garden. It shattered his thigh bone.

The bad guy has disappeared. He's gone.

All hell breaks loose after that. Every police car in the general area shows up. They can't find the guy. I don't know that all this has happened to McGuire because I'm back down the street with this guy that I shot. He's screaming and shit. Finally when help arrived and I went up to this other detective—the guy that ran over McGuire—and I said, "Where's McGuire at?" He didn't say anything to me, so I figured that McGuire is still out chasing this guy. I head down to where the rescue squad is taking care of the guy I shot. He survived. We didn't kill him.

I see this group of people up behind this house. I thought, "They must have found the guy that McGuire shot at." I get up there and I see McGuire laying there on the ground. I said, "What the fuck are you doing?" He don't say nothing. Then I can see that there's something bad wrong with his leg. I piece it together from the other guys.

We had an asshole captain at that particular time. A real asshole. When I came back to the station that night—

we'd gone out about eleven-thirty, the shooting took place at twelve-thirty and we got back about three-thirty—the first thing this asshole captain said was not "Is your partner all right" or "Are you okay?" He says, "What the fuck were you doing out there?"

They ended up putting a big steel thing in McGuire's leg because the bone had shattered. They tried this to get it to heal back together, but of course that didn't work. He was off for nine months. That leg is now three-quarters of an inch shorter than the other one. He walks with a limp. He'll never be the same again. We still tell him he should have been given a ticket for leaving the scene of an accident.

The guy that hit him really felt bad. In fact, he had a drinking problem for about six months afterward. We kind of rehabilitated him and got him back together. We tease him about it. But it's kind of a touchy subject.

*

My first post was a foot post, four till midnight. It was a dead-end block and at that time there were probably two thousand people living there. I walk the block. There's six crap games.

I was there for about an hour and a sergeant and his driver came by. I threw him a high sign. Suddenly he realized I was there and stopped to sign my memo book that he had seen me on my post. He started to drive away, but he stopped and got out. He said, "Do you know where the firehouse is?" I said yes that I did.

About an hour and a half later they drove by again and said, "Are you sure you know where the firehouse is?"

"Yes, I know where the firehouse is."

Two hours after that, they came by again. The driver gets out and he says to me, "You're making the sergeant very nervous. The firehouse is over there. That would probably be a good place for you to be."

It just didn't occur to me. I just assumed that these were all nice people. The people on the block weren't terribly threatened by me. Later on, I realized how unflattering that was.

The culture that pays and maintains the police department is not the culture that we most often supervise. Very often people in a ghetto neighborhood do not want police protection. Most of the time they do, but in subjective terms. If you are there you have to be aware of what they are talking about and of their standards, because you can take a bad situation and make it worse. You can also get yourself hurt when you shouldn't.

This was to be my steady post. Not long after I started there, a fight broke out in the street between a guy and his wife. In less than a minute there had to be two hundred people there. In my own stupidity I jumped into the middle of this thing to try to straighten it out. They both had knives.

But, I was rescued. I was holding onto the husband and out of the corner of my eye I saw a radio car drive right into the crowd. An arm reached out of the passenger side and grabbed me by the neck. I held onto my prisoner. The arm threw us both in the back of the radio car. The sergeant then proceeded to chew me out. "What the fuck are you doing?"

*

They were always shorthanded in that department. I still had two weeks to go in the academy and the chief got me out ahead of time to go to work. They were giving me fairly simple things to do, like deliver messages, go get the cars gassed up, that type of thing. The lieutenant was eating dinner and the other patrolmen were doing something else when they got a call that a man needed to talk to the police. They said, "It sounds like he can handle it. He's a policeman and he can talk."

I go to the residence and there's a guy out in the front yard. I pull up and say, "Can I help you?"

"Yeah," he says. "Alphonso is in the house and he's dead." I didn't have any idea what was going on, so I go into the house and Alphonso was laying in the front room, sure enough dead. He'd been stabbed twenty-seven times. There is blood all over the walls. So I get on the radio and I called the lieutenant and gave him the signal for "You need to meet me at this address." That's all I told him. I thought I'd done pretty good.

I could hear him coming with his siren on, down the road, 90 miles an hour, with the blue lights flashing. He comes sliding up there, runs up to the front porch of this place and sees that we, in fact, have had a murder.

Alphonso had had a homosexual relationship with some guy he'd picked up and carried home. The guy he'd picked up was into a little more bizarre stuff than Alphonso was prepared for. It started back in the bedroom when the guy cut him and then they had fought all the way up the hall. Then he killed Alphonso out in the front room.

Here I am a rookie. He's laying on his stomach with nothing on but his Jockey shorts. He's got stab wounds all over him, but there's generally not that much blood. There's got to be something wrong though, because the front of his underwear is totally soaked in blood when we turn him over. Everybody is thinking, "We know what happened to this guy."

The chief is standing there and they say, "Well, who's going to check?" Naturally everybody looks at the new guy. I didn't want to do it, and I imagine it was obvious that I couldn't do it. So the chief goes into the kitchen and gets him some of these spaghetti tongs and uses this kitchen utensil to pull the elastic out. The guy was still intact. We all breathed a sigh of relief.

Later on, when we'd gotten the processing taken care

of, we were talking about it and I asked the lieutenant, "How did you know that something so bad had happened that you were getting here so fast?"

"Your voice was cracking on the radio," he said. "And you could barely talk." I hadn't even noticed it.

*

Sergeants turn into shitheads pretty quick. Lieutenants are not too bad, but once you get above a captain, you can forget it. They no longer have anything to do with you. They're administrators. Everything that the group does is reflected on them and they don't want to stand behind an individual unless that individual is 1000 percent right.

I had an inspector come over to me once and tell me that I'd done something that he thought was pretty terrific. He was very straight and very honest. A tough old cop is what he was. He looked at me and he said, "If you ever get in trouble and you're 100 percent right, call me."

"Fuck you," I thought. "What'd I need you for if I'm 100 percent right?"

They'll never intercede for you if they think there's a chance—not that you're probably right—but if there's a chance that you're wrong, no one's going to stand by you.

Cops expect to be backed up by people even when there is a chance that what they did was wrong. Most cases they're wrong as far as the rules and regulations are concerned, as far as the law is concerned. Morally, in almost every case, they're right. There are those cases, of course, when they are not. But the situations where most cops get into trouble, usually from a real-life perspective, they're doing something that's okay. People understand it. They say to themselves, "I would have done that same thing." That's how cops base their opinions. They say to themselves, "What'd he do that was so terrible?"

But you can't expect the administrators to say, "Okay. That's all right."

*

I was walking foot post just rattling doors, checking the glass. We had this lieutenant that used to hang signs on the door handles of stores saying, "This is a simulated burglary, contact the desk." The whole thing was just a way of catching you loafing. If you don't call in when he thinks you should have found the note, he comes down and wants to check your book. "Where were you at such-and-such a time? I planted a sign on this store. You must not have picked it up. You must not have been doing your job." I was pretty new on the job, so I didn't need threats. I was out there busy, walking and looking all night long.

The car man pulls up and says, "Hey, Mack. Over there on that store, there is a sign. It says, 'Simulated burglary.' You're supposed to contact the lieutenant when you find it."

"Oh, yeah? Don't worry about it. I'll take care of everything. I'll do just what it says."

"No," he says, "I don't want you to call in."

"What do you mean? Don't call in? He's the lieutenant. I'll get in trouble. I got to call in."

"Don't worry," he says, "I'll take care of everything. In fact, don't call in for the note and don't make any of your rings for the rest of the night."

I was torn between getting in trouble with the boss and being accepted by the other guys on my squad. I debated a few minutes in my mind. The car man had been on the job a good while and he kept reassuring me. So finally I said okay and I didn't call in.

About seven-thirty we meet at the relief point. The lieutenant pulls up in his squad car. He's mad, really angry. "Where the hell were you all night?" he yells at me. "You didn't make any of your rings. Not one. I also had a note posted on a door on your beat and you didn't find it, because then you would have called. Where have you been all night?"

With this, the car man comes over to the lieutenant and says, "We found your simulated burglary, all right. But the foot man here was simulated shot. He never called in or made any of his rings because he was simulating a possibly fatal wound." He looks the lieutenant in the eye and he says, "What took you so long? From two o'clock to seven-thirty you never found the guy. He could have bled to death in the alley. You made a simulated burglary. We made a simulated death. That's all."

*

Before I used to think, "Their doing this is a direct attack on me because I'm a black woman." Then I found out that when you are a new police officer you are prime vegetable for every piece of meat that wants to beat you. Even I have had the opportunity to get some of these new recruits and it's a satisfactory thing.

Two girls came in going to do a strip search on a female junkie. They brought her in and I happened to be in the station. I asked them if they had ever done a strip search before and they said no they hadn't. So I offered to show them how to go about it.

I gave each of them some rubber gloves to make sure they didn't touch her body. She was swollen all up and you could see that she was a bad user. I told them, "You got to make sure that there are no vials up in there in the vagina, see?" They were a little shocked.

This woman must have weighed a good two hundred pounds. I told her to bend over and spread her legs and grab her ankles. Of these two recruits, one was a short girl and the other was a tall girl. I told them, "Now you got to bend over and look and make sure she doesn't have anything up there. If she has got something up there, you got to take her to the hospital and let them take it out."

The real tall girl, she stood up straight and she kind of squints her eye and is looking real hard but from a good distance away. But the short girl, she gets bent down and she's looking right up there and I said, "Watch it, before she farts!"

This girl jumped up in the air. It was the funniest thing. I rolled around the room. I almost peed myself laughing. The woman prisoner was so mad at me. I had to explain that I wasn't laughing at her, but she should have seen the look on that girl's face.

But it was a very satisfactory thing, because I had five years on and had been getting zung myself. It was a good feeling to zing somebody else.

*

We once had an old sergeant who liked to sleep on the midnight watch. That's against our rules and regulations. We're not supposed to do that, but being an old-timer like he was, he didn't seem to understand that he couldn't sleep. He would pull up under a streetlight out by a Pic 'n' Save. Lock his car up, lean back and start sawing big trees about an hour or two into the midnight shift. He'd set an alarm clock, I guess, because the next morning he'd be awake and away he'd go. If you called him on the air, he'd finally answer after a couple of tries.

One night some of the guys got together and decided it was time to get the sergeant's attention. They took a hydraulic jack and some cinder blocks. When he went to sleep, they jacked up the back end of his car and put cinder blocks under the rear axle. Took the jack out from under it and left him there. Nobody called him during the night.

The next morning, it came time to check off and he awakened to the jingling of his alarm clock. He cranked his car up, put it in gear and didn't go anywhere. Put it in reverse and it still didn't go anywhere. So he tried forward again. Without getting out of the car to see what might be wrong with it, he got on the radio and called for a wrecker.

*

You come into the precinct and there's a long desk that the lieutenant used to sit behind all the time. This cop comes in to sign out with no clothes on. Just a gun belt. I mean naked, no socks, no nothing.

The lieutenant looks down, figuring if he doesn't acknowledge this is happening, maybe it will go away. The guy will sign out and that will be that.

But naturally, when you're naked, you have no pen to sign out with. So this guy said, "Hey, lieutenant, can I borrow your pen?" The lieutenant doesn't look up, just hands him a pen out of his shirt pocket.

*

Lieutenant Stobb—bad-ass Lieutenant Stobb—Small Paul we called him. He was about five-seven and had a Napoleonic complex from being a little guy. He was an overbearing son of a bitch and an irritating bastard. He went out of his way to make things aggravating for the fucking troops. So needless to say, the troops did the same thing for him.

Larry would walk into the station, flexing his muscles and the lieutenant would say, "Hi, Lawrence, how are you?"

"Fine, Lieutenant." Right next to the fucking front desk is a pay phone. Larry drops in his dime and calls the station. He gets the desk clerk, Eddie Forno.

"Station 11. Forno."

"Lieutenant Stobb, please."

Forno knew who it was. "Lieutenant, phone call for you."

"This is Lieutenant Stobb."

"Fuck you, you baldheaded prick." Larry would hang up, walk out of the pay phone, look the lieutenant in the eye and say, "How are you, sir?" Larry is doing this four or five times a night five nights a week.

Now Forno would get the residuals from the phone call because the lieutenant would slam the fucking phone down and start hollering at Forno for what Larry did. So now Forno gets smart. When Larry calls up the station, Eddie says, "Fuck you, Larry. I'm not telling him anything and I'm not calling him to the phone."

So we're over to the hospital and Larry is saying, "I got to get that little prick lieutenant one more time."

"Yeah," I said, "but Forno won't give him the fucking phone. As soon as he hears either of our voices he knows what's going on." Sara, a little nurse, is standing over there, so I said, "Sara, how about doing us a favor? Give Lieutenant Stobb a call."

She knew him and she says, "Well, what are you going to do?" We told her what we were going to say and she says, "I'll do it." She picks up the fucking phone and calls the station.

"Station 11. Forno."

"Officer Forno, could I speak to the lieutenant?"

"Certainly, ma'am. Lieutenant, some girl on the phone for you."

"This is Lieutenant Stobb. May I help you?"

"Is this Lieutenant Stobb?"

"Yes, uh, this is Lieutenant Paul Stobb."

"Fuck you, you little baldheaded prick," she says. We were positively fractured.

*

The first thing about supervising other cops is you shouldn't fraternize too much with your subordinates, because sooner or later it's going to make it harder to drop the hammer on them. You got to be tough, you got to be firm, you got to be fair. All those things are right. But in police work, if you don't have some familiarity with what these guys are going through, if you don't know something about their backgrounds, their family lives, and in some cases their social lives, they'll do everything they can to make your fucking life miserable.

I tried to play it by the book for a little while. But I found out I was losing somewhere, because they would give me nothing but the facts, the old Jack Webb syndrome. Nothing but the facts is fine in some respects, but you can't run a tight ship in that way. You got to keep tabs on what's going on.

So I changed around. I got involved and tried to deal with people's personalities on a one-to-one basis. I became very helpful because I figured one of my strengths was my ability to talk. I tried to establish a bond of trust. I'd tell these guys what I was going to do and then I'd go tell my superiors exactly the same thing.

What I didn't really understand was that the responsibility of looking at somebody else's performance goes way beyond just what they produce as far as police work is concerned. You find yourself in the middle of disputes with investment companies, in the middle of their marriage problems. Guy's drinking too much and his wife calls you and says, "You're the boss. What are you going to do about it?"

I thought, "I'm getting a promotion and I'm finally getting out of the street shit," which was frustrating the ever-living shit out of me and I'd had enough of it. I got promoted with a decent pay raise. I have my own car now and I'm a supervisor. All I got to do is make sure these guys do the work. All of a sudden, it becomes much more frustrating in a whole lot of different areas.

A lot of these things that the wives were calling me

up about—hey, that's me. They're talking about me and my family. "The guy's staying out, he's running around with this dude and he's hanging out there." I start thinking to myself, "Holy fuck, that's me." I got to go home right away and figure out who the hell my wife must be calling. Is she calling the lieutenant or what?

Jesus Christ, these people want me to handle their fucking problems and, God damn it, I got the same shit. So now you're not on the street getting shot at any more, but your level of frustration dealing with problems hasn't stopped. It's increased. If you have three guys, you have three times as many problems. If you have fifteen guys, you have fifteen times as many problems. It's a heavy thing to deal with and it's not easy.

I had one guy call me to come get him out of a restaurant because he's there having a meal with his girlfriend and on the other side of the partition his other bimbo has come in. So he's eating two meals and telling them both that he has a urinary infection and has to go to the men's room every few minutes. He was literally out of breath calling me to come down and tell this one broad that he had to go home sick. He wanted me to finish dinner with her, so he can go home with this other one. He calls me at home with this shit. I told him, "Fuck you. Pick the one you like most and leave the other one there. I ain't going to fuck up my life telling my wife I have to go downtown to help you with your two bimbos."

I had this other guy who was never where he was supposed to be. He was always screwing off. After a couple of counseling sessions that did no good whatsoever, I called him in and told him, "Look, I'm going to recommend that you be transferred and that you be stripped of your detective grade. And that you be monitored because of your lack of productivity." The guy didn't say anything, just gave me a blank stare. That's it. He got up and left.

After lunch, he walks into my office and his exact words were, "You know, if I didn't fear getting locked up, I'd pull my gun out and I'd blow your brains out right now." If you'd seen the look in this guy's eyes and heard the tone of his voice, you'd know that he was dead serious. He scared me. I was sitting there sweating because I knew he meant what he said.

He knew he was in the gin mills when he should have been working, but who was the guy who had to come down on him all the time? Me. It was me. I was the guy who had to ream his ass out.

*

It was bitter cold, four o'clock in the morning on the late tour. Not a soul on the street. So a guy on the adjoining post says to me, "Hey, I got this girl I'm seeing on this beat and she's got a sister. They've invited us up."

"That's great. Let's go."

We're so careful not to get caught. We go up in the building next door to the sisters, climb up to the roof, then down the fire escape in the back of the building to their apartment. We get inside. One thing leads to another and we pair off into separate rooms and have a good time.

Now it's an hour and a half later. We get dressed and go back out the way we came into the building. We're watching and listening all the time. As soon as we hit the streets a sergeant drives by and he hits the brakes. He says, "Where the fuck have you two been?"

"On our posts, sir."

"Don't give me that shit," he says. By this time I could see the sergeant's driver laughing his ass off, but I say, "What do you mean?"

"Just look at yourselves." I turn and look at my partner. His navy blue overcoat is covered with pink fuzz. I look at me and my overcoat is covered in yellow fuzz. We had put our coats down on the sisters' crummy blankets when we took them off. We were caught. What are you going to do?

*

Somewhere there's always a broad or two who stop you and want to give you a blowjob—not for any other reason than that you're a policeman. Back when I worked the streets, there was a couple of girls like that. They had a little Mustang. They would spend the night taking care of everybody. They'd be out cruising and they'd find you. Sometimes, you'd find them—whatever.

We had a big party one night, and these two gals were the main attraction. This thing had started in a bar for a couple of hours. We took the place over and drank everything. After we left the bar, we were moving to an officer's house. His wife had left for the night. It was supposed to be a stag party for all the policemen changing shifts. We were going from day shift to night shift, so we would get off at 3 A.M. and we wouldn't have to be back at work until the next night at eleven-thirty. If we partied, we'd have time to recover.

I had a brand new car then—nice car, too. So this one gal I was with, me and her were going to the party house. When we got to the house, this broad is taking off all of her clothes, so I just kept driving up the street. But she had been drinking heavy, and I mean mixing everything. All of a sudden she said, "I'm going to be sick."

"You're not going to be sick in my new car." I reached over, opened the door and shoved her all the way out the door. She starts yelling and screaming. All the porch lights come on in this neighborhood. There's this broad out there with nothing on. I just put the old car in drive and go to the party. No way was she going to get sick in my new car. That was a good party, too.

*

I worked with a guy who went through a whole string of crazy girlfriends. He was buying a box of bullets every month. He was afraid to be in the apartment with them and a loaded gun. So every night, before he'd go to bed with them, he unloaded his gun and flushed the bullets down the toilet. He's going to go broke buying bullets.

*

You see policemen with coyote dates. When you wake up in the morning and she's laying on your arm, you chew your arm off so she won't wake up as you leave. That's a coyote date. Who do you think a guy meets in topless bars and strip joints and hooker bars?

*

I've had a few casanovas approach me on the job. I had one guy say to me, "I'd like to take some off-duty time with you."

"Oh, yeah? Take some off-duty time and get lost, buddy. I'm your co-worker. Your uniform doesn't impress me, because I wear one, too. I do my late cruise at home with my family. I'm not here for 'The Dating Game.' " They all call me Bitch because of the attitude I have with them. I tell them, "I love you. If you ever need to talk to me, I'll talk to you. But I'm not here to date you. My personal life is my personal life."

Some guys think the bosses are more partial to the females. "Yeah, she's driving the sergeant because she's a girl," one guy said to me when I first came here. "You're probably driving the sergeant because you got dirty kneepads."

"Not really, dear," I said to him. "Are you shotgun

qualified?" He said he wasn't. "Any sergeant's driver has to be shotgun qualified. Number one: I am qualified. Before the qualification came down you used to drive the sergeant. Did you have a patch over your ass? Was he giving it to you up the ass?"

"You can't even take a joke. I was only kidding," he says.

"You're damn right. That to me is not a God damn joke and don't ever mention that shit to me again." Now he won't even dare speak to me. "It can't be that maybe the sergeant likes the way I drive better than you? I had a good activity record maybe?"

*

One particular guy switched to my squad about a year and a half after I started. He stood back and watched for the first six months to see what I was made of. After that time he came to me and said, "I want to help. Anything I can do, advice, questions you've got, whether it's concerning the guys, law, traffic, anything, ask me. I want to help."

We worked real well together. Max is one of these real fired-up, aggressive kinds of cops. I'm more laid back. I do a lot of talking. I'll talk my way out of a fight before I'll punch my way out. We complemented each other. I cooled him down and he made me a little more aggressive. It worked beautifully.

"Making friends with the girl cop" caused him considerable problems with the other guys. They didn't take what they saw as his defection very well. They started all kinds of rumors that he and I were going to bed together which were totally untrue. The most I've ever touched the man is I've shook his hand maybe three or four times. That's it. But some people have to put other people down to make themselves feel better.

If I'd been doing all the things the guys said I'd been doing, I'd be too sore to walk. It was all bullshit. Before

I even got out of the academy, I promised myself that I would never date an officer that worked in the same department that I worked in. And I haven't.

His friendship with me caused Max problems at home, still does, I think. One time we were both working second shift and we stopped into a restaurant for supper. His wife walks in with their youngest boy, who was seven or eight at the time. She's not saying anything. I said hello and asked her how she was doing, because I had met her before. She wants to talk to him. Okay, so they go over near the bathrooms and I'm left with the kid, which I like to talk to kids anyway.

They come back and they're arguing. They're starting to scream at each other in the middle of the restaurant and he's in uniform. She looks at me and she says, "She knows what she's done." She's screaming at him. He smashes out his cigarette in the ashtray and says, "Cancel my dinner order." He walks out. She walks out. He tears out of the parking lot. I'm sitting there going, "Oh, shit." In full uniform they are having a family fight in front of all these people and I am the subject of the argument. I canceled both dinners and left.

He still cannot mention me in her presence. She still doesn't believe him. There's absolutely nothing to it. I care for him as a partner would care for a partner, but other than that, forget it.

One of the other guys used to have coffee with me quite a bit until the other guys started teasing him saying, "Hey, we'll have to call your wife and let her in on this." He quit having coffee with me. I have coffee and supper alone a lot unless I meet an officer from another, neighboring department.

*

We had these two police officers who rode together for two or three years. They were real close friends. One of them lived across town, but the other lived on that beat they patrolled. When they were on the shift from ten-thirty at night to seven-thirty in the morning, they would go by his house about five o'clock in the morning, wake his wife up, and she would make coffee and maybe scramble some eggs and make them some toast.

One night the partner that lived across town called in sick, so they assigned a new man for the fellow to ride with. Ordinarily, this man never did take a new man by his house, because he didn't want anybody to know that he was stopping on city time to eat and drink coffee at his home. This particular morning, he decided to go by his house for a cup of coffee anyway, because he wanted one so bad.

As he rounded the corner he saw a light on in the back of his house where the kitchen was. He pulled up and across the street from his house there was a car that he thought he recognized. At first he thought, "Well, that's my partner's car." Then he thought to himself— he told me this later—"Naw, my partner is off sick, so that can't be his car." He dismissed it and went up on the back porch. He knocked and his wife come and let him in. As he walked into the kitchen, there was his regular partner sitting at the dining room table with the husband's housecoat on.

Now, his regular partner was a person who could lie and make you believe it. At first this man said he really got perturbed about the whole thing. But his partner talked to him and swore up and down that he had been out all night and he had just come by ten or fifteen minutes before, all wet and nasty and the wife had let him take a bath and put on that housecoat. It sounded so good that the husband didn't think nothing more about it.

About six months later, he went home and found everything he owned on the back porch. On top of the pile of his clothes and shoes was his shotgun and a note that said, "Goodbye, don't you never darken my door again. I want a divorce." He couldn't understand it. His wife left town. Six or eight months after he got the divorce, she came back and her and his former partner got married.

*

One of the things that really violently upsets me is some of these television programs like this "Hill Street Blues." I've had too many police officers and other people say to me, "Oh, that's the most realistic thing to what it's really like." That's not true. One of the things I really resent is that just about everybody on that program is sleeping with somebody else's wife.

I've been a police officer for twenty-five years and married longer than that. I have never stepped out on my wife and I resent the fact that they paint us all with the same brush, that all policemen are doing this.

I admit it's a heck of a temptation and I'm not homosexual by no means; but I love my wife. She has to be a special person to be a policeman's wife. I don't like everybody labeling us as being that kind of person with our morals. I may be in the minority, but I am a basic believer that our whole society is based on our families. Without a good sound family our morals are going downhill. That's the way I really feel. We need to safeguard that.

*

I just left my ex-wife a few years ago. I didn't have a vehicle except the patrol car to get around in, but I left her one morning and I came to work that night.

Les and I were riding together. Les had a real bad problem about falling asleep at the wheel. But it was his night to drive because we alternated driving. I came in and hadn't been to bed all day. I was goggle-eyed and emotionally strung out. But I got into the car with Les and he drove around for about an hour and a half while we talked it all over. Then I just got real, real tired. I lay my head back on the seat and said, "Les, I don't think I can keep my eyes open any more."

"Just go ahead and go to sleep," he said. "If I need you, I'll call you." So I laid my head over to one side and I died. Out of this world.

I must have slept at least five minutes, I guess. It may have been an hour, but it was probably five minutes, if my recollection is correct. I woke up with a semi-truck in my mouth. Les fell asleep and drove under a parked semi. The undercarriage of the truck had sheared off the windshield and front post and was resting up against the side of my nose. My eyes came open and I looked both ways, but it was stopped and my head wasn't coming off.

"What happened?" Les said. "Oh, God. I hit a truck." We climbed out and created a fictitious dog that had run across the road in front of him. Then we called the sergeant to come write the report about how this dog had run us into this semi-truck.

Of course, nobody believed it, but that didn't matter. The point was, we weren't going to admit that we were asleep. I had glass all over my face and hair and down in my collar, but otherwise I was fine.

*

David is a good friend of mine. We lived three blocks away from each other when we were kids. We grew up together. We went into the state police together. We're still very close to each other.

Christmas Eve a few years ago, we're working out of the same station. They made the decision that everybody will meet back at the station house, we'll have some pizza together and we'll sit down and bullshit. Then we'll go to sleep, leaving one guy on the desk. The next morning, we'll work it up so that two guys can go home at a time and see their family. So about eleven-thirty a couple of guys had stopped off to get some pizza. Everybody's headed in.

I call the station and say I stopped a hitchhiker and I'm giving him a ride. I get out of the car. Here's this guy walking on the shoulder of the road. I say, "Hey, I'll give you a ride. Where you going?" I figure I'm going to be real nice. It's Christmas Eve.

"Get the fuck away from me," he says. "You don't know what the fuck I'm going through. You fucking cops are all the same."

"No, I just want to give you a ride wherever you're going."

"Get the fuck out of here."

I go back to the car and he keeps walking. I get on the radio and say, "I may need backup. Send a car. I have this person and he's being a little irrational." In the meantime he runs right across the highway. I pull behind him with the lights going. I get out of the car and say, "Pal, there's no problem here. I just wanted to take you for a ride. It's no big deal. Are you okay?"

"You cops are all the same," he says. "My girlfriend threw the ring back to me. She's going with a cop. You cops suck. You're all fucking around."

I thought, "This poor guy, he hates all of us. This girl could have waited until after Christmas to dump him." So I got him by the arms and say, "I'll take you anywhere you want to go. You're going to get hit out here in the middle of the road. There's cars going by here at 55 miles per hour."

All of a sudden he goes into a rage and he starts to hit me. I just grabbed his hand and I hit him. As I hit him, we went down. Now I'm on top of him.

David had been back at the station unsaddled, he had all his gear off. He knew I needed backup, so he just threw his jacket on, stuck his gun in his belt and comes out. He rolls up. Here's my patrol car on the inside lane with the lights flashing, the door's open. It's a four-lane highway with a treed area breaking up the north- and south-bound lanes.

I'm in the grassy area and from my headlights all he can see is my legs. I'm laying on the ground. And they haven't heard from me at the station for a good three or four minutes. He can't see the guy underneath me. David starts calling, "Chuck. Chuck! CHUCK!"

I turned around and looked at him and he was white as a ghost. He thought I'd been shot. I said, "David, give me a hand cuffing this guy, will you?"

"You prick, my heart is going into my throat!" He's yelling at the guy. He thought it was all this guy's fault because he got so scared and he thought I got hurt.

"David," I said, "I'm all right. It's okay. I just pushed him down. I had him." I picked the guy up, but his shoe was off on the ground. David picks up the shoe and throws it at him. Now he hit him in the freaking face. Now the guy's got blood all down the side of his face. I said, "David, this guy is going to go to court and charge us with assault." At that time everybody was signing complaints on us.

So we get this great idea. I'll get my tape recorder and we'll ask him to tell in his own words what happened. We're stopping the tape every ten seconds you could hear the stops, then we're telling him what to say. We thought we had this great statement, so that if anything came up in court about this kid being slashed in the face, we're covered.

*

Every cop can tell a story about some guy throwing himself in front of him. I had one. A guy pulled a gun on me in a hallway and I never seen the gun. I was nose to nose with this character that I had chased a few times. I was so hot and angry that I wasn't even paying attention to him. I was young. But I could hear from the back, "He's got a fucking gun."

It was dark in the hallway and I froze. My partner just threw me to the side. The guy pulled the trigger twice and it didn't go off. We took it to ballistics later; they pulled the trigger once and it went off, exploded. It was a tear gas gun. If it had gone off, I would have been dead and full of tear gas. But my partner never hesitated. He saw the gun and he pushed me out of the way and went for the guy.

*

One time we were just waiting outside this door. It looked like a real heavy door. So I decided to kick it in. When I kicked it I knocked one of the panels out and my foot went through the door. I was half in the apartment and half outside. It was pitch black in there and I couldn't see shit. I knew that there was supposed to be a wanted killer from Florida and Louisiana in there. He's a Cuban and no one can take this guy. He's got a life sentence waiting for him in federal court, so he'll kill you in a fucking minute. I'm straddling the middle of the door thinking, "That's it. I'm like a fucking target here. Backlighted by the hallway."

As afraid as I was, my partner was twice as afraid. I saw the expression on his face. He was petrified. He started screaming, "Please, please, don't shoot." It wasn't him that was going to get shot; it was me that was going to get shot.

With all this screaming and yelling and everything else, we put the light on in the apartment and the guy was sound asleep in the bed. Never woke up. Kicked the fucking door in and everything and he's snoring away. He had his gun there, but he wasn't awake to use it.

*

So many police terms are picked up from the street world and become incorporated in police mentality. A lot of it has to do with the Mafia. A lot of policemen will say, "He's a stand-up guy."

What's that mean? He's a fucking policeman. That doesn't make him a good guy. What do you mean a stand-up guy? Do you mean that what makes him a good policeman is that he's brave; if he sees a crime being committed in his presence he's going to do something about it? No, not necessarily. If it's his partner who commits the crime, he won't do anything about it. That makes him a stand-up guy.

Had a case where a bunch of cops went to a family fight. There was nothing to it and they were coming out. There were six cops coming down the stairs. It was the middle of the night, but in most ghettos the middle of the night is just like the middle of the afternoon. The street was filled with people. The stoop was crowded with kids.

The kids move up the stoop as these cops were coming down. One kid walked over to one of the cops and said something to him. The cop pulled his gun, shot the kid in the head and killed him. Outright.

Now you got five cops standing there going, "Holy shit! Why'd you do that for?" The guy said, "I don't know." Twelve- or thirteen-year-old kid. They all got together and they figured, "We got to do something. We'll say the kid had a gun or he had a knife or . . ." They came up with all these stories.

Later on a couple of the cops said, "Fuck this. Here's what really happened." They all ended up getting into serious trouble. The cop that did the shooting they sent off to the funny farm. They found his memorandum book and inside his book he had notations that were clearly written by a guy who was mentally unbalanced. He was having a breakdown and they read about it in the book. "Another night in the zoo. I don't know if I can take it anymore. It's making me crazy. These animals." He had written it right in the book. No one had even looked in his memo book.

Nevertheless, these cops felt that kind of bonding relationship with him to protect him. So they all lied. They didn't have to say that the kid had a gun. But they wanted to protect their brother, because he was one of them.

The end result was that he went to the hospital and kept his pension because he was crazy. The rest of the guys got fired from the job and a couple of them went to jail for committing perjury before the grand jury. But they're all stand-up guys.

That mentality is an organized crime mentality. It is to be respected in some ways, but it has to be respected from the perspective of criminality, not from legitimate law enforcement. The culture that we come from and the kind of country that we live in, we do respect that kind of camaraderie. But it's magnified in police work.

It can go too far.

*

Eventually forty-three people that I worked with were arrested. One guy they caught taking money from a peddler on the street. He had over twenty years on the job. Here's what they did. "You're caught. You will be off the job. We might prefer criminal charges against you. You lose your pension. That's it. . . . Or we could give you a choice. We're going to put a wire on you. You go back out there. Don't let anybody know. If you tell anybody, we put the cuffs on you. No questions."

He says to himself, "There's no choice to make. I'm going to lose my pension. I'm not going to get a penny for all this crap. Oh, my God." They all go for the wire.

So this guy puts the wire on. What else is he going to do? The first day out with the wire, he gets his partner.

They grab the partner and say to him, "Tell us every-

thing you've ever done and don't let us catch you lying."
This guy is pouring out his heart. "We want you to tell
us everything you know and anything that's gone on
whether you were in it or not. Anybody you know,
anybody you gave money to, anybody gave money to
you."

The thing snowballs. Guys start getting caught. That
was a traumatic time. I was afraid to talk to the guy I
rode with. You could be together for ten years. He's
off one day and you're riding with another guy. You
get caught and you're put in this position. Then the next
day your partner is back again. He's your best buddy,
the guy you hang out with before, during and after
work. You know his wife and kids. Everybody's friendly.
Now you got to sink him.

And they did it. They did it. They sunk everybody
to save their ass. There was one sergeant that stood up.
Everybody else gave everybody up. That was an ugly
time. It was just cold. Police work was secondary.

So what did they do? They transferred the whole
precinct out. It made all the papers. I'm home at my
house and my neighbor says, "Oh, ho, you're from the
precinct in the papers. You fucking crooked cocksucker
you, taking all that money. Where you getting transferred?"

"Hey, that ain't fair, man. I been doing a good job
there. I ain't crooked."

"Yeah, sure. You been doing a good job. You bought
a new car last year. Now I know where you got the
money from."

What were you? You were just another number. It
made you very defensive. That makes you wake right
up to the reality about the camaraderie. But that's also
how organized corruption was stopped.

We have what's called field associates. Very interesting people, these field associates. He's a police officer
who for whatever reason has a number he calls and

talks to a lieutenant. He doesn't have to give his name. He will report any sort of corruption that he feels is going on in his precinct.

Sometimes you go into a restaurant and the guy only charges you half price. Maybe it costs $1.50 and the guy only charges you a dollar. The field associate reports this back to his guy in IAD. They send IAD out to the restaurant and he says, "I'm going to lock your ass up if you do it one more time."

Every precinct has at least one of these guys. Nobody will ever know who he is. He will not get any monetary gain. He can't be uncovered. It can't help you when you retire. It can't help you get promoted. It can't help you do nothing. But all your life, all you do is rat out your friends. There are hundreds of them all over the department.

Corruption is ready to rear its ugly head at any time. Still that's a tough way to live, knowing that the guy you're working with may be a field associate. Or the guy you're working with may not like you, so what he does is tell everybody that you're a field associate. Then you're stuck with that.

Okay, you handle rotten DOA's, you handle emotionally disturbed people, you make rotten arrests, you go to court. But what you really hate doing is ratting on another police officer.

*

IAD's is following us around. We could spot them following us around our beat. I got in the habit of holding back waiting for a light to change from green to red and then racing ahead to make the light. Then running up a block and turning to disappear and lose them.

So they got in the habit, when I started getting up near the light, they'd get right on the ass of my car, so that if I ran the light they could chase and follow me. I let them do that a couple of times. Then one day when they were getting ready to do it, I made like I was going to go for the light, but when I got to the intersection I jammed on my brakes. They plowed into the rear end of the radio car.

I jumped out, "Let me see your license and registration." The guy didn't want to show me no ID because he doesn't want to blow his cover. I say, "I'm giving you a ticket for following too closely."

The bosses come down, the captain. I says, "I know who they are. I know who they are." I just was sick of it. I was an honest cop and I wanted to teach these assholes that I'm not some stupid schmuck they could follow around all day and I don't realize who they are. I taught those motherfuckers a lesson, man. Plow into my car!

"He gets a ticket for following too closely," I said. He ended up showing me his license and getting the ticket and that's the last I heard from IAD.

*

Top level job from the police commissioner to the chief of Internal Affairs to the captain, my boss. He says to me, "Robert, go interview the mayor. There was a party at the mayor's mansion last night and it made headlines in the *Herald* that a drunken cop wrecked the place. The mayor wants to know what's going on." When you go in the organizational table of assignments and duties, it says at the end of the list of all your assignments and duties, "And whatever other thing as directed by the police commissioner." This is it.

Now the case was handled through normal channels by a unit in the precinct. I'm the overseeing agency as a representative of Internal Affairs, the big umbrella unit over the small unit. It's got a lieutenant and a sergeant. Then there's me and my sergeant. A whole crowd of us.

At the mansion, they had a party. The mayor was

entertaining dignitaries. I forget who. Anyway in the mansion, if they have a big sitdown dinner—a buffet— they have a big room and then to the side they have a press room. Whenever they have important people, maybe twenty guys from the press come in there, so they got to entertain the press, too. So they got beer, the liquor, the hors d'oeuvres. They got good beer, imported beer, top drawer. This is part of the expenses of government.

At the mayor's mansion there's a detail of three or four cops to guard it around the clock. One guy at the gate, one guy to walk around the grounds. Nobody goes in or out without going through the gate. The allegation in the paper was that after the mayor's shindig, the cops had a party with the remains from the original party. During the course of this, somebody dirtied the rug in the press room and broke the windows in the guard booth. The cops were loaded. This is the way the re- porter had set it up.

Okay, we call up the private secretary, make an ap- pointment and we go interview the mayor. He's a funny guy. He's fast with the quips, very enjoyable to be around. In the one hour I was with him, he changed my whole attitude toward him. He's got charisma.

"What the hell's going on," he's saying. "Who's minding the store? They send all this brass over to find out about a rotten party? Who's that stupid reporter that wrote that story? What's the matter with him?" He didn't like it. He didn't want that kind of publicity, so he's making light of the whole thing.

I had to sit there and laugh. We got the police com- missioner worried that the mayor is mad and he's not. He says, "I know that you got to do what you got to do. I don't like these guys drinking my beer. I give them enough while they're working. What kind of beer were they supposed to be drinking? Heineken's? They're going back to domestic."

All right, we make our notes. Now we go back to the reporter and get more of the story from him. More than he wrote in the paper. What happened was, one of the reporters had a fight with one of the cops. Now he wants to zing him. While they're having their press room party, the cop is in there having a beer with the reporters. This reporter takes offense, tells the cop to get back to work, to do what he's supposed to do. The cop tells him to go take a walk. This triggers the whole business. That's the basic background of the whole thing.

Now we go interview the cops who were on duty that night. We have to take statements. These are statements that could be used against you in a department trial and maybe criminal trial if it turns into it. But this is the Internal Affair's function. We interview the sergeant on duty. We interview each of the cops.

One of the cops is a very nervous type of person. Very high strung, worried sick because Internal Affairs is going to interview him. I could see. The guy was getting me nervous. He was no kid. He was like forty something years old. He's scared he's going to go to jail for ten years.

End the interviews. We make out our report. I tried to tell my boss that the mayor isn't really mad, so maybe he can tell the police commissioner that he can take it all with a grain of salt. If everybody had just shut up, nothing would have happened. That report in the newspaper the day it all came down would have been the end of it. But these people in Internal Affairs are hard to describe. It wasn't an important thing, but to them it was. They want their ounce of blood.

I gave them the report. We pinpointed the guy who threw up on the rug. We pinpointed the guy who had the fight with the reporter. We showed them that it was the reporter's fault as much as the cop's, even though the cop wasn't supposed to be there and he knew it. He's not supposed to drink on duty, he knew it. Those are the things he was hanging himself with saying, "I was in there. I had a drink." Somebody's got to get hung, got to be in trouble.

That's about the time I decided I was going to try a new business. I was planning on using the Internal Affairs job as a stepping-stone to an assignment that I wanted. But I really didn't like it there. I didn't pass the captain's test. I had an opportunity to go into business with a friend of mine, so I retired and took my pension and went into business.

Turns out that cop—the one I said was so nervous— he killed himself about six months later. Over that. Over nothing. I read in the paper about his suicide. That's a tragic end for a silly nothing.

CHAPTER 6

The Borderline, the Bad and the Ugly

As YOU are driving down the highway, suddenly there are flashing lights in the rearview mirror and the whoop of a siren in your ears. A small dose of adrenaline surges into your blood stream. Your heart beats faster; your palms sweat. You feel guilty whether you've consciously done something wrong or not. Everyone is afraid of the police.

There is really little to fear, especially if you are white and middle-class. The police officer will be civil and efficient. He will finish his business and have you back on the road in a matter of minutes. If he gives you a ticket, you can probably afford to pay the fine. No real damage is done, just a slight inconvenience and perhaps some minor bruises on your ego from being told you were wrong.

However, the officer who stops you does have some extraordinary powers. On his belt there is a pair of handcuffs. He can arrest you and take away your liberty. In the holster on his hip is a pistol. You know it's there and he certainly knows it.

There on the side of the road, miles from a courtroom and judge, isolated from any support you might receive from friends and neighbors, removed from the moral restraints witnesses might impose on the officer's conduct, you are at his mercy. A little fear is in order. Courtesy and a touch of humility are usually the best course to follow. Most people slip automatically into a "Yes, sir—No, sir—Thank you, sir" form of communication. Offending a person with a gun is almost never a good idea.

A police officer is well trained to deal calmly and coolly with the public. Even when he is confronted with abusive language and disrespectful behavior, he must suppress his personal prejudices and wield his authority with fairness. He is taught to hold his temper and to act in a detached, professional manner. And he does— most of the time.

But a cop is only human. Every police officer has had a bad day—a hangover, a fight with the wife, a screw-up with the bosses—and has taken it out on the citizenry. He is rude, insulting, intimidating. Many a cop has given in to temptation and has misused his discretionary powers to gratify his own ego, tormenting some civilian like a cat toying with a mouse.

It is a frustrating job, admittedly. There is so much work to do. For one example, recent statistics estimate that an assault occurs in this country once every forty-nine seconds. In the minds of most police officers, our system of laws and the constraints placed upon law enforcement by the Constitution give all the breaks of the game to the criminals. They feel impotent and ineffective. It is easy to understand the urge to circumvent all the red tape, to just get out on the street and take care of business. Cops figure they can tell who's the bad guy and who's not.

But for all the glorification of vigilantism in the movies and on television these days, it is not a noble impulse. It leads to illegal search and seizure, planted evidence, perjured testimony and a subsequent perversion of justice. A cop who makes himself judge, jury and executioner tramples over the fragile rights that protect the liberty of each of us. The next time you are cheering on Dirty Harry, imagine this: The suspect in Harry's clutches is you or a member of your family and is, by some quirk of fate, an innocent victim of circumstances.

Fear and the anger it arouses are the most common causes of what is labeled police brutality. An officer is put in mortal danger and his hormones and emotions take over. When he finally gets his hands on the suspect who forced him into this precarious situation, his gut reaction overrides his brain. It is an explosion that is regrettable, but uncontrollable. One officer described his experience this way:

"There were six of us in four units chasing these guys at a high rate of speed. I thought I was going to die more than once, and I was sure some bystander was going to get clobbered by these maniacs or by one of us. It was totally hairy. The driver finally lost control and smashed it up. Our four cars all come sliding up sideways. The first officer to the suspects' car yanked open the door, jerked a guy out and punched him a good one right in the face. Then he handed him to me. I punched him one, too, and threw him spread-eagle on the ground. I was so mad I wanted to just throttle one of these nuts. I slapped a cuff on one wrist and grabbed the other arm around behind him. It came off in my hand. The guy's got a fake arm. I just stood there with this arm in my hand wondering if anybody seen me punch out a one-armed guy."

The ugliest of all police brutality is the kind that amounts to vengeance. But this is really a sort of vengeance by proxy in which the victim may have little or no connection with the act for which vengeance is exacted. The pent-up frustrations, anxiety and rage come pouring out of a cop. One offender becomes the scapegoat for all the bad guys who got away, for all the humiliations, for all the cuts and broken ribs, for all the cold sweat and creeping flesh. The violence that results can maim or kill. It may start as a reaction to an emotion-charged incident, but it might also be set off by something much more minor—an insult, a curse, an obscene gesture. As one cop told me, "I've seen guys brought in and the entire outgoing platoon—who have no idea what's going on except that a cop has a guy in the back room and he's beating him up—and the entire platoon, forty guys, go in and take a shot. Everybody wants a piece. The guy's half dead. What'd he do? Well, he spit on a cop. He doesn't deserve six months in the hospital for spitting on a cop."

Minority-group members are most often on the receiving end of abuse and brutality. It would be expedient to blame this state of affairs on economics and the statistics of probability: Blacks and Hispanics and other ethnic minorities are generally poor and living on the fringes of society where they are more likely to be involved with crime and therefore more likely to become involved with the police. But the plain fact is that there is racial prejudice among police officers. Minority-group members are more likely to be verbally or physically abused by cops and to be denied their rights than are whites. Is this situation likely to change? One ray of hope is that police officers seem more willing to admit their personal prejudices than most of the rest of us, judging from the interviews I conducted.

When asked about such abuses of their powers, though, most cops throw up their guard and back off. They act as though every civilian they meet is just waiting for the opportunity to scream, "Police Brutality!" into a cop's ear. But they will talk about brutality and abuse, admit that it happens, sometimes even tell about some incident they have witnessed. A good cop is perhaps more outraged by the misdeeds of a fellow officer than the general public is, because he knows his reputation and character are besmirched just because he and one bad cop wear the same uniform.

"A few bad apples spoil the barrel" is the old saw that all cops repeat. Generally speaking, it applies. One lazy cop sleeps on the job and they all look like bums. The power to arrest people is put into the hands of a bigot, and racist acts are committed. A greedy cop will be corrupt, a bully will brutalize. No amount of screening and testing will eliminate these kinds of people from the ranks of the police. A few bad apples always end up in blue uniforms. Innocent people and our system of justice suffer because of them.

The bigger problem is that bad apples are not always thrown out when they are discovered. Individual cops are all too willing to look the other way when another cop does something wrong. It's easier and safer to tend to your own business and to ignore someone else's petty abuses, laziness or corruption. Police department administrations often tacitly condone less than professional behavior rather than stir up bad publicity or incur employee animosity by actively prosecuting cases of misconduct.

One officer described the danger of this "hear no evil, see no evil, speak no evil" approach: "In any department, anywhere, you can take 5 percent of the cops and they will be honest under any circumstances and they'll never do anything wrong. They are the priests of the department. Five percent on the other end of the spectrum would have been criminals had they not become policemen. They are, in fact, criminals who happen to be cops. The remaining 90 percent will go whichever way the peer pressure goes."

Racism, corruption, brutality can slowly become institutionalized throughout a police department simply because so many officers are willing to be indifferent, to let the standards erode from inattention, to go along and follow the crowd. Slowly the pendulum swings toward criminality. A locality gets a reputation for its dangerous or larcenous police officers. Those cops who are unwilling to participate are overruled or driven out and replaced with individuals who are attracted by the prospect of living above the law. The community, the people the police are sworn to protect, must live in fear.

IT WAS a rotten night and all I wanted to do was get through the shift. I've got about three hours to go and I'm really pissed.

We got a call of a guy and his girl that ran out on his check at one of the nicest restaurants in town. We're talking $50–$60. I find him hiding in this little alcove area in a service station restroom next to the restaurant. The guy is bent over with his head between his knees. I was given a clothing description. It was very obvious that this was the guy. For one thing he was right next to the restaurant, nobody else in the vicinity.

I just want to get rid of this thing, go back to my car and drive around. I go over and tap him on the arms and say, "Are you awake?"

He shrugged me off with this big macho thing, "Get the fuck away from me." I felt a little better right away. I'm going to get a chance to work out a little frustration. I said, "I don't want to hear that. Just stand up and turn around and put your hands on top of your head. You're under arrest."

"Fuck you," he says. "You ain't big enough to take me, motherfucker." He stands up. He's got his fists clenched and he says, "Come on. Just come on. I'll kick your ass."

Before I knew it, I've got all this frustration pent up and I hit him one time with my stick. I don't think I've hit ten people in eight years with this thing. But all that frustration came through in one shot. That would have been a 450-foot home run. Reggie Jackson never connected so well as that. Good follow through. Hit the sweet spot. I felt real good after it was all over. I forgot what I was pissed about. It took the fight out of me. It stunned him. It didn't hurt him—didn't break his bones, didn't break his skin or anything like that. Took care of the problem. I thought to myself, "It's a very therapeutic job."

*

It's common practice to get stuff thrown at you from the rooftops. You always expect that sort of thing. You're walking down the street and some fucker throws a brick or a Pepsi bottle from six stories up. A brick dissolves when it hits the street from that height. If I get hit with that, I'm a vegetable for sure.

I once was walking along and I got hit in the center of the back with a flashlight battery. I thought I was shot. Knocked me right down. Owww! Everybody laughed on the street. Some guys pull a gun and shoot up on the roof. No big deal. I get crazy. I went up on the roof and I pulled down every TV antenna on top. Fucking guy probably didn't even live in the building. But I had some sense of getting even. I knew guys who would throw pigeon coops full of pigeons off the roof if they got hit with something from the roof.

There's no way to condone that sort of thing, but you can understand it. People will say, "I don't understand it and I think we have to eradicate it."

That's great. That's just verbiage. It doesn't mean shit. It doesn't mean dick, because nothing is going to change. People are what they are and they're going to behave the way they're going to behave in stress situations. Period.

Nothing will change until we turn the whole society

around and in a sense it's getting worse. It's not getting any better. There's more anger. There's more unemployment among the people we police. The cities are boiling pots with the lid screwed down tight. Guys are waiting for the factories to reopen. That's never going to happen, and if it did, there won't be any jobs for these guys.

For them the representative of the society is the cop. He's got a job, he's there and he's fucking them around. The government is paying him and keeping them out of work. He works for the bad guys. So he's going to catch the shit.

He always does. During civil unrest in this country, the only ones people can put their hands on is a cop. "He represents everything, so let's fuck him around." That kind of pressure on the police creates the secret society. They turn inward. "Hey, fuck these people. It's you and I against them." The system is self-perpetuating.

*

See, if you do something really insane, no one believes it. Throughout the country, there are certain guys that if they stop you and you give them a hard time, they'll eat your driver's license. That's it.

There's a guy in motorcycles, big monster of a guy. Any time he gets hassled, if the guy starts calling him names or whatever it is, he takes the guy's license, puts it in his mouth and starts chewing. "I'm going to give you a ticket now for driving without a license," he says.

The guy would go to court and scream at the judge, "This cop stopped me, took my driver's license and ate it!" No one would believe that.

"I don't know about this guy," the cop says. "He must be nuts, your honor. He didn't have his license with him."

*

We were out in the park. A bunch of people were shooting craps. They, of course, scattered when they saw us, so we were writing tickets for parking on the grass. While I was writing this one guy a ticket, this black dude is sitting in his car behind me. He honks his horn and says, "Hey, you honky motherfucker, get the hell out of the way. I want to move my car."

I couldn't believe he said that to me, so I told the guy I was writing the ticket to, "You wait here." I went back and I said to this guy, "You got a problem?"

"Yeah," he says, "I got a problem. You're in my fucking way. Why don't you move, so I can get the hell out of here?"

"Nah," I said. "One of your wheels is on part of my grass and I'll have to write you a ticket." There was about an inch and a half of his tires on the grass.

I wrote him the ticket and gave him his copy of it. I went back and sat in my cruiser and tilted my side mirror so I could watch him. I knew what he was going to do. He rips up the ticket. He smiles at all the dudes out there and he throws the ticket on the ground. I jumped back out of my car and snatched him out of his. "You're under arrest," I said.

"What for?"

"Littering." I picked up the ticket and put it in my pocket and took him back to the cruiser. I'm frisking him down. He takes his hand off the top of the cruiser and I said, "Ah, resisting arrest."

"Man, if I had my shit with me, I'd take . . ."

"Ah-ha, menacing threats." That guy started out with a parking ticket and it took him $5,000 to get out of jail. "You going to screw with me, I'm going to screw with you. But, buddy, I know how to play the game a little bit better than you do."

*

COPS

I saw one guy arrested once for speeding and the police officer lost his temper. Of course, this highway patrolman brought it on himself, because he was bad-mouthing the guy. Finally—he's a man, too—the guy lost his temper and spit on the highway patrolman.

Right on the side of a U.S. highway on a Sunday afternoon, the highway patrolman wrestled the guy down, took a handful of hair and held his head down in the dirt and started packing the guy's mouth full of sand. The guy was choking and spitting and this patrolman was shoving sand in his mouth. "I'll teach you to spit at a trooper, boy." Those were his exact words. I'm standing in the background, watching the cars go by, slowing down to stare at this event. It looked bad.

*

We got a call on the radio and they said they'd found this woman and her child dead in Phoenix. Her relatives lived in our precinct and would we go down and notify them that their daughter had been found dead. I told my partner, "I can't do that."

"What do you mean?"

"I can't go up and tell somebody that their kid is dead."

"You're not going to get out of this one. I did the last one and you're going to do this one."

"I can't go up there and tell them. I can't."

"You're going to."

"Okay, but you'll be sorry."

I went up to the house and knocked on the door. Man opens the door and I said, "Is Mrs. So-and-So there?"

"Yeah."

"I'd like to talk to her." So she comes downstairs and I said, "Ma'am would you mind coming into the living room? I'd like to talk to you. You'd better have a seat."

I'm standing there and she's looking up at me and I started smiling. I kind of put my hand over my mouth. I asked her, "Do you have a daughter named So-and-So?"

"Yes." The grin is starting to really grow across my face and my partner is looking at me real snotty like. I started laughing and so I bite my hand and try to hem and haw. Her husband's sitting across the room and he says, "She's dead!"

"You're right!" I yelled. "Excuse me, I have to leave." I went out into the kitchen and I was hysterical. I don't know, ever since Vietnam, I got in the habit of laughing at a death to keep from going nuts. When something like that happens, I just can't keep a straight face. My partner says, "You weren't kidding. You really can't do this."

*

There was a deal we did one night that we thought was funny as shit at the time. But when you think back about it you say, "God damn, we could have got in trouble for a lot of reasons."

There was a compound about 100 yards square on a lot that was open street to street—you could see completely across it in both directions. No trees. The guy that owned the property had built a concrete block construction of eight rental units. It had a pine bark parking lot and driveway. Spotty weeds and grass covered the rest of the lot. There was a 12-foot-high fence all the way around it—a big fence—with only one opening in it, just big enough to drive a car through.

The people that lived there at this point in time were drug dealers. They had fires going outside in twin 55-gallon drums. They sat around on little benches thrown together from lumber and concrete blocks. It was impossible to sneak up on them and jump them. No cover. Only one way in.

We conspired and conspired and talked about it and thought about it from every angle we could. We actually did get an undercover man in and made a buy on them and put one of them in jail. But then they got real suspicious after that boy got busted and they wouldn't sell to anybody except people they knew. We couldn't get any more of them.

So we said, "Let's start scaring them." We started wolf-packing. We'd get four or five cars and we'd zip up there and run into the gate and chase them all over and laugh and have a good time. Sometimes, they'd really get scared and they'd throw their shit into the fire. We thought, "What the hell, we're making them burn their dope about every other night, so this is great sport, right?"

But that wasn't enough. We got greedy. We said, "Let's *really* scare them."

So one of the guys brought an Uzzi that he owned from his house—an Israeli nine mm machine gun. He loads his own shells, so he loaded a thirty round clip of blanks. No one wanted to actually shoot this thing off . . . so I did it.

We only had three cars this time. When we rounded the corner, there were a good ten or fifteen guys sitting around the fires. Well, they started running. The two cars circumvented the area and started catching the guys climbing out over the fence. Where they saw them ditch the dope as they jumped the fence, they caught them coming down on the other side. We actually made a couple of good cases.

But the big man was sitting there with his hand out over the barrel ready to ditch his shit in the fire. Calm as can be, but on Start, ready to run.

I skid into the lot, which is dry as a bone, and just a big cloud of black dust goes everywhere. All you can see is this red flashing light on the dust particles hanging in the air. Around me it's lighting up like an auditorium.

I'm laughing like a motherfucker already, because I see the expression on these guys' faces as I bail out of the car with this weapon.

I squeezed down on this machine gun—Budda-budda-budda! This son of a bitch is only fifteen feet away from me. He is looking straight into my eyes. He grabbed his chest and his knees buckled. He just knew he was hit and he was going down. I stopped and thought to myself, "The motherfucker is having a heart attack. Oh, God damn. What have I done? Scared this man to death?"

It turned out that he recovered. He hadn't had a heart attack. It just scared the shit out of him and he fainted dead away. We made two arrests out of this thing and not a swinging dick out of that whole place complained. If they had we'd have been up the fucking creek.

*

We do some things on the street that would probably be frowned on if it was common knowledge that we did them. But the people it happens to, they're not going to go complaining because they are escaping jail. One of the things that I enjoy when it gets boring is busting crap games. Bust those crap games.

We usually get four or five cars together and completely circle the block and then converge on the game. A lot of times, you get real close on them before the first one sees you. By then, by God, it's too late, buddy. You run and chase them, but you never try to catch the bastards. Because then you're going to have to do something with them. It's funny as hell to chase them. And they run, boy. They run good.

The idea is to get as close as possible and jump either on the pile of money, or on the guy that has the money, before the rest of them get out of there. It's like a chess game. You have to get close enough to see the pile.

We'll get there, converge on the damn thing, dive on

the money and cover it up. They'll grab it right from under your body and run, because they know there's twenty of them and you're not going to catch them all. So you have to literally tackle that damn money and cover it good while they haul ass.

They don't run far, because they know you can't identify them for shit from anybody else on the street unless they got a red polka dot shirt on. They mingle with the rest of the people on the street and wait and watch.

We take the money and go cruising down the road. The kids know what the hell is going on. They get ready. We get all the money and shit together and you look around and here come the kids, like seagulls when you show up at the beach with a loaf of bread. You don't know where they come from, but the seagulls start coming from somewhere and in droves. That's just the way it is with the kids. We hand the money out the window of the cruiser to the kids.

Choong! They haul ass. They know they're fixing to get their butts fixed, because the players see what's going on and they want their money back. It's great sport. The sport of kings. It's beautiful. Those are some of the best times I've ever had.

*

You get somebody in here that's a real hard ass and you treat them halfway decent, you know that somewhere down the road they're going to come back and say, "Hey, you were halfway decent to me. I'd like to do something for you." Then there's some people that come in here and you might as well talk to the door knob.

They brought an eighteen-year-old kid in here one night that come in with a hard-on. I mean, he was raging. "White motherfucker!" and all that shit. He had whipped some old man up on Cleveland Avenue, robbed him of about sixty bucks and put the old man in the hospital. Cruisers just happened to be in the right area and got the guy. He had the man's wallet on him. The old man had a broken jaw and his ear was messed up. The kid had kicked him in the head a couple of times.

This kid is really wound up. He's wanting to fight. It's a lot simpler to talk to somebody without handcuffs and stuff than it is with. After about fifteen minutes of motherfucker this and motherfucker that, he seems to calm down a bit. So we say, "Well, we'll get started now." We take the handcuffs off him.

I say something to him and he jumps up, swings on me. So I took the telephone and hit him in the head with it. I'm not going to mess up my hands for nobody. I've seen too many guys do it. Then you have to mark off on the injury to your hand and all that shit. So you use something and not hurt yourself.

The telephone is pretty hard. When I smacked him in the head with the phone, it seemed to take a little bit of the fight out of him. We kind of wrestled around and I said to him, "Are you going to start acting like a human being and not a God damn nigger?"

"Yeah," he said, and quit fighting.

Now the sergeant's got to come in because I've used force. There's got to be an investigation about whether it was excessive or whether it wasn't—which it wasn't. They have to interview me, the prisoner and everybody else in the room. There were two other officers in the room, so they interview them separately. I don't know what they say. I only speak to what I can say and I told the truth, because if you lie and get caught in a lie, it's just that much worse. Then the sergeant goes and interviews the prisoner.

The prisoner says, "Yeah, I swung on the officer and he hit me with the telephone and we wrastled around. I deserved it. But he called me a nigger."

The sergeant comes back to me and says, "Did you

call the prisoner a nigger?" I told him I had said, "Are you going to start acting like a human being and not a God damn nigger?"

That was a Thursday. I'm off on Friday and Saturday and I come back to work on Sunday. The sergeant says, "John, I'm going to have to give you an oral reprimand for using the word 'nigger.' " An oral reprimand is basically, "Don't do it again and everything will be all right." I screwed up and I knew it, so I said, "Let's get on with it."

He writes the whole thing up and tells me. Then he has to send it through the chain of command from the sergeant to the lieutenant to the captain to the deputy chief to the chief. It got through the lieutenant and the captain. But then it went to the deputy chief who's black.

"That's not enough," he says. "He deserves more punishment." So he changes it to a written reprimand that will stay there in my permanent file for three years. But even after three years, it will still be around. It comes back down the chain of command as a written reprimand even though it went up as an oral.

"Wait a minute," I said. "You can't give me two reprimands for the same incident." I filed a grievance with the fraternal organization. The grievance officer says, "No problem, we'll get it taken care of." So the sergeant he waives his comments, the lieutenant waives his comments and the captain waives his comments.

When it gets to the deputy chief, he's pissed. He writes this two-page thing that the black citizens of our city will not withstand racial abuse from the white officers. If it ever happens again, I will be fired and all this shit. I didn't get anywhere with him, so I went to the chief. Of course, the chief has to concur with his deputy, so he did.

My little incident came out in a federal discrimination trial brought by the black officers of the city. My reprimand was brought out as evidence—the fact that I had called a prisoner a nigger. It was in all the newspapers. I didn't even testify.

I'm not denying that I'm prejudiced. But if all you deal with for eight hours a day is the assholes of society, you do get a little prejudiced. You get cynical. My wife says I'm hard. I'm hardened. There's a lot of things that don't bother me and a lot of things that do.

*

The highway patrol was having this big push to hire minorities. They had this black trooper who had just graduated from the academy. His assignment was going to be about a hundred miles away, but he hadn't been issued a patrol car yet. He was being relayed from highway patrol troop to troop to his new post.

I'm at the station house. There were a couple of troopers I liked to go on duty with because they were real levelheaded and good law enforcement people. I was trying to learn as much as I could at that time. But those guys were out. So Bert turns around to me and says, "Want to ride?"

"No, I'm waiting for Hunter."

"Aw, come on, come on." I finally said okay. We go up to the county line and meet the patrolman who has brought this new black trooper to us. We're to carry him south. I get in the cage in the back and Bert puts the black trooper in the passenger's seat.

We start heading south. Bert's not going down the main drag, he's taking all these back country roads. His intentions are that he's going to show this black trooper what it's all about—scare him a little bit and have some fun with him as Bert gets him where he's going.

It was a Plymouth Grand Fury we was driving, one of the last of the good 440 Police Interceptors. We're rolling along this narrow country road past cattle ranches and farms and we're doing about 110. Bert is driving sitting sideways in the car with his right arm on the back of the front seat looking at this black trooper and driving with his left hand. He's watching the road out the corner of his eye, but he's trying to make it look like he's not, see? He's zipping along at 110 and he starts in on the black trooper. He reaches down and finds a country and western station on the radio and he says, "Say, boy, you like country music?"

The black guy is scared, you know. He's thinking to himself, "I'm stuck in a car with a maniac." I'm sitting in the back of the car clutching onto the cage watching cows whiz by at 110 miles an hour. I am scared. Old Bert is saying again, "Do you like country and western music, boy?"

"Yeah, I like it fine," the trooper says.

"I'll bet you listen to all that nigger jive, that boogaloo and all that. Don't you? You like that, boy?" He just keeps eating at him with this "boy" business, that southern cop routine.

There's only one little narrow road going into this one-horse town. Bert's still trying to impress this trooper and the road kind of snakes and everything. They have these things called goats which are vehicles they use in orange groves. It's usually some old chopped up vehicle like a flatbed truck. Sometimes it has a little like crane on the back of it to lift pickers up into the trees. Well, here's this goat ahead coming out of the groves on one side of the road to go into the groves on the other side of the road. He comes shooting across.

I'm hanging on the cage in the back and Bert didn't see the goat. So I hollered, "BEEEEERRRT!"

Bert hit the brakes and just locked them up at 110. The nose of that patrol car is dipping down almost eating the pavement like something you might see the stuntmen do on "T.J. Hooker." It has took the black trooper and got him slung up against the dashboard, his face pressed against the windshield. I'm pressed against the grate in the cage. The car comes to a stop and we've done left yards and yards of rubber.

Bert starts laughing and he turns around and says, "Did that scare you, boy?" and just grins. Hits the gas and with a squeal of tires off we go again.

*

He was a good trooper, but he was a redneck. He'd been brought up rough and hard. He and his daddy poached alligators to put supper on the table and shoes on their feet. All these are hard-luck stories, but he lived it.

He hated blacks. His favorite thing to do was to patrol some of the back countries and wherever there's a creek or something back in there with a bridge over it, you always find black people in there with cane poles, fishing. His thing was to hunt these places up. He'd go stand on the bridge—and I have seen it—he would pull out his revolver and commence to shooting the corks off their lines. Of course, the first thing they would do was drop their cane poles and run for their cars and get the heck out of there. He thought it was great, this was his bag. He'd get with me and say, "Let's go see if we can find some corks to shoot." I'd say, "Oh, no, here we go again." He had his own flair and style.

*

This one lieutenant would marry and divorce people. All police departments all over the country have a guy that does that shit, especially in the ghetto. Some old Irish lieutenant that has something special about him. He has winos coming in and out all day long, all kinds of wackos going and coming, so after a while it affects his brain. He also gets into it.

"Oh, fine. You want to get married? Bring her over here." He makes up some kind of ceremony. Maybe he gives them their Miranda warnings. "Do you swear to love and honor each other forever and ever? You're married."

I remember coming into the precinct one night and a couple were there screaming that they wanted a divorce. The desk clerk says, "I can't give you a divorce."

"I don't want no more of this bitch, man. She's driving me crazy."

"But I can't give you a divorce. You got to go downtown and all this other shit. You really married?"

"Yeah, we're married."

"Where'd you get married?"

"We got married here."

"What?" the desk clerk says.

"Yeah, we got married here. That lieutenant, he married us. Ten-dollar wedding."

"Well, it's going to be a ten-dollar divorce, man. Put your ten dollars here. You are officially divorced."

"Okay, get lost, bitch. We're divorced." And the girl walked out crying.

That stuff is happy farm. It's crazy. When you think of the very professional modern police department—the computerized police department—you don't see a whole lot of that. But the fact is, in the old precincts in the really tough neighborhoods, that's what goes on.

*

Me and another guy had pulled in and were gassing up our cars. Some guys were stealing gas at the time, but we weren't. I was in a sector which generally was busy, but it was midnight shift and everything was fucking dead. I said, "I'm fucking bored."

"Yeah, I'm bored, too," he says. We talked a little and he said, "Hey, you ever been to the races, the stock car races out at the track?"

"Yeah."

"I used to drive in those years ago," he says. "Yeah,

we used to have a lot of fun. We used to burn tires all the time."

"Burn tires?"

"Yeah, we ignite the tires to get traction."

"No shit."

"I'll tell you what. Back up here and I'll show you." So we back the two Chryslers up to the gas pump. We took about 25 gallons of gasoline, fresh from the nozzle, and squirted it on the tires and all underneath the back tires.

He gets in his car and he's looking at me. He turns his hat around and puts it on backwards. We're revving up the two patrol cars in neutral. "When I give you the signal," he says, "drop it into drive, spin your wheels and we'll take off from here like a bat out of hell." We had big engines at the time.

I don't know what the fuck possessed me to do this. I mean, what the fuck am I doing this for? We're doing this because we are bored. That's why we were doing it.

He drops his arm, we peel out of the lot. Look into the rearview mirror we see—BOOM!—flames shooting must have been forty feet in the air. He takes off now. My car is on fire. The paint's burning right off. I'm afraid my gas tank is going to blow. He jumps out with his fire extinguisher and starts putting out my fire on the back of my cruiser. The paint is a mess. Ah, fuck! I got to get this car painted. We're not paying any attention to the flames that we let go in the back.

I'm out of my car and I said to Alan, "What the fuck . . ." At that, the gas pump blows up. The housing goes up. It was like you went down to Cape Canaveral and watched a rocket go up. It had to fly a hundred yards straight up.

Now what are we doing? Now what's going to happen? All Alan says is, "Follow me." He calls up his buddy in the next town and got him out of bed. He reported back in that I had mechanical trouble.

The desk sergeant inside is an old guy. He sees fucking flames and he's going bananas. He thinks some electrical spark started it because he didn't realize we were out there. The fire departments from all around the area show up. The thing burned for like two hours.

While they got the fire under control and were calling everybody in, Alan got this guy out at 2:30 A.M. who owned a body shop. By 6:30 A.M. the bumper was off, the entire trunk of the car had been taped and painted, the bumper was back on and the lettering was redone. I was back on the street and nobody ever found out about it. And that's how out of boredom you can get yourself fucked up, especially if you get yourself killed.

*

Most police officers don't like to talk to the press. I enjoy it. I like the notoriety of it. When everybody else walks away, I take advantage of that. I walk up to the front. Nobody else wants to be on TV? Shit, I'll do it.

I tell them, "TV cameras will not hang around a scene where there's no action, because the newspapers can snap that. So what you got to do when you get on the scene is, you got to move around a lot, do a lot of action. If you're constantly moving, that shows up on TV real nice." The other officers don't think of things like that.

One time we had an incident where a guy had stolen a taxi, hit a couple of cars and injured a few people. Then he smashed up the cab. When the TV cameras got there, they went right over to one of the victims. The medics were working on this person that had been hit by the cab. On the news that night, you see me grabbing the end of the stretcher and I'm putting the victim into the back of the ambulance. Then the shot changed to the front of the ambulance on the news for the next clip.

I'm standing in front of the squad, looking into the camera and taking names. Then the next clip, I'm walking the suspect down and putting him in the back of the wagon. It was a one man show.

One night somebody called in and said they thought they had spotted a baby hippopotamus in the river that runs through town. They were sending the cruisers out and I told my partner, "Man, this has got the makings of a good TV appearance."

"Oh, no," he says.

I call on the radio and tell them that we will respond and see if we can spot this animal in the river. "Get ahold of the director of the city zoo and get him out here. Also, you might want to call the fire department. And water rescue, we might need them down there."

My partner is going, "What the hell are you doing?"

We get down there and all the newspapers show up as well as the TV guys. But we can't find no damn animal. The zoo wasn't missing one. Some drunk was seeing things and called in the report, I guess. There weren't anything in the damn river. This newspaper guy comes up to me and says, "What was it?"

"It was the Mysterious River Monster."

"What do you mean?"

"Every hundred years, it pokes its head up out of the river, laughs at Mankind and then dives back down. It probably won't surface again for another hundred years." It was such a farce.

The next day on the front page: "Mysterious River Monster reported seen by city police Officer Johnson."

When I say I like to be on TV, I mean I really like it. I was riding a cruiser and we were going on a robbery call running with red lights and siren. This woman busts a stop sign, runs right into the side of us and runs us right into a telephone pole. That knocks both of us out.

I come to and the car is on fire. All this radio equipment and shit is laying down in the floorboards. We can't get the car doors open. My partner and I were finally able to knock out the windows and crawl out that way.

The rescue squad shows up. They're taking us to the hospital, when I look out the back end and see the TV cameras have showed up.

"Stop the ambulance," I said. "I want to get back in the police car. We'll get back out and they can get us on film."

"Are you serious?" the medic says.

"Yeah, he's serious all right," my partner says. So they stopped the ambulance and they put us back in the car and then they loaded us back into the ambulance.

I'm a frustrated actor. This is the only way I can get on TV.

*

We were walking around in the park and it was late. There was this big black guy wearing a bedspread as a wrap. He's carrying a long square iron rod. He's a weirdo. We see him walking around the parking lot so we decided we better check this guy out.

I said to my partner, "You distract him and I'll throw this iron thing into the lake, out of his reach, so he doesn't have a weapon. We'll see what goes on from there." My partner distracted him. When the guy stood up and faced him, I walked over, nonchalantly picked up the rod and threw it in the lake. I could barely lift it, but I got it away from him. The guy got really mad, but he didn't try to attack us or anything.

"What shall we do?"

"He's not breaking the law or anything, so let's leave him alone."

"But sooner or later, we're going to have a problem with him. Sooner or later something is going to happen with this guy. You watch," I told my partner.

About two weeks later we were working back in the park, but it was early, still daylight. Some woman comes up and says that there was a man chasing women along a foot path just south of the theater. We go down a little further and another woman describes him to us. She says, "He's a big black man with a bedsheet." We know it's the psycho. I say, "Oh, shit, John. We've had it. I told you we were going to run into this guy."

Maybe a hundred feet further, we see this guy. Right away, he must have recognized us, because he starts yelling, "I'm going to get you. You fucked with me before!" He's by a tree in a little clearing.

"This is how we'll work it," I tell John. "You go off to the side and distract him again. Poke him with your stick, but hold your stick loosely. Let him get your stick. When he gets your stick, I'll blow him away. I'll just shoot him. That way we'll have a reason: He got your stick and you were in danger. There's no way we can just tackle this guy, the two of us alone, without getting hurt." He was big and he was strong. He was mean and he was crazy.

John circles off to the side and starts talking to this guy. His voice is lowered, but I figure he's egging the guy on. I'm waiting. I got my gun out. I'm planning to blow this guy's brains out, splatter them all over the field. I'm maybe twenty yards away, but I'm sure enough of my shooting that I'm going to get this guy. I'm not going to shoot him in the leg. He's not going to go down if I shoot him in the leg. I'm just going to blow this guy away. John is circling and talking to him.

The next thing I know, the guy's putting his hands behind his back. John signals for me to come over and put my cuffs on him. They barely closed on his wrists. I couldn't believe it. I was stunned. I said, "John, how did you do it? What did you say?"

"It was easy," John says. "I just kept telling him, 'Hey, nigger, you see that guy over there with the gun out? He's going to blow your fucking brains out.' He took one look at you and put his fucking hands behind his back." He believed it and he believed it because it was true. I was going to do it. I wasn't going to get hurt and I wasn't going to allow my partner to get hurt. It didn't make any sense.

But after we got the cuffs on him, he started to fight. He kicked my partner in the balls. I had him from behind and was wrestling him over toward some rocks to knock him out. I pushed the guy down. I look up and my partner is taking a swing at where the guy's head used to be. He's swinging with all his might, but now my head is in the way. So I pulled the guy back up again and when the stick hit him in the head it shattered. The guy went down, we took him into the house. Maybe that was excessive force or something, but it didn't seem to do any damage to him or really subdue him. When he came to, he was just wild.

He was crazy, but he wasn't that crazy. We got him into the station and now he figures he's safe. What can we do to him with all the witnesses around? He starts going berserk, kicking stuff around and trying to throw things. Cursing and spitting.

He spit on the sergeant. The sergeant just looked at me and said, "Harry, I know that you'll take care of this." He walked into the back room. Up till then I had never hit a prisoner, somebody that was already subdued, but this guy wasn't subdued. This guy was still causing a big ruckus. I didn't hit him and I didn't beat him, but I threw him around the back room a little bit. That calmed him down a little bit to where he was going "Yes sir" and "No sir." I wasn't going to put up with his shit. I knew that he was rational enough to go through the processing.

We took him down to court charged with assault on an officer. The lawyer tried the defense, "Your honor, my client was drinking. He didn't know what he was doing."

The judge said, "Intoxication is no excuse for trying to strike a police officer." The guy went berserk in court. The court officers tried to hold him down. They were getting nowhere. So I hit him. That's a no-no. You don't hit prisoners in court. I knocked the guy out. The judge just smiled at me like, "Now I know why you did what you did."

At the time I knew a girl who was an admitting nurse at the hospital psycho ward, so I used to take all the psychos down and she'd hustle them through. Normally it took hours for the processing. But she'd hustle them along. Then from midnight till four in the morning we'd be up in her room enjoying ourselves. Around five o'clock I'd call the station and say, "Gee, I just got finished with this psycho. Will you sign me out? I'm going home from here." I'd have been getting laid.

*

These young kids want to be a bunch of PR people. I told them, "If you're going in there and talk, you got to talk their language." When I go into a bar in a black area where there are fights going on, I just climb up on the bar, walk down it and kick everybody's drink off the bar. Then I says, "Okay, motherfuckers, the Man's here. Let's take care of business." All these sons of bitches look up to where I'm standing. The go-go dancers is standing next to me and the crowd is wondering which one of us is going to put on the best act.

We had a couple of suspicious persons on the lot next to this bar. When I ran a check, one of them had a warrant on him for a traffic ticket or something. So my partner and I put him into the wagon.

A crowd of people started gathering out of the bar. One of them says to me, "We're not going to let you take our brother to jail."

The guy I was arresting had a fifth of MD 20–20 on him. So I took the bottle of wine off him and said, "I'm going to auction off this bottle of wine and the proceeds are going to go to the NAACP." They gathered around and I climbed up on top of the wagon out there on the street. I said, "Okay, we will start the bidding at ten cents. Who will give me ten cents for this bottle of wine?"

"I'll give you ten cents," says this wino over to one side.

"Do I hear twenty cents? Who'll bid thirty cents?" I bid it up pretty good. Finally I got down off the wagon and set the bottle of wine down. I said, "I'm going to set this bottle of wine down on the ground here. Then I'm going to turn around and check on my prisoner there. I hope nobody takes this bottle of wine." As soon as I turned around somebody in the crowd grabs the bottle and takes off.

When I turn back around I said, "Man, wine evaporates fast. Even the glass is gone." Everybody is laughing, cracking up. I told my partner out of the corner of my mouth, "Get in on the driver's side and start this thing. Soon as I jump on, get the hell out of here." He gets the thing started and I jumped in the back of the wagon and I said, "GO!"

This brother is sitting in the back of the wagon and he says, "I'll tell you, man, that's class. I seen a lot of cons in my day, but that was fantastic. I enjoyed that show so much, I don't even mind going to jail. Five minutes ago, they were ready to kill you. Now look at them back there. They don't even know what the hell happened. They'll be telling each other about tonight for years to come."

*

I'm a light sleeper. I heard somebody out messing with my car outside my apartment. I got up very quietly. He was so engrossed in siphoning the gas that I walked right up and stuck my gun in his ear. I said, "Swallow." He swallowed. I went back inside, called the local police and told them where they could find him. He was outside gagging, sick. I went back to bed.

I got arrested for terroristic threats. I got a lawyer. I got grilled. "Two wrongs don't make a right. Blah, blah, blah." The son of a bitch had a record as long as my arm and he was only nineteen years old. I got a suspended sentence and a $300 fine. Fortunately that was all that happened.

About two months later the bastard broke into my house again and took about $200 and a television set. Six months later while the son of a bitch was out on bail, he got shot in another incident. He robbed the wrong person.

*

We got the call that there was a disturbance in progress at the ABC Lounge and we go roaring up there. A bunch of other highway patrolmen come roaring in and city policemen and county deputies. The county helicopter is hovering overhead flooding the parking lot with the spotlight. The people are being contained and those that are blowing up at the police officers are being arrested for disorderly intoxication. Everything is taken care of. No problems.

Here comes this highway patrolman roaring up the avenue. Slams on the brakes and slides sideways into the parking lot. He jumps out. You remember the old Dodge Boys commercial on television that featured the epitome of a southern cop? Jackson looked the part. He had little bitty eyes, sunk back in the folds of flesh in his face. Jowls hanging down and this big pot gut. He stood about six foot three, I guess. Big old redneck-looking guy.

Jackson comes jumping out of his patrol car and he's

got his sap gloves on and he's clutching his riot baton. He looks like he's dressed in a hurry, see. He's got his riot boots on, but they're unlaced and his pants are kind of shoved down into them. He's looking around and he can't find anything to do. This guy comes walking across the parking lot heading for his car. Jackson ran up to him and said, "Weren't you told to get out of here, boy?" Jabbed that riot baton in the guy's ribs, doubled him over and drug him off to his patrol car.

We all sort of went, "Oh, my God," under our breath. Jackson had on his helmet and the straps were dangling. It was kind of funny, but it was sad, too, if you think about it.

Here comes this car down the avenue, this guy and this girl. The girl leans out the window and she sees all the blue lights and the cop cars and the helicopter in the air. She hollered something out the window. I never made out what it was she said. But Jackson did. He ran, jumped into his patrol car, puts it in gear and burns rubber out of the lot after these two.

Me and a trooper I was with said, "We got to go with him." We jumped in our car and took off. By now, Jackson pulled the guy over a couple of blocks away. He has got that guy out in a parking lot, making him dance. He made him dance on his left leg, then he made him dance on his right leg. He made him do the Twist. He was standing there with his riot baton, getting his kicks, making this poor guy Twist all over the parking lot. The guy's girlfriend is in the car watching all this and the guy is crying.

We get ahold of Jackson and say, "That's enough, Jackson. This is all taken care of now. Let's go." We managed to get Jackson back in the car.

Jackson had been sitting in his house listening to the police scanner. When I'm home, I don't listen to a scanner. When I'm on the job, I monitor the police frequencies, because I like to know what's going on around me. But when I'm home, I turn the damn thing off, pop open a beer, prop my feet up and watch TV just like everybody else. Jackson was sitting at home and heard this call come over the scanner. He's off-duty, but he's got to go get involved in this big situation.

*

Our sector turned out to be the bridge plaza. It is known for its whores, 99 percent of which were men, usually ex-cons who did five-dollar blowjobs in cars. They wore wigs and tied their cocks up with pantyhose back toward their ass, so if the guy reached down he couldn't feel the swanz hanging there to give the guy away. They were all ugly as sin, but did they do business? Oh, man. They're making $100 to $150 in a night turning five-dollar blowjobs.

We also had the bridge itself as part of the sector, so there were a lot of accidents to take care of. Other than that the sector was quiet. It was factories. In the daytime it was busy with traffic, but not much crime. At night, everything was closed up and there was nothing but the hookers.

Something possessed the captain to tell the lieutenant to tell the sergeant to tell us to clean up the hookers. Being the literal-minded cop that I was, when they said, "Clean up the hookers," I said, "Okay. You want it done, we'll do it." I cleaned them up. Me and my partner did it. We got some reputation, but we did it.

I'd drive around the sector and we'd see a hooker. I call them all women even though most of them were men. It's easier in your mind and it's easier when you point at somebody who looks vaguely like a female to say "she" instead of calling it a he and having to explain that it's a guy dressed up like a girl. We'd drive up to them and I'd say, "Okay. That's it for tonight. Go home."

"Yeah, yeah. Okay, okay," she says. So you drive

away. You come back five minutes later and she's still there.

"Didn't I tell you to leave? Leave."

"Yeah, okay. I'll leave. I'll leave."

Ten minutes later she's still there. It's frustrating. It's aggravating. I said, "Hey, I told you to leave, man!"

What are you going to do? Lock them up for loitering? The courts were throwing that out right and left. The hookers were laughing at us. The desk didn't want you to bring them in. They want you to clean it up without doing anything. The captain was giving lip service to this, but I guess he wasn't really expecting us to do it, much less to succeed. He expected us to do what everybody else ever did that had ridden that sector— drive by occasionally and say, "Get lost!" Then you were supposed to put up with the affront of somebody throwing the authority of the badge in your face. That is what they would do by not leaving when you said to leave.

So I started becoming a psycho. I'd tell them to leave and they wouldn't leave. I'm working the midnight shift. It'd be five o'clock in the morning and this hooker would still be standing on the corner after the tenth time I told her to leave. I started slow in the beginning and I'd only chase them down the sidewalk at 5 or 10 miles an hour. But after a while, I was hitting 30–35 miles an hour with lights and siren down the sidewalk. If they didn't move, I probably could have stopped without hitting them. But they moved.

I put the fear of God into them. No, I put the fear of me into them. I was the one guy who, when he said move, you moved or this guy was going to do something weird. They'd see me coming and they'd start to run.

I'd come rushing up at them, jump out of the radio car with my stick and I'd be screaming, "I'm going to kill you. I'm going to break your legs, you son of a bitch. I told you to get out of here." They'd never had a guy try to do this shit to them.

I'd make them come over. They'd shuffle over expecting to get yelled at. I'd say, "Put your leg on that fire hydrant." They put their leg up on the fire hydrant. I'd reach into the radio car and bring out one of those big, old-fashioned fire hydrant wrenches. I'd go to take a swing like it was a baseball bat at their leg. "I'm going to break your fucking leg, you fucker. I told you not to come back here. I told you last week and the week before that. I'm fed up with this shit. I'm going to fucking bust your leg!" I'd swing it at the fire hydrant in such a way that even if they didn't move, I'd miss their leg. Almost invariably, they'd pull their leg away.

I terrorized them. The only one that got hurt was one who fell down and skinned up his knees and hands and got a scratch on his face while running from us, but I didn't touch her.

They used to call my partner The Nice Guy. I had a mustache that I grew into a Fu Manchu down past my chin about an inch and a half and I'd twist it. The hookers called me The 'Stache.

They were afraid of me, but my partner they could look to for shelter almost. He would protect them from my wrath. That was the act that we put on. He would say, "Aw, 'Stache, don't break her leg."

"I'm going to kill this bitch."

"Now, 'Stache, take it easy. She's going to go away and she won't come back. Isn't that right, honey?"

But we still had some who would keep coming back or new ones to replace them. You get tired of doing the same thing every night. I thought, "How are we going to do this? How often can you threaten to break their leg and then not break their leg before they realize it's just a sham? It's not going to work forever." I had to figure out a way to escalate it without causing real damage. It had been basically scary, but nonviolent. A show. A facade.

We picked three of them up one night, took them to the railroad yard and locked them in a boxcar. We were going to let them out in the morning when we got off work. When we got back there in the morning, they'd kicked out the screen on one of the little air hatches and escaped. In their minds, they were going to Oregon. Only one of those three ever came back to our sector.

We took three girls in the car one night and we drove down under the bridge. My partner and I get out of the car and start looking around as though we were looking for a body and shining flashlights around in the water.

"You see her?"

"Nah, I think she hit the water. I don't think she landed up here."

"Yeah, we don't have to worry about the body. She's out in the ocean by now."

This was all for the hookers' benefit in the back of the car. Word got out that we had thrown a girl off the bridge. "The 'Stache threw a hooker off the bridge." In some versions she was dead before we threw her off. In others she died from the fall.

I ran into one of these girls one night and I threatened to hit her with the stick. It didn't seem to faze her. Nothing seemed to faze her. For some reason, I don't know why, I took out the gun. I was standing like two feet away from her and I stuck it right between her eyes. I said, "If you don't get out of here, I'm going to blow your fucking brains out."

She just looked at me. So I cocked the gun. Her eyes sort of revolved. They seemed to almost change places as they followed the cylinder rotating. Then she just dropped like a stone to the sidewalk.

I looked at the gun. It was still cocked. I let the hammer down and broke it open. There's no fired shells. For a minute, I thought I'd shot her. When you're hyped up, maybe you pulled the trigger and didn't even realize it. I had to look to make sure I didn't blow this hooker away. But I hadn't. She'd just fainted.

Oh, shit. My partner looked at me. "What'd you do?"

"I think she fainted," I said. So I put my gun back in my holster; we got back in the car and drove away.

There's another hooker around the corner. I told my partner to stop. I get out and I says, "Wait a minute, I need you to do me a favor."

"What do you want," she says. She's scared. "Come on, 'Stache, what is it? What do you want?"

I walked her to the corner and I said, "I just shot that girl down there and I want you to take her to the hospital for me." She looks and halfway down the street she sees this body laying on the sidewalk. She screams and runs the other way.

This added to our reputation. Threw a hooker off the bridge, put them in railroad cars, breaking their legs. When they get together and talk, it's not, "Oh, I pulled my leg away and nothing really happened." They tell each other, " 'Stache hit me, he broke my leg." "Put me in a boxcar and I ended up in Florida." "Yeah, I saw them throw the girl off the bridge. She was a friend of mine." So we got a reputation for being killers.

Things got so bad—or good, depending on your point of view—that I could get in the radio car at the beginning of the tour, drive around the sector one time and look at all the girls and let them see me. Then we'd go to the diner and get coffee, drive someplace and have a roll. When we'd drive around the sector again, there wouldn't be one girl on the street.

Later on, it bothered me, because there was a part of me that had the feeling that what I was doing was wrong. But I was told by my superiors to do it. I had to do it. I'm not the type of person to do a halfassed job. I didn't hurt anybody. I scared the hell out of a lot of people and broke a lot of rules. But I got my job accomplished. I cleaned up the sector.

*

Downtown precinct has some really elegant detectives. In order to work downtown, you had to dress and look good. Generally they were excellent detectives, but they also had to present a good appearance.

I had an arrest in that area so I was in the downtown precinct. They were interrogating a bunch of people. Finally they got to this guy who turned out to be a child molester. Like everyone else, police get really angry at child molesters. Most cops get crazy over it. Some cops are maybe a little more educated and understand that this guy has a very serious problem. They'll deal with it much more professionally, but there is a certain group that if they get a hold of a child abuser, the guy is in a lot of trouble.

I saw this guy. He's a big, big fat guy, looked slightly brain-damaged. He was sitting in the corner. They had him for a number of child molestation cases.

This detective sergeant, an elegant guy, looked like a movie actor, he came in after all the other guys had finished the interrogation of this character, taken statements from him and fingerprinted him. They'd done the whole bit. He read all the reports. He'd been out drinking, so he was also half in his cups. But he's looking at all the paperwork.

I had a prisoner and I was sitting at a desk near him. He calls to me and says, "Have you got the prick cards?"

"What do you mean, the prick cards?"

"You know, the prick cards," and he gave me a wink. "I got to print this guy."

"Oh, yeah, yeah," and I picked up a fingerprint card and I said, "Here's one."

"All right." He looked at it. "You. Come over here." From the way he looked and the way he dressed and spoke, you'd just respond to him. He looked like he was used to command and he was clearly not a crazy. "Sir, what's your name, ah, Mr. So-and-So. Sit here. I'm in charge of this section. In a case of this kind, what we do is, we're maintaining a record of all the people arrested for child molesting. We're keeping prints of all their pricks."

"I've been arrested for this three times before and I've never heard of this," the fat guy says.

The detective sergeant replies quietly and calmly, "It's a new procedure. I'm afraid we're going to have to print your prick. You see, it doesn't matter whether we print your thumb or your fingers or your prick. Sometimes we have semen stains or marks inside of kids' mouths or the ass of somebody's kid. We want to be able to check the cards for possible identification. Especially if someone kills a child."

"I don't know what you're talking about. I don't think that's possible. Besides I would never kill anyone. I've never done anything to anyone who didn't want it done. I paid them for it."

"Yeah, well, that may be the case, but we're going to have to take your print. So stand up and come over here." He had this little portable print board on the desk—generally, they're up on a table, bolted down. He sets it up. He had the card folded over and all this shit. He goes, "All right, drop your pants."

I couldn't believe this guy. Everybody in the room stops and looks. "What the fuck is this guy doing?"

"You guys by the door," the detective says, "make sure no women come in, because I'm going to be taking a prick print here." So there's witnesses all over the place. There's cops and there's a couple of prisoners. The child molester drops his pants. The guy tells him, "Now take your prick out and put it out here on the desk." The guy takes his prick out and lays it on the desk. The detective grabs the guy's prick in his hand.

Under the desk he had a blackjack in his hand. He came up with a slapper and gave this guy a shot that went through everybody in the room. Everybody grabbed their balls. Boom! He hit him in the prick. The guy screamed and doubled over.

My prisoner was a dope dealer. He got up and said, "He deserved that. Fuck him."

The cop said, "Okay, now you can go back in the cage." Where my head was at the time, I wouldn't have had the balls to do it. Excuse the pun, but I just wouldn't have had the balls. I would like to do that to somebody like that. I probably would. But to have the chutzpah to grab hold of this guy's prick and hit it with a blackjack, that was bad.

The guy went to court later on and he told the story to the judge and the Legal Aid had the guy show his prick and the judge said, "He must have done this to himself. I can't believe a police officer would behave that way. I mean, a cop told you he was going to fingerprint your penis and then he grabbed it and hit it with a blackjack? Come on."

*

Some guys need a beating. In the street or the back of the precinct, there's a guy who needs a beating. And you got to do it. If you don't do it, the next situation that a cop runs into this character, it's going to be bad.

It's hard for people to understand or believe that. But the fact of the matter is, if this guy runs into a cop, gets into a fistfight and really beats the shit out of him, he believes he can beat up all cops, if you arrest him without working him out. He's got to know that the next time he does this, he's going to get his ass kicked in.

So I have no problem with that. Neither did any cop I've ever known have any problem with that. As long as you don't do it in public, as long as the guy really needs it, and as long as you don't carry it too far. Give him a beating and that's it. Don't break his ribs, you don't knock his teeth out, you don't crack his skull and give him a concussion.

It's simple. Have a guy hold him. You rap him in the shins a couple of good times. Let him know that he's going to get his ass kicked and it's going to hurt.

But how do you stop these guys. There's a very thin line between giving a guy a couple good shots in the mouth and giving him a couple good shots with a nightstick across the shins. The problem is that you can't stop guys once they get started.

I went into a precinct once and seen a guy hanging on a cage. He looked like Jesus Christ. What they did was they put a handcuff on either hand and hung him up on the cage with his arms spread. They cut out a crown of thorns from a piece of paper and tacked it to the back of his head. Put his feet together like Christ and tied them with a shoelace. The guy had a beard. I genuflected when I walked in. Christ on a Cage.

It was early, like seven o'clock in the morning, and the sole person in the squad room was this old Irish detective, smoking a cigar and doing paperwork—ton of paperwork. Here's this guy hanging there. I was there to get some forms. I stood in front of the detective and he didn't even look up. I says to the guy, "That guy alive or what?"

"Fuck him."

"What happened?" What happened was that this guy was involved in a family fight and some cops showed up. He had made a Carolina pancake. A Carolina pancake is a mixture of lye, Crisco or bacon grease. Fat and lye. They cook it up and then they throw it on you. The lye will burn right through you. You mix lye with grease and you can't wash it off. It happens a lot.

The cops had responded. This guy came to the door and splashed a cop. Caught him on the side of the face and it ran down his overcoat. They couldn't get the overcoat off him fast enough and the stuff burned right through it to him.

This guy was psycho, he ended up burning three or four guys. So they beat the hell out of him and then they hung him up. This old guy looks up at him hanging there and says, "He's not going to do that again." That guy deserved a beating. Whether he deserved to be hung up on a cage like that all night . . .

*

I ran into a different kind of cop that I'd never met before, the cop who got off on brutality. Got off on degradation, got off on putting people down. They stuck me with this guy named Gray. He was fat, sloppy, out of shape. He was a pig, physically and mentally. He was a mental pig. Apparently this guy had problems with other partners so they would put people with him that didn't know it. I said, "Okay, I'll try it for a while." I discovered why people didn't want to work with this guy.

You start out the tour with him saying, "Are you catching?" That meant if you came across a crime and made an arrest are you willing to be the one who makes the arrest and has to do the paperwork. He didn't like to go to court. He didn't like the hassle of it.

If I said yes, he'd say, "Good. I don't have to be nice." Then he'd go out of his way to be nasty to people, to cause problems, to push people around. He'd be arrogant for no cause.

I was the type of person that if I took a dislike to somebody, I could turn a traffic ticket into a felony collar just by the way I treated them. I didn't have to be insulting or pushing people around or brutal to get a guy to lose his temper and take a swing at me. If the guy came out of the car when I stopped him with, "What do you want, motherfucker, money?" I could turn that kind of attitude into a felony real easy. Assault on a cop, just by the way I smiled at the guy and yes-sir'd and no-sir'd. Check the depth on his tread. "You got a bad exhaust system" and "Let me hear your horn. Now the lights." You'd be surprised what you can do with people's heads. But I didn't make a habit out of it unless they came on to me first.

Gray got off on doing this. He liked doing it. That was his thing.

One day he told me while I was driving, "Make a U-turn." I made the U-turn and he tells me where to stop. He calls this girl over to the car. I didn't know if he knew her from somewhere before or what, but he starts rapping with her. She's leaning on the car. He's looking at her tits and he says to her, "Are those real? Are they really all yours?"

"Of course, they are," she says.

"Let me feel." He puts his hand out and starts playing with this woman's breasts. I'm sitting there flabbergasted. He just picked her up at random on the sidewalk.

The next thing I know, he's got her head dragged inside the radio car through the window, her tits are resting on the car door and he's squeezing her tits. I can't believe this is happening to me. What is this guy doing? Is he nuts? But this is where this guy's head is at.

Gray loved to treat people like garbage. You'd go to family disputes. He liked to push around husbands and try to get them to swing so he could lock them up for assault—if I was willing to make the arrest. Then I'd get stuck with the assault or some other bullshit arrest.

I started being a bounty hunter, which is a guy who gets a lot of arrests. The system being what it is, you can get overtime if you make the arrest. They had sent me to school for forged licenses, so I started using that to advantage. It's a bullshit collar, but it's a felony.

I'd stopped some guy driving down the street and looked at his license and saw that it was forged. I said, "Okay, you're under arrest. It's not a big deal. You go down to court and you'll be out tomorrow morning. I make a hundred dollars overtime."

While talking to this guy, a kid walks past us and in his back pocket he's got these sticks attached with a piece of chain between them. Those are not classed as dangerous instruments but as deadly weapons, meaning that just carrying them is against the law. I figured, "While I got the guy with the forged license, I'll take the young guy with the sticks, too." It's eight o'clock in the morning and he ain't going to karate class. He's carrying them as a weapon.

So we put him in the radio car and I told the guy with the forged license to take his car and follow me to the station house. "Don't run on me. Just follow me like a nice guy." The guy with the sticks offered no resistance, but my partner was unnecessarily rough, pushing him into the radio car. The other guy followed us to the precinct.

We got there. We're walking them into the station house. For no reason, Gray grabs this guy with the forged license and just shoves him. In doing so, he injured his thumb. He sprained it, badly enough to damage the ligaments. Now he's injured "in the line of duty," and he wants me to tell somebody a bullshit story that he got injured by subduing the kid with the sticks. He wanted me to lie and say that this kid resisted arrest. He wanted an excuse for the injury and maybe get a medal out of it, plus get time off.

By this time, I couldn't stomach working with this guy and I'd been asking out for months and months and been getting stalled. I hated his guts. Just being in the car with him turned my stomach.

I told the sergeant, "That's not how it happened. I'm

not going to say it happened like that. He did it by pushing this dude for no good reason. Fuck him."

They wrote it up that he sprained his thumb while he was helping the prisoner with the sticks into the radio car so he wouldn't hit his head on the top of the door. To save face for him, because I wouldn't lie and add onto the charge. That motherfucker retired from the job with three-quarters pension on a medical disability because they operated on his thumb and further fucked it up. He got out with 75 percent of his full pay, tax free, plus social security for being a scumbag. But at least I got rid of him as a partner.

*

I got stuck with a bad guy. If you're the new guy on the block, you get stuck with the guy nobody else wants to work with. When I first started narcotics, all the partners were established. You got to get the guy who had no partner. But how bad could the guy be?

I had this wonderful Irish lieutenant, a beautiful man. My first day in the division he said, "Look, I'm assigning you to this guy. He's an outstanding cop and a good detective. He's a little bit kookie, but you'll calm him down a little bit."

"What do you mean by kookie? What does that mean?"

"You'll see. The guy has a little hand problem and most guys don't like to work with him."

"I worked with a lot of guys who were tough guys. I don't mind working with guys like that, as long as he's not a sadist or crazy. I don't need to work with a crazy," I said. A hand problem means that he beats up on people. I can usually deal with that because I don't do it at all. Generally a guy like that will only behave that way if the guy with him will back him up. I wouldn't. I just didn't like it.

So I call the office, they give me this guy's home

phone number and I call him. The guy sounds like he's from West Point, very direct, very official. He's a very, very square guy, I can tell. He says, "We're doing ten to six tomorrow. I want you to meet me at the precinct. I have some paperwork to do there. Then we'll go out and take a look."

This guy seemed really nice. He says, "Look, you have to be careful around this area. It's a zoo. The animals are loose around here. What you do is, park your car across the street in the gas station. It's the only safe place around here. Keep your car next to mine. I got a black Oldsmobile. I'll be there before you."

"Maybe I'll get there before you," I said.

"No," he says. "I'm always there first."

All right. He was there first. I got there at a quarter to ten and his car was already in the parking lot. I put my car next to his and I walk up to the squad room. He's typing arrest cards and telephone cards. He's a big blond Swede. I say, "How are you doing?" And we started talking about the narcotics division.

"You're going to love it here," he says. "It's a really nice place to work. If you don't mind working with junkies, it's the best place to work in the whole department. Nobody bothers you here. Nobody wants your job. You do what you want to do as long as you give them four arrests a month. I give them four." He led the group in arrests, always the most arrests in the group. "I give them four and I want to give them eight a month as a team."

"I'll give them ten a month. I don't give a shit," I said. "I like making arrests."

"Terrific. You're going to like working with me. You look good. I'll use you as an undercover guy." And all this other business.

"By the way," I said, "what are you doing with the arrest cards?"

"Holy shit!" he says. He gets up and he's running

out of the station house. I'm running after him. We run across the street into the gas station. He opens the trunk of his car and there's a junkie in his trunk. He pulls this guy out of the trunk. I'm thinking, "The guy's got to be dead." It's the middle of the summer, a black car with the sun beating down. The guy could barely talk.

"Who is this guy?" I ask him.

"This is my informant."

"Your informant? Aren't we supposed to treat these guys nice?"

He pulls the guy out of the trunk and the guy is crying and begging him. He tells the junkie, "You're fucking going to jail. I'm locking you up."

"What'd the guy do?" Turns out my new partner went to meet this informant before he came to meet me. When he went into the guy's apartment, he found a set of works on the table and a bag of heroin. My partner says, "He knew I was coming and he didn't clean the place up. He embarrassed me and I'm locking him up for that junk."

"But he's your informant. He's a junkie. I mean, you got to know the guy's going to shoot dope."

"Fuck him. He embarrassed me and he's going to jail."

The guy is pleading with him, calling him Mister, "Please Mr. So-and-So. I'm so sick. Please, let me shoot up my skull."

"I don't believe this," I thought to myself. Even if you were real straightlaced, if you locked up a real sick junkie, you let him shoot up if he had any junk. You didn't want to put up with him throwing up all over your car and the precinct. Let them shoot up before you take them in. Not this guy. He enjoyed it. Loved it. Loved to see them sick.

I worked with him for nearly two months. After the first week I started begging to get away from him. He did things that were fucking indescribable. The guy would never take a dime. Never take a free meal. This guy would do nothing wrong. But he was the most sadistic, bestial person I'd ever met and I had met some bad guys. This guy made them look like pikers. He was incredible.

He was the most prejudiced, bigoted person. He hated everybody. But blacks really suffered the brunt of his hate.

We had a search warrant for a guy we watched for a long time. Finally we did get into the house, caught the guy in bed, got him cold and executed the warrant. Girlfriend was there. We searched the apartment, let the girlfriend go. Then we had the guy alone.

I could barely get my handcuffs on him, but I did get them on. As soon as I got the cuffs locked, my partner started beating on him, kicking him, hitting him. This guy was a big guy and he didn't budge. He just took it. Finally he looked at my partner and he said, "Sooner or later you're going to have to take these cuffs off of me, you know."

The cop was like six-two and ran about 170 pounds. Tall but thin and wiry. He says to me, "Go down, get the car and meet me out in front of the building." So I go get the car. He's coming down the stairs with this guy and he yells to me, "Can you hear this?" Bong-bong-bong. He's hitting the guy with a blackjack as he's going down the stairs. "Listen to the way his head sounds. Listen to that conk." Bong-bong-bong. "Listen to that. It's hollow, man." The guy comes down and he's all lumped up.

This prisoner was only about six feet tall but an easy 230 pounds. We barely get him in the car. Head shaved, one of these triple X guys. He was pulling on the handcuffs behind his back. I thought, "Oh, boy."

We get him into the station house. My partner is throwing the guy around. The guy falls down and he's kicking him in the legs, in the balls, all over. Cops saw this. They're walking around saying, "Fuck this guy." They didn't care.

Get up to the squad room and now we got to do the paperwork. Who's going to print him? My partner says, "I'll print him." He takes his gun and puts it away. That's procedure. I turned to the guy and I says, "Look, there's just the three of us here. I know how you feel, but you took your beating like a man and . . ."

"Fuck you. When he takes these cuffs off me, I'm going to kill him."

"Oh, Jesus, you do that and I'll have to kill you. Someone's got to kill you if you attack that cop."

"I don't care. I'm a man. I ain't no animal and he can't treat me like that. I'm going to fucking kill him. It's as simple as that." He was not excited. He spoke calmly. He wasn't mad with me. "You want to try and stop me, you can try and stop me. But I'm going to kill this motherfucker."

This guy's eyes were going round and round in his head and I said to my partner, "You're going to have to take the cuffs off this fucker. I'm not doing it." I put the guy in the cage and I finally took the cuffs off in there. I figured I'd best take them off, because he wasn't going to come at me—at least I didn't think he would. I get the cuffs off of him and he's rubbing his wrists. He could have torn us both apart.

I said to him, "Look, go through this shit, get printed." I printed him. He acted like my blond partner didn't live. He wouldn't acknowledge his questions. He just said to him, "Come near me and I'll kill you, motherfucker."

I told my partner, "If I were you and I saw this guy on the street in the future, I'd either run for it or shoot him. You either got to kill him or you're going to have to hide, because this guy is going to kill somebody someday, and it will probably be a cop."

About two weeks later, we ran into some woman in

the street and this partner pulled the same shit. A black woman walking down the street. We have no idea who she is. She has nothing to do with what we are up to. People find it hard to believe that someone would behave like this. She was pregnant. He walked up to her and said, "What black prick did that to you." He thought it was funny. The woman conked him on the head with a wine bottle. She really whapped him. He ended up going into the hospital.

Turned out this woman was an assistant principal at one of the local schools. She wrote a letter on him.

Right after that, he got into a fight. I told the bosses, "Look, I can't work with this guy. I can't be near him. He's crazy. The guy's nuts. Let the next guy who comes in worry with him."

That's what they did. The new guy would work with him for two months and then the next new guy would work with him for two months. I saw him years later. I was going into a precinct and he was coming out with a prisoner. His prisoner looked like he'd been through a meat grinder.

CHAPTER 7

Hardening of the Heart

"YOU COME into the job with a lot of preconceived notions. No matter how worldly you are or knowledgeable you are, your body of experience has expanded exponentially because of the job.

"Whatever sacred cows you may have been feeding all those years are usually slaughtered after a very little while. That's probably the greatest single tragedy that every cop faces. You find out that nothing is on the level. You find out that people die for nothing.

"Whatever it is that drives people to religion is what you experience. And yet you're in a position where you can't accept religion, because you can't function that way. The job runs against every good impulse you ever had." These are the words of a thirty-eight-year-old detective describing the slow descent into cynicism and self-doubt that most cops experience sooner or later.

Police officers are face to face with the evil in humankind. They see daily the worst impulses of men and women driven by blind passion as well as the broad spectrum of brutality the human intellect can concoct.

COPS

In the wake of crime, insanity and pointless maliciousness, they are constantly confronted with grisly reminders of man's mortality. The longer they study our culture, the more deeply they probe into the dark side of American society, the more pessimistic they become. Here is a profile of the perpetual offender from a retired New York City cop who spent most of his twenty years on the street dealing with narcotics cases:

"What people don't understand is that there are street criminals out there now who are irretrievable predators that just get off—it's a sexual experience—on people's pain and on people's crying and begging and pleading. They get off on it. They love it.

"You're not going to scare them. There's nothing you can do with them. You've got to defeat them somehow. To talk to them about any sort of sense of morality, they don't have any sense of morality, they don't have any sense of right and wrong. Their sense of right and wrong is, 'Do I have a few bucks in my pocket to do what I want to do?'

"It's a major misconception having to do with drug addicts that this screaming, crazy junkie is going to go out and rip off an old lady. Heroin addicts are sick most of the time. If they're not sick, they're high. When they're sick, they don't feel like beating up some old lady. When they're high, they don't beat up on anybody.

"The real street shit is generally somebody who doesn't use drugs. I've known a lot of those guys. They have a life story just like other people except their life story changes at the age of ten. They are extortionists by eleven. By twelve, they're untreatable. Forget it.

"These guys are out there and they'll take your head off without blinking an eye. Your pain doesn't register with them. The blood, the shock, nothing registers."

Policemen hate and fear the criminals. The cops in turn are feared and hated by most of the people they police. The establishment they serve seems to hold them in contempt. In the cop's opinion, the press is a mortal enemy, ready to chew up an officer's entire career just to spit it out as a sensational headline or a news update.

"You meet people and all they want to talk about is how this policeman who was a real bastard gave them a ticket. You go into a restaurant and everybody stops eating and they stare at you. The people at the next table are talking about the time they got a ticket and look at the cops in here eating when they should be out saving people and arresting criminals. You either weren't there soon enough or when you got there you handled it wrong. Aw, man, I'll tell you, you'd think you'd get just a little respect for what you do, but you're not recognized for that. You're not even paid for it especially around here," one officer told me.

Cops feel as though they get no support from their colleagues in the judicial system. Cops see the system of justice, including the judges and attorneys who operate it, as a broken-down machine, spinning its wheels over solipsistic arguments rather than turning out clear-cut decisions based on the elemental concepts of right and wrong.

It doesn't take a cop long to decide that his own administration, like all bureaucracies, is more interested in maintaining the status quo and its own integrity as an institution than in protecting the rights of any one officer. Patrolmen are numbers, interchangeable parts. Even the police brotherhood usually dissolves when an officer is in trouble—under investigation or indictment.

Finally, a police officer looks inside himself. He sees the callouses growing thick and hard over his ability to feel. He reconsiders his own motives with his newfound cynicism. If he is honest with himself, he sees how tarnished his ideals have become, how hard his heart is. The last disappointment is with himself.

At this point in their careers, most cops simply resign

themselves to a fatalistic view of their lives and their work. They just try to do the job and not think about it too much. As one officer expressed the attitude, "The most important thing to remember is this: The street is there now. It's been there for a hundred years. It'll be there a hundred years after you're gone. It's not going to change. You're certainly not going to change it. The street rubs off on police. They never rub off on the street."

FROM THE time a guy puts on the uniform and steps out of the academy, an erosion process begins to take place. Some guys are able to deal with it and cope with it fine. They pop out the other end no worse for wear. That's very, very rare. The vast majority of policemen are eroded by their environment, by the people and the places they work in. They become reflections of the people they police.

There are some police who never have that experience, because they're working in areas where they never do anything—they're administrators, special investigators, students, teachers. But policemen who work in a real combat situation cannot help but be affected by what's going on around them. It's not humanly possible to come away from that without being touched by it. How much you are touched by it really affects what you end up as.

After a while a cop becomes a judge, a juror and an executioner. If the rest of the world knew that a whole lot of cops—the most decent kinds of guys—would drive down the street in the ghetto and just spend the entire night shooting dogs, what would they think? "We're going to kill ten fucking dogs tonight because the whole neighborhood is running wild with dogs. The ASPCA ain't going to come up here if their lives depended on it. We're going to shoot, you should excuse the expression, nigger dogs, because they are all over the fucking place."

They're vicious, they run in packs. They kill kids. You're talking about big-time dogs—German shepherds, Doberman pinschers. People who own the dogs let them run loose and they get wild. So you get a bunch of decent guys who say, "Hey, enough of this shit with these dogs. I'm going to go out and shoot some dogs tonight." Two or three o'clock in the morning, it's quiet. A blue and white sails down the street. They slow down. Pow! Pow! Pow! They take off and there's three dead dogs on the corner. "Hey, who killed my dog?"

It's not a big deal, but people don't know that cops behave that way. Cops never talk about it. That is the type of thing they don't talk about a whole lot. They don't talk about the guy who goes inside a bar and has a few beers and comes back out and shoots out a few streetlights. A guy'll do that. Go in a bar and shoot it up. These kinds of things will happen. People will say that guy is a weird guy.

I worked in a unit that was sixty average guys. They were good detectives and of the sixty, 100 percent in one way or another did something that was criminal— not corrupt, but criminal things. "Well," people will say, "water seeks its own level. These guys found each other and kind of formed an alliance."

That's not true. They came from units all over town and they ended up working in an environment that was totally out of control. They were told, "You go out and do the job. We don't care how you do it; just get the job done."

They cleaned it up. They did a better job than was ever done before, but what happened was they became reflective of the people that they were taking out. "If we're going to catch these guys, fuck the Constitution, fuck the Bill of Rights, fuck them, fuck you, fuck everybody. The only ones I care about are my partners."

So you have all these decent guys all doing something wrong. My feelings after a lot of thought about it is this: I know what kind of guy I was. I was the kind of guy who wouldn't cross against the light. I wouldn't break the laws. I was afraid if I did. I didn't like taking on a cop. Had I been out running free in the '60s I don't know how I would have been. I know my own history up to that point was that I was a very straight guy. I carried the flag in the classroom. I find myself years later, kicking people's doors down, beating up on people, stealing people's money. I don't know how it all happened.

It's an erosion process. After a while you throw up your hands in the air and say, "Fuck them. This is the way to be and I want to be with these people. They're the ones I care about. And I'm going to do what they think is right."

*

The bottom line in police work is riding around in a radio car answering calls. There's nothing after that. You're in the basement. What are they going to do to you? The only thing they could do to you is transfer you to another place which is the same as working here. And they don't want to do that, because they'll be transferring a problem they had to another guy's precinct. So what you have is guys who whenever they are encouraged to do their work say, "What are you going to do? Transfer me?"

You're on patrol in a precinct. There's a guy over at the big building they call headquarters. The guy's got an inside job, right? He's trying to get more out of you. He comes up with a computer. I can go downstairs right now and push in the number of any radio car in the city. There are seventy-three precincts and there are ten cars in each precinct. I can pick one at random, press a button, it comes up on the screen what the car is doing right now. I'll find out if he's on a job or on patrol. If he is on a job, I'll find the exact location. There'll be a phone number where I can call him. At the end of the tour, I can press some buttons and it prints out what he's done. It comes out on a sheet what time he took each job, what time he came back on the radio and the disposition of each job. Now Big Brother is watching us.

Over at headquarters when this guy came up with all this stuff, they said, "This is great, man. Look at what we can do."

The guy on the bottom of the barrel is thinking, "What are they trying to do to me? The guy over at HQ is whipping me to death and they're telling that guy what a great job he did because he squeezed a little more sweat out of me." But how many of them are out there on the street dealing with the public? There's 24,000 officers altogether. There's got to be less than 10,000 on patrol.

Let me tell you something. This has been part of the job since I came on and to this day everybody from the police commissioner on down knows it. They still use the number of summonses you give to determine your productivity on your activity report, because it's a number. You can't put down the number of times you prevented a burglary by parking the radio car in the right place and questioning a guy in the street. It's not on paper. It's not on the radio. It's never known. You can be out there being a diligent guy. It comes the end of the month, "How many parkers you give out? None? Five? Three?"

Some guys can give a parking summons in a minute, a minute and a half. A moving summons is going to take you five or ten minutes. You got to talk; you got to fill out all the details. Every precinct has a summons man. He goes out and gets a book a day. Twenty or 25 tickets a day. That's 125 a week. That's 600 a month.

"Fantastic. Six hundred a month at $25 to $35 a pop. Promote that man immediately!"

What's he doing? He's spending twenty-five to forty-five minutes out of an eight-hour day giving out summonses. They don't care what he does with the other time. The guy's a hit.

You got a guy on patrol who has said, "Hey, fuck this job." He don't answer the radio or he's slow on giving a disposition on a call. He spends an extra twenty minutes in the place and in the meantime other cars are picking up the jobs that are starting to back up. You work with twenty guys. After a year, you know who's fucking who and who's not. But this guy here, he gives out 50 parking summonses or 10 moving summonses at the end of the month and the sergeant thinks, "Whoa, this guy is great." He doesn't know how many radio runs he handled. He doesn't know what he's doing.

To this day, believe it or not, you go into the captain to ask him for a favor and he'll say, "What're you doing for me, you fucking hump? Let's see. You got no tickets."

"Yeah, but I been working with the community. The kids all respect me and the shopkeepers aren't calling all the time." That don't matter. It comes down to summonses.

The other guys on a squad, there's nothing they can do about it when one guy fucks off. It's like playing a basketball game and there's two referees, but they're not calling shit. After a while you're getting jabbed and fouled and so you go, "Fuck you." And you start jabbing back and it turns into a brawl. The sergeant knows who is working and who's not working. He's not saying anything. Why? It's tough to be a sergeant. Being sergeant means not having any friends. And what's he going to do? Transfer the guy?

At the end of the day we get the proof back from the

computer. Here's one guy's got twenty jobs and the other guy's handled three or four.

There's this one car that goes to get gas at two-thirty or a quarter to three every day on the day tour. They don't want to get stuck on any jobs at the end of the tour and it's a busy time of the day. I was working this shift one day and the guy I'm with says, "There's these fucking pricks. Watch this guy. I guarantee you at two-thirty he's going to go for gas." Sure as shit, the guy makes the call and goes for gas on the button. And then they brag about it the next day. They come into roll call and I said, "Hey, you going for gas again at two-thirty?"

"You're fucking right, I'm going to go." And they do. The sergeant, he's oblivious to the whole thing. He could care less.

A guy realizes, "I got to go fend for myself out there. Cover my ass and don't get caught. Try not to work my ass off and be a fucking idiot. I'm going to start getting stuck at the end of the day or I'll be making all the arrests and waiting all night at night court."

*

When you first get out there, you have to make yourself a reputation as a cop, not as much with the people in the street as with the other cops that are out there. "Wow, look at this guy. He's got that collar, he's got this collar. He's in on that collar." You're pushing yourself a little more out there.

As you're established, you pick your shots. You find out that you get the same amount just without really risking it. Without chasing this guy down the block. Now I say, "I know this guy. I'll get him tomorrow. He's not going anywhere. I know where he is and I'll go out there and grab him."

When you're looking for it, you never find it. You come back in and your eyes are like two cigarette burns in a blanket, sick of looking for people to do something. You wish mayhem on some poor little old lady walking down the street. "I wish this guy would grab her purse and knock her down so I could get him." You get a strange attitude out there. "Gee, he only stabbed him once. If he stabs him again, it's a second-degree assault."

I don't expect people to understand this unless you're out there. I'm not talking about for a weekend or a week. I'm talking years and years. You see a lot of your friends burned out. They've had enough. They pack it in and go out to the suburbs. Or if they're fortunate, they get promoted and go on to a different level.

*

It takes eight men to man a sector around the clock, seven days a week. So there's me and my partner and six other guys. A member of the six other guys comes up to my partner and says, "We have a number of contracts. There's money to be made. There are arrangements that are in order. Now, do you guys want in on them or not?"

My partner came to me and told me, "One of the guys came to me and wanted to know what we wanted to do about the contracts." We talked about it. Should we go in with it or what? We thought and we said, "No, we want to stay clean. We like not having to worry about being crooked."

A lot of guys transferred out of the sector. We killed the contracts. Now I'm starting to realize that there is really corruption in the department, something I didn't think existed.

I had three years on the job now. I used to eat hamburgers and drink coffee in the sector for nothing. You didn't go in and order steak. You didn't order the guy's best meal. You got a sandwich. They wouldn't charge you for it and they got insulted if you tried to pay for it. So you leave a big tip for the waitress. You go in and have a buck and a half hamburger and a soda and leave a dollar tip. This was the only corruption that I was involved in.

Was it corruption? Yes. The owner of one diner used to park his car on the street. That was essentially his private parking lot. There was a fire hydrant in front of the place and people used to park there while they ran in for coffee and we didn't hang tags on them for that. In that sense, maybe we were corrupt. That's not totally neutral. If we had hung tags on every car that double-parked in front of the place, somebody would have accused us of trying to shake him down for money.

They moved my partner and I out of that precinct and into a residential community.

*

When you've been on the street for ten or eleven years, you know what it takes to make a good case and what doesn't make it.

You go out on the street and here's a car with the side window busted out. You look up the street and there's a kid running up the street with a paper bag. You fire up there and snatch him up. It turns out that, yeah, he's got a paper bag and in this paper bag he's got four cassette tapes, and an AM-FM radio and tape player. That's it. That's all you've got.

Most of the time, you can't find the victim—the guy who owns the car. If you do find the guy who owns the car, he says, "Oh, yeah, I had such and such tapes and a portable AM-FM cassette player." So you take it to court and the first question out of the public defender's mouth is going to be, "Did you see the defendant break into the car?"

"No, sir."

"Did you have sight of the suspect the whole time?"

"No. He ran around the corner."

307

"So is it not possible that, as my client says, he found that bag on the corner when he ran around there and just happened to pick it up as you came around after him?"

So you go ahead and you chase them down. You do what you're supposed to do. But the main thing you're after is the property. You'll take it to the property room, so the victim can get his stuff back. To hell with the arrest, because you know it won't make it in a million years.

We had a robbery of a sailor downtown at one of the topless bars. The sailor described the suspects and the van they left in. Me and my partner put the sailor in the backseat of our patrol car and drove him around to see if we could find them. All of a sudden he says, "That's the van there."

We run up with our guns drawn and we're dragging them out. The sailor goes, "That's them, that's them. Those two there, the tall one and the short one." So we take the sailor out of the backseat, frisk these guys down and put them into the backseat. We got positive identification of the vehicle. He points it out as it's going by. A positive ID of the suspects—"These are the guys who hit me over the head and stole my wallet."

He gives us all this information about what was in his wallet. He had $50—a twenty, two tens and two fives. We search the van. Down in the back of the van where the spare tire is, I found the twenty and the two fives. I leave them right where they're at and get the evidence technician down there. He comes and takes pictures of where the money is at. Then we pull it out and he takes pictures of the money itself. I initial the bills and put the serial numbers in the report. We take them to jail.

We no sooner get in the car again when we get a call from the jail. One of the suspects when given a complete search before being placed in a cell, they found two $10 bills in his shoe. Ah-ha! We had the missing $20 out of this deal. We go down there and get the two $10 bills. I initial them and we put the $50 in the property room.

The thing goes to court. I'm sitting up on the stand. The attorney comes over and he's got the money laid out there with my initials and my ID number on them and he has the pictures that were taken by the ET. "Do you recognize these pictures? Is this the way it was?"

"Yes, sir."

"Are these the bills that were recovered?"

"Yes, sir."

"Can you tell me which bills were where?"

"We found the twenty and the two fives in the back of the van and the two tens were found by the officer at the jail."

"Who found the two tens?"

"The corrections officer."

"Who was the corrections officer?" I referred to my notes and said it was So-and-So. "Are you sure these are the two tens that he found?"

"Those are the two $10 bills that he handed me at the back door to the jail on the night of the robbery."

"But you don't know where he found these two $10 bills. These could have been two $10 bills that he took out of his own wallet."

The corrections officer didn't have his initials on the bills showing that he had turned them over to me and so the chain of evidence was broken. They threw out the whole thing. That was the only thing we had on the suspects other than the victim's testimony to prove that they had taken the money.

You spend time and get what you consider a good case and something like that happens. Then the next time it happens and the sailor says, "That's them." You say, "Who gives a fuck. What's the sense?"

*

We had a little dope dealer down there named Benny Jefferson. Nat had a very special relationship with this dope dealer—like every time he saw him, Nat jacked Benny up to see what he was holding. We'd end up in internal about twice a week on that, because every time Nat would see Benny, we'd stop him. Nat would say, "Benny, what are you holding?"

"You just fucking with me again," Benny would reply.

"Nah, we ain't fucking with you. What you holding?" We'd then use the old stop and frisk to find it. About one out of every three times, you'd catch him holding some horse. Jack him up, bring him downtown, put him in jail. But I said, "Nat, you're going to lose the case. The district attorney is not going to file them. This is illegal search."

"I don't care," Nat said. "It may be illegal, but I'm taking the stuff off him and he ain't getting to sell it." Nat may not have been making good cases, but in reality he was right. He was cutting into the guy's profit real hard.

We finally made some good cases on Benny. We caught him with three or four ounces of heroin and brought him down. I don't remember how we had stopped him this time, but we'd had a good reason. The state attorney's office naturally dropped it to possession instead of possession for sale. Then they let him plead to a lesser charge. So he ended up convicted of a second-degree felony.

We were horribly depressed by the fact that, even when we did make a good case, we couldn't make it go anywhere. The attorney's answer to us was that Benny had never been convicted before of any charges.

"Yeah," Nat said. "I've arrested him forty-two times and every time you failed to prosecute him. I finally get a good case on him and you still don't prosecute him."

*

The first thing that really struck me was plea bargaining. People are out there doing really terrible things to each other and just fucking each other up. We're there just after it's happened. You see the victim, this hysterical person. You lock up the suspect and file charges. And then all this cools down. The person becomes healed.

Then we get down to the judicial part; that usually takes place weeks and weeks later. There have been two or three or four continuances and maybe a motions hearing, trying to get the guy off on some technicality.

If by some dumb luck, the person who is initially harmed during this thing has gotten all our subpoenas and makes all his appearances, then you might go to bat. What usually happens is this: The case load is so incredible that once the prosecutor sees that the defendant, the defense lawyer, the victim and the cops are there and all the witnesses are there and he's got to do something, then it's—Ta-da-Dah—Let's Make a Deal. "You let this guy off on a misdemeanor and we'll plead him guilty," the defense lawyer tells the prosecutor. They work out a deal that makes both their work loads lighter.

That kind of bothers you but then—surprise—the judge turns around and gives him this incredible sentence. "Six months in the workhouse and a $1,500 fine."

"Wow," you go.

"And I suspend the sentence and I suspend the jail term."

First of all, you've seen this terrible thing happen. You've been down there to the courthouse umpty-ump times. Finally you walk out of the court and you go, "Nothing fucking happened to nobody except me. And here we are."

You know the fucker is going to go out and do it again. We go after all these bank robbers and stick-up artists and murderers. The one thing that is 99 percent certain is that when you go down to the ID bureau to look for the guy's records, they've got his picture and they've got his rap sheet. He's been in trouble before. It's a certainty. If you go down there and the guy has no record, you shake your head and say, "Jesus, he's never been in trouble. I've got a virgin here." It's an event.

To me it's a totally screwed-up system. It's always the same guys. They just graduate.

You've got to really screw up to get sent to the penitentiary in this state. First you've got to screw up a couple of times in juvenile. Then you get to be eighteen and you get to start all over again.

You get caught for doing one burglary you get probation. You get caught doing another burglary, you may do some time down at the county jail. Maybe the third time you get caught, you might get shipped to reformatory. To get to the big house, you've got to have been going and getting hit for a long time, doing some nasty stuff.

Armed robbery carries a penalty of five to twenty-five years. If you get convicted of armed robbery—if you don't get it plea-bargained down, which is often the case—and you go up for the crime, you're looking at two years and you're out. It's a revolving door. It's job security for me if you want to look at it that way. But it ain't right.

They all know it as well. They know what the risks are and they can tell you. You've got the cuffs on them, taking them downtown, and most of them can tell you what kind of penalty they'll get when it's all said and done. "So what, man! I'm going to do two years. So fucking what? So what, motherfucker! I'll be seeing you again." They don't care. They're telling you what they're going to get and they're usually right.

*

California has the highest number of lawyers per capita in the United States, and the United States has more lawyers than the rest of the world combined. They have to make money. One of the best things you sue is a municipality, because they have the money to pay off. Within that structure, the police department is a good thing to sue, because they're always getting into things. Even if you can't win, they'll settle out of court for some money just to get rid of the case. That's an ever present thing.

Most cops want to know, "Where do I stand on being sued? If I'm over here, am I safe?" But it doesn't work that way. You can do everything absolutely right and still get sued and still lose.

An officer sees a motorcyclist. The registration is expired. He turns on his light to initiate a traffic stop. The motorcyclist looks over his shoulder and just hits it—accelerates. The officer goes in pursuit down an alley. The cop is going 25 miles an hour.

The motorcyclist cuts out of the alley into a major street and runs broadside into a car. He is killed. The passenger in the car is a ten-year-old boy. The impact causes glass to go into his eye and the boy loses his right eye.

The driver of the motorcycle is a 2.5 blood alcohol, a drunk driver with three priors, a suspended driver's license. He is pending sentencing on another charge of drunk driving.

The parents of the little boy sued the city, saying the officer chased the motorcyclist and caused him to run. The whole chase amounted to about a block. The wife of the motorcyclist is suing the city, even though she and her husband were estranged.

I had arrested the same man three months before for running into three parked cars because he was so drunk. He's dead. He was a dirtbag. No money. No insurance. No job. Just a dirtbag.

What did the officer do wrong?

You're before the jury. Here's the little boy minus

an eye. He's traumatized for life. You've got the bereaved widow who's going to come in there and sob, sob, sob. The only reason he ran was because the officer was chasing him. Why was he chasing him? Just because he had a registration violation. That's all he knew at the time. The policeman has got to lose this case.

Okay, say the motorcyclist is driving 90 miles an hour and the officer doesn't chase him. Well, you're liable then, too. That's wrong. You're obliged by law to do something about it. If he runs into somebody and they know you were there and saw him and you didn't chase him, they can sue you. You failed to take action, so you get sued for negligence.

*

We just did a search warrant the other day and kicked in the wrong door. The informant for the anti-fencing unit told us there was a bunch of counterfeit money that had been stashed in this one apartment. It was being marketed at three dollars each for a $20 bill. If we didn't move quick, it'll be all gone. It was a very reliable informant. He'd turned nine felonies in a row.

We got the Treasury people and we got the search warrant. The guy pointed out Apartment D of this address. They called us in on it because there were supposed to be a bunch of guns and bad actors in there. We went to the door, knocked and gave them twenty seconds to open the door. No answer. Boom! Down comes the door.

The counterfeiters are supposed to be a family of white people. We go in and we find one lone black sixteen-year-old in the house who is first thrown up against the wall, searched and terrorized a little bit— shivering in his shoes. Then we realized that we'd made a mistake. We started apologizing profusely and telling about how the city is going to take care of the damages to his house.

314

The detective goes and finds out that the family that we're looking for lives next door. He's admitted to the house. The occupant says, "Go ahead and search." No guns, no nothing, no screaming, no yelling. But these people started seeing dollar signs and made up the most incredible, preposterous story for the newspapers about our conduct.

The black family told the truth. We busted in on the wrong address and then had to beat a hasty retreat behind a barrage of apologies. The white family made up this story and the press picked up on it and turned it into one of the biggest scandals we ever had. According to them, as soon as we realized we had made a mistake, we went and kicked in their door. We pointed a gun at their retarded seventeen-year-old son. As we kicked in the door we had knocked over their other son and stuck a shotgun in his face as he was thrown on the floor. We held them at gunpoint against their will for twenty minutes without a search warrant. When the other son arrived home in his car, I yanked him out of the car, twisted his arm up behind his back and slam-dunked him on the car face first. None of it happened. None of it.

We have an investigation that's coming to a head now, including eight civilian witnesses right there in the apartment complex who have verified everything we've said. They're probably not very fond of the police down in that part of town, but at least they're verifying us down the line. The federal agent who was with us there said, "The only reason I know the story I read in the paper and what happened out there were the same thing was the correspondence of the date, the time and the address."

That shit upsets me. They interviewed the woman of the household. She was on her couch with all the news teams around, half hysterical about all the shit we'd done. My wife was waiting for me at one o'clock in the morning when I got home. She'd seen the news and came running down the hall. She asked me what in the hell I'd been doing to that poor woman that day.

My neighbors are calling me. They don't ask me dead out what's been going on. They go, "How you been doing, Jeff?"

"Fine," I go. "How about you?"

"Fine," they say. "What have you been up to?"

"Oh, not much."

"Anything exciting happen lately?"

"No. Not really."

"Well, you were out there on Garden Place, weren't you?"

"Yeah, sure."

"Well, how much trouble you going to get in? You going to get fired?"

"That's really nice. Thanks a lot."

I explained to my wife what happened. She has faith in me. She knows that I'm a dedicated policeman. She knows how hard I work. I'll have maybe a month of burn-out every once in a while where I just don't give a shit, but mostly I go on and on and on. When it's budget tightening time and no overtime slips are approved, if I'm working on something important, I just stay with it.

The newspapers will print your name, address, the whole bit. The other kids at school know what's going on. Right now, my five-year-old is just as proud as he can be. I go to his preschool with my uniform on and hand out the coloring books about bicycle safety and traffic lights. My kid is in the front row and he's beaming. But I know it's going to change.

*

You have to understand that you are, in fact, the good guys and they're the bad guys. As long as you're not doing something criminal, it's okay. Just be careful and protect your ass, because the guy you're going to lock up or testify against isn't worth getting in trouble over. You make sure that the case you make is good enough. And if it hasn't been good enough out on the street, you make it good. Or you make it good when you tell your boss about it. Or you make it good when you talk to whoever could hurt you.

Policemen are taught very early that truth rarely, if ever, can be helpful. If a case or a situation is clearly without problems, you take whatever action you have to. If that action is justified in all sorts of ways, then there's no problem. You can tell the truth. For most policemen 99 percent of what they do is legitimate. In some cases 99.9 percent. The problem for policemen these days is that they don't really know what they can do and what they can't do, what their rights are.

They don't know how much force they can use, so they lie to protect themselves. Because they've been told by unions, by fraternal groups, by older cops, "Everybody out there is going to try to hurt you. You open your mouth and they'll use it against you. So you tell them shit. Don't tell them anything. You don't remember."

Of course you remember. Nineteen witnesses say that this guy got beat over the head by this cop with a nightstick. The cop gets called into a review board and they ask him, "Did you hit this guy?"

"No, I didn't hit him. I never hit him. Nope. He may have hit his head on the car when we were putting him in the radio car. Maybe he tripped and banged into something."

"There's nineteen witnesses here who say you were doing a number on this guy in the street."

"Who you going to believe, those people there or me? Fucking creeps. You fucking crazy? Is there a pro-cop among that whole bunch or what? They're just looking to hurt me."

His PBA lawyer and his PBA delegate are sitting there with him. Before they went in to talk to the investigators on the review board, he spoke to these two guys and he said, "Look, I banged the guy. I didn't particularly want to, but the guy was robbing an old lady and he gave me some shit and I hit him."

"You can't tell them that," the lawyer and the delegate say. "No way. You can't punch him. You can't hit him with your nightstick."

"Then what have I got a nightstick for?"

"You got a nightstick so you can probe with the nightstick. You can't hit somebody over the head with it. Hit them over the head and—shit—you're trying to kill them. So just say he's lying."

But that cop has every right to use that nightstick. He has every right to hit someone in a situation where he feels threatened or the guy is threatening him. The cop has the right to say, "Hey, I'm five-nine and I go 145 pounds. I got somebody here six-four and two-thirty or -forty. He's going to take me apart. So, yeah, I beat him up. My partner grabbed him and I hit him. It was great." That's okay, that's not bad. You're allowed to do that. But they'll never admit it. Instead they make up all sorts of stories.

*

Search and seizure, the Miranda decision, all this kind of stuff, police have never cared about any of that. That's all bullshit. They testify however they want to.

"Did you give him the Miranda warning?"

"Yeah, sure I gave it to him." Who's there to say he didn't give the prisoner the Miranda warning? The prisoner? That's a joke.

If the cops do give the Miranda warning, they give it at times when it's very self-serving. They have a camera and a guy in a very serious case. "You're going to confess; we're going to put this on tape. We'll do the

Miranda warning first. You'll have your lawyer present."

But probably 80 or 90 percent of the cases that are made aren't made on camera. They're not made in a nice room someplace. They're made on the street, in a hallway, on a rooftop or in the back of a precinct.

It becomes very complicated for most people, but it's not complicated for the police. Even though they say it is in public. Policemen know guilt from innocence. There's no such things as technicalities of the law on the street. Either you've got the smoking gun or you don't have the smoking gun. This guy either did it or he didn't do it. He had the gun or he didn't have the gun. "What difference does it make where the gun was when I found it? Whether it was in view or it was hidden? Whether I had a search warrant or I didn't have a search warrant? I'm there. I can see it clearly. I see the spreading pool of blood. I know who the good guy is and who the bad guy is. It's simple." It doesn't matter to the policeman, which is the way most of our justice should be run. The bottom line is the smoking gun.

Now the case gets to court. "You're telling me that you're going to let this guy go because I didn't give him the Miranda warning or I searched him when I shouldn't have searched him?" Now it gets down to a one-on-one situation. Essentially the police officer wants to beat the defendant. "This son of a bitch ain't going to walk out of here smiling at me and giving me the finger. I'm going to put that fucker in jail. I caught him. I got him. I know he's guilty. He knows he's guilty. He knows that I know he's guilty. He's going to jail. Don't give me this shit about how I didn't see the bulge under his coat. Of course I saw the bulge."

"What do you mean, you saw the bulge? You couldn't have seen the bulge. The defendant had on an alpaca coat, three sweaters and all this other stuff."

"No, I seen it."

The judge and the lawyer and the prosecutor say to themselves, "This cop's lying." They know the cop is lying because from earlier evidence his story can't be true. So the bad guy gets away. And unfortunately there will always be one bad case where the cop will lie and not get caught and the guy is really innocent. That's why all these rules come down in the first place.

*

Most of the things I do as a cop have to do with drugs and a lot of them have to do with either buying drugs or somebody else buying drugs. In those cases, you almost never have to be concerned about your testimony. The only time testimony is a problem is when you make application for search warrants or wiretap orders.

I go into an assistant district attorney and I say to him, "I want a search warrant for this particular location." You have to make out an affidavit. Based on that they decide whether or not they'll let you have the search warrant. They have a form and you just fill in the blanks all the way down. Observation, information, type of drug and all this kind of stuff. You fill it in: "Two observations on Monday, two observations on Tuesday, two on Wednesday, all between such and such hours."

You made the observations. You go, you sit and you watch. You see whatever it is that you see. You know damn well that the information is good based on an informant that you've known for a while and who you trust. He's telling you this guy's selling drugs. You see people—junkies—that you know coming in and out of this building. So you fill in the blanks on the affidavit.

The D.A. tells you, "Oh, that's not enough. You're going to be going into a specific apartment, not just the building. I can't give you a warrant for the whole building."

"Well, I was down the hallway and I saw them going into this apartment."

"How did you get into the hallway to make this observation?"

"I was sitting in a refrigerator box, one of those big giant ones. Somebody delivered a refrigerator that day and the empty box was sitting in the hall. I got into it and put a little hole in it and I saw them go into the apartment."

"Okay, that's good. That's what you have to testify to. Remember that. You got it? You were in the refrigerator box, right?"

"Right."

"Saw them go into the apartment through the little hole, not just into the building, right?"

"Right."

"Okay, I'll give you the warrant." He knows you're full of shit. You don't care. As far as you're concerned, you're not doing anything wrong at all. You know absolutely what the truth of the matter is. Junkies are going into this building and they're going into that apartment to buy heroin.

You get the warrant, you go in there and you find the dope just where the informant told you it was going to be. Everything is just the way it's supposed to be.

So you get into court and the judge asks a question like, "Well, officer, we don't care whether this guy had the drugs or didn't have the drugs. We don't care if the guy is guilty or innocent. What we care about is that in your application for the search warrant, you said you saw people going into the apartment. We find that hard to believe. How did you see people going into the apartment?"

Now I've got to worry about—not whether the guy is guilty or not—but how did I see people going into the apartment? What kind of box was it, a washing machine box?

"Give me a fucking break," the judge says. "The last four warrants, you guys were in boxes."

"That's the way it was."

"I don't believe you." The judge will throw it out.

That is what cops call just crap. It doesn't make any sense to them. "If the guy didn't have any dope or if my informant said the guy was a black guy, forty-eight years old, and the guy turned out to be a white Jewish teenager—okay—my information is bad. But I found the dope, look."

They can't understand—along with the general population—who are we benefiting here? Who ultimately gains by this sort of behavior? The only ones gaining are the people who are breaking the law, because an innocent person is never going to be in trouble. If that person is innocent, there wouldn't be dope in the apartment, there wouldn't be guns in the apartment or there wouldn't be a kidnapped person in the apartment.

*

They send you out there to do a job and they tell you not to get emotionally involved. You'd have to be superhuman not to get emotionally involved. But you try to keep your wits about you.

If it goes bad they say, "Why didn't you use any discretion?"

"You told me not to use any discretion. Just the facts. Do the law, Sergeant Joe Friday."

"Why didn't you show any compassion?"

"You told me not to get emotionally involved before."

It's baloney. There's no way you can help but get emotionally involved. I used to go home thinking about the kids. You go to house calls where the family is fighting, beating each other, beating the kids. We walk in and the kids would be so relieved to see us. When you're five years old and your family is fighting, killing each other, you think your world is coming to an end. The kids come up and hug your leg.

Then you're useless, because there's nothing you can do and we're leaving. They look at you like, "You're it. If not you, then we got nothing."

I remember getting into the radio car and thinking, "Holy shit, I can't believe I'm doing this." But we couldn't do anything.

*

I was riding with another officer and he had a CB radio in his patrol car. He hears this girl come over the air on Channel Nine, screaming that a kid had been hit over on the bridge. So we go roaring up through town. We were only a couple miles away.

Here's traffic backed up in both directions. Right at the north end of the bridge was this mother screaming and yelling and crying, holding this kid who had just been hit by a car and knocked 180 feet. Chaos, you know.

The other officer grabs the woman and tries to pull her away. Of course, she tries to clutch onto the kid a little more. I get her arms off the kid and the other officer walks her off to the side of the road. A couple of women who are there get around her. This officer comes back to me and we took one look at the kid and he said, "Bob, I don't think my first aid is as up as it should be. I'm going to go back and call for help. You take care of it here."

"Okay, Russ." The kid—must have been about six years old—would come and go. He was bleeding from real severe scalp lacerations and bad abrasions on his back and his rear end. One pupil was dilated and the other was like a pin head.

Here we are in this tragic situation, and all of a sudden, this guy comes running up there and he starts snapping pictures. The mother is crying over there and

I'm huddled over the kid. Russ comes back from the radio car after calling for rescue and sees this guy with a camera. Russ asked him, "What are you doing here?" About the same time the mother is screaming, "That guy is going to take a picture of my baby!"

"I'm a member of the press," the guy says, "and I have a right to be here."

"You going to take a picture of this?" Russ said.

"Yeah, it's news," the guy says.

"No, it isn't," Russ said. "It's a tragedy. I'll tell you what. You snap one more picture and I'm going to throw you off this bridge and I mean over the rail and into the water."

The guy got a picture of Russ in his uniform. So it shows up in the newspaper the next day, "Newsman Accosted on Bridge."

I hate a news cameraman. They thrive on sensationalism, blood and gore and bad happenings. That's how they make their living. They're like buzzards.

*

The smell was so bad, the building emptied out. It was in the middle of the block and the bar on the corner had emptied out. People thought it was a sewer backing up in the basement.

We get there and open the apartment door and there's this mound on the floor. It wasn't hardly recognizable. The stench was so incredible that you didn't breathe in the room. It's something I can't describe. I can't say it's like rotten eggs or anything. It was like nothing I ever smelled before. It was wintertime and the apartment was hot. This thing on the floor was a nineteen-year-old kid covered with maggots and blown up all over the wall.

The story we found out was that the mother had a heart attack and he took her to the hospital. He came home and shot up. Died with the needle in his arm and laid there for two weeks while his mother was in the hospital. The body began to decompose. Since there were not breaks or punctures or wounds, the gases of decomposition made the body bloat. There was nothing for this expansion to come out of. The body blew up. He was on the walls and all over the floor and when you rolled him over he was nothing but a pile of maggots.

We had to guard the body for the medical examiner to come pick it up. You're supposed to literally sit in the residence. We sat out on the street.

That shook me up a lot. It thickened the shell I was developing since I got on the job. As the shell thickens, you become more and more out of touch—not with the world, but with yourself. So that when you walk in on a scene like this, you just shrug your shoulders. Another messy thing.

When you get a dead body you have to search it. If it's got any jewelry or anything in its pockets, the clothes stay with the body, but anything else is supposed to go as evidence to the precinct.

We had a DOA that was partly decomposed and it had a gold ring on it so I had to take its ring off. When I pulled the ring off, all the soft flesh pulled off the finger and just left the bone. But I had the ring. I started carrying rubber gloves around in my briefcase along with my accident reports and other forms.

Some guy fell in front of an elevated train and Emergency Services gets there to go on the tracks to help this guy and get him out from under the train. For some reason, they couldn't find his foot, so they told me and my partner to go under the tracks of the elevated train and look for the foot.

I found it in the shoe and picked the guy's foot up. You build up a thing where you just don't feel it. Where a normal person might look at that foot in a shoe and puke, you can't do that. You can't vomit and run away from it. So you pick it up and carry it back to the Emergency guys. They tell you to throw the whole she-bang into the morgue wagon and off it goes. You get another layer on the shell, so you don't feel things.

Before I started seeing so much death, the job was like a game. I played a cop and I chase the robbers while I'm at work. Then I started getting down to the other business of being a cop, which is driving around for eight or nine hours and not having anything to do, running up and down stairs for nothing, getting into family disputes where no matter whose side you're on, they're both against you. I got exposed to the routine of boredom.

Once they sent me over to this bar where a guy had just keeled over on his bar stool and was dead. He had a bad heart or liver or both. We had him declared dead at the hospital and then they sent us to notify the parents.

We've just washed up this guy off the barroom floor and we've taken him to the hospital where he has been pronounced very dead and we're now walking up the stairs of this building to notify the next of kin. The guy was in his late thirties or early forties, so the parents have to be at least sixty. We're joking. I say, "Here's how we'll do it. We'll knock on the door and then when they come, we'll SING, 'Your son is dead, your son is dead. He drank too much and now he's dead.'"

While I'm singing this, a man is walking down the stairs. He walked past us. We get to the apartment door and this older woman answered. "Hello, are you Mrs. So-and-So?"

"Yes, I am."

"Is your husband home?"

"No, he's not. He just left. He'll be back in a moment. What's the problem?"

Oh, God, he was the one who just walked by me. The older man who had passed us on the stairs did in fact come back in within a minute or two. I thought he must have heard me joking about his son dying and singing my little ditty about the kid.

"I'm sorry to say that your son was in such-and-such a bar when he had a cardiac arrest and was taken to the hospital and declared dead."

They took it pretty well. "It happens. That's life." And we walked out the door.

Another layer goes on the shell to help shut out the grief and not let it affect you. Go down and get into the car. I felt bad. Stupid and bad. But I just let it become part of the scene.

*

The part that really caught up with me was seeing the death. A lot of people say they don't see a lot of it. I saw a lot of it. You go to somebody's house. She's crying because her husband died at the dinner table. The police are the first with everything. You're involved with her screaming, her crying. She wants you to play God. She wants you to bring life back into that person. You go through the motions. It really catches up with you.

Let's say that you got to knock on the door of this woman's house and tell her the husband just died down at the square. I sit down at the table with her and break the news to her very slowly and naturally. She goes into a state of shock. What people don't realize is that I'm picking up the feeling, too—unless you're a callous, cold-blooded drug addict you can't help it. Now they train you with different techniques about how to do this stuff. You don't go in and say, "Are you the Widow McNamara?" But nobody tells you how you're going to react. They don't train you how to deal with your own emotions.

The next thing you know is that you're kicking kids off the corner or you're getting the newspaper for the sergeant or lunch for the guys in the back room or you're going to a barroom brawl and you're the bouncer. You're breaking up this fight. You're not Superman. You can get knocked on your ass. When somebody punches you in the mouth, you can feel it, too. You're scared.

You're always scared. I don't give a shit who the cop is that tells you that he's not scared, that's a lot of shit. He's scared all the time. He's scared of looking like a fool, of being weak, yellow, of being a coward. Afraid he's going to say the wrong thing and get in trouble with the department. Fear is a policeman's life. It's impossible to go out on the street day in and day out and not have fear.

*

I had a two-year-old kid raped once and I took him to the hospital. The city doctor wasn't on duty at that time and not one of the doctors there would deal with it. They would examine him for damage and that would be it. I said, "Somebody has to examine this kid. This is crazy."

"Okay," one of them says, "I'll examine him, but I'm just going to make sure the kid's going to live. That's as far as I'm going to go." They didn't want to get involved in the court case or anything. They won't get into testifying about whether there is semen in there and tear marks and fingerprints on the baby. You say to yourself, "What the fuck. You ain't a doctor." But the whole system is like that.

*

Here's a guy who lives out on a tree-lined street in a lily-white area with his wife and a couple of kids. He gets on the train or he drives into the center of the city to a ghetto area and he just deals with blacks. You don't see a white face all night unless it's your partner. Not that there's anything wrong with that, but he's living in two worlds.

He gets more work in one weekend than some entire towns get. Even if he's a racist and a bigot, you'd have to have a heart of stone to go into an apartment house there and take a look at babies without diapers, just laying there, filthy, no mattress. The kid's having trouble. And it's not just one. There's thousands of them out there.

He goes to a family fight and one of them is knifing the other one. He sees the kids are in the apartment during this whole thing. People are drunk and overdosed.

He does that for eight hours a day, forty hours a week. He goes home to the wife. He walks into the house and she says, "You better take the day off tomorrow. I've got a PTA meeting and you got to take care of the kids."

He just saw like five people die tonight and she's worried about the kids need shoes. "I seen kids without clothes. They needed food!" He don't say that to his wife. He can't say that to his wife. He don't say, "Leave me alone. I got all these problems to think about." What does he say? Nothing.

*

After eight hours of this shit, you're supposed to go home and be a human being. I say that you can't do that. You witness these things and you can't go home and be a normal human being.

You don't know how to express them. Do you alarm your family? Do you tell them that you're dealing with this type of stuff all the time? They can't understand it. How do you relate this type of stuff to them? Subsequently what you do, what I've done over the years, is to say little or nothing to my family about my job.

That has an advantage and a disadvantage. The advantage is trying to answer the questions they would ask me that I can't answer would be frustrating for me, and when I get frustrated, I get angry. When I'm angry I make a miserable husband and father for my wife and kids. So it's good for me and them that I don't tell them.

The negative thing is, my family feels like they are cheated. I'm out in an exciting job, but I never related any of it to them.

The disadvantage for me personally is, Who do I talk to? You talk to other cops.

*

How do you get this out? Your wife or girlfriend will give you all kinds of heat about doing what you do for a living. The first Christmas you have to work or one of your kid's birthdays you have to work and all the neighbors and relatives are there and you—the father—you're not there, they start blaming everything on the job. They don't realize all the good you got from the job. They just look at the bad. They start giving you heat about being on this job. So, you don't bring the stories home, because you know what's going to happen.

Plus how do you tell your wife that you were scared. You're supposed to be this big, brave guy.

*

The job is like a mistress, too. If you have a serious relationship going, it's every bit as threatening. Aside from the obvious—the fact is, if you work around the clock in this kind of irregular atmosphere, the opportunities for actually fooling around are much greater—aside from that, a lot of cops screw up their relationships because they don't want to track that dirt into the house. There are things they're not talking about. A perfectly good woman feels cheated. Because she knows that something is going on. She knows that there are major parts of your life that you're not talking about. It can be bad.

*

I just recently was divorced. It's been a year since he left. I think my marriage was a typical police marriage. He is the public relations officer for a neighboring police department. It's kind of a nice job because he gets to work eight to four Mondays through Fridays. He spends his time talking to kids about protecting themselves and how to prevent crime. He doesn't see the stuff that I see. He doesn't have people calling him pig because he's the good guy.

I didn't realize it at the time, but in our marriage, I was the police officer and he was the normal person. He had regular hours on regular days. I was working weird shifts and couldn't socialize with our friends. I brought my work home. I was the one up in the middle of the night saying, "Darn it, this guy won't confess." I brought home the bad feelings and bad attitudes. I think it affected me and that might have been part of our problem.

I'm just at the point now where I'm getting somewhat normal so I can start dating again. But the people I have most in common with are other police officers. I see it here, I see it in all the other suburbs: Most of the married police officers have at least one girlfriend on the side. We call them police groupies. Somehow I never had that problem when I was in uniform. Men aren't attracted to women wearing men's clothing. They don't exactly set off your figure. Hell, I had hardly started wearing a bra and I had to start wearing an undershirt.

I'm definitely a one-person person. I couldn't condone something like that and yet I know that most police officers are like that. I know a lot of their wives, too. I'm a little in the middle, because I know that he's seeing a girlfriend. I think to myself, that could be me. It's kind of a dilemma for me.

*

A lot of cops really want to believe that they're the type of guy that can do the things the cops on TV can do. They want to believe that they can talk people into confessing and they'll fall down at their feet, instead of having a guy whipping out his cock and pissing on you or spitting in your face. Nobody knows what it's like until you're talking to a guy and there he is smiling at you, but you're just looking at his face. Now watch his hands, because he's taking out his cock and pissing at you.

So you lock him up. So what? "Punch me again." He doesn't give a shit. The fucking guy has an IQ of two. That's what it's all about.

Once you find out and you're comfortable with that and you can deal with that, then you can be very successful.

*

I worked the streets for a couple of years. Then because I was a photographer in the Navy, I applied for the photography section of criminal investigation. I even used politics to get the job. After I had the job a few years, I said, "Why did I ever use politics to get this fucking job?"

I was photographing winos who died and their throats were chewed up by rats. In cold water flats, babies that just died. A family that was wiped out by a deranged father who killed all his kids and his wife and then himself. I had seven kids and everything you get involved with reminds you of the needs of your own family.

A lot of anxiety comes in. You have an image, this macho image, that nothing is supposed to bother you, that you're a hard robot. You're out there and you have a job to do and people expect this of you. What people expect, what society expects and what you expect of yourself, it's too much. It's too much. You can't hold up to it.

My job was photographing dead people, and taking their fingerprints. Holding dead hands, breaking off the fingers when they're too stiff to manage or having to cut them off, inking them and feeling them, putting them back in bags. Seeing that this is how people end up.

We're in there with the smell, the roaches all over us, for two and three hours. We're also in the other rooms, trying to tell the people, "Please, we're doing our job." They don't think you are. They don't think you give a shit. It's their husband that was just stabbed seventeen times and they're screaming that they want justice.

The very first thing that happens to most of us—and I don't give a shit what anybody tells you—is that we start to lose touch with reality and you really start to believe that there is no God. You get very mad at God. You want to know, "Why does God allow this?" You see one side of life. You see the seamy side of life— the corrupt politician, you see the homosexual priest, you see the deranged guy who wipes out a young woman. You see so much of it, you start to believe that's mostly the whole world. That it's all a sewer.

We go in on the tail end of things when it's too late. It's sad when you see a fifteen-year-old girl who committed suicide or died from an overdose and there's nothing you can do about it. You get frustrated.

By the time you even get some of the maggots and get them in court, because of some little infraction of justice, they walk free. More walk free than are convicted. It's a tide coming at you all the time. No matter what you do, it keeps coming at you. There's too many of them out there and not enough of you.

*

People are emotional creatures. I was sent to a call. It was a despondent subject. It was daytime. I went to a house in a middle-class residential area, knocked on the door by myself. A woman comes and says to me, "I want you to talk to my husband. He's just really been depressed and I think he may be suicidal. I'm really worried."

"Does he have any guns that you know of?"

"He's just been off work. He's got a medical problem, and I'm just worried because he's so down."

"Where is he?"

"He's sitting out in the garage." She told me his name, which was Tim. So I walked around there and I see this man sitting in the garage on a stool, slumped over.

"Hi, Tim. My name is Daniel. Can we talk?" He doesn't say a word. He just kind of looked at me. He had a strange look inside. All of a sudden, he got off the stool and jumped on me. He was trying to take my gun. He was making horrible noises. Kind of a moaning scream. The guy was six-four, two-seventy-five and he was quite strong.

We were fighting over my gun, which was still in my holster. We went down to the ground and I was trying to get out my portable radio. I was losing. He was stronger than I was. I realized that I was losing. I got out one word on the radio: "Help!" I was supposed to send one of our code things, but at the time my brain didn't work like that. He kicked the radio and broke it.

I managed to get over and get my arm around him where I could choke him. He starts biting me on the arm. I could see blood coming and I knew it was my blood. I had this real strange feeling. I yelled at his wife, "Call the station. I need help." I'm trying to beat him off and he's still trying to get my gun. He ripped my shirt completely off.

The nearest unit took three or four minutes to get to me, which doesn't sound like a long time unless you're on the ground fighting. The unit gets there with a female officer, five-foot-two, a hundred and ten pounds. She comes up with her gun. By this time I had sort of gotten the upper hand. I was in better shape so I was outlasting him. I said, "God, put that gun away." I was afraid she would shoot me or him or both.

"What do you want me to do?" she says.

"Just sit on him." I was really running out of gas bad. About thirty seconds after that one of our detective units came in with two officers. I remember hearing the brakes squealing out front when they pulled up. With their help, we got the guy handcuffed.

He goes unconscious. The wife comes out and says, "He has a heart condition." I can't believe it.

Here I am. I've got blood all over me, which is mine, my uniform is torn, my heart is thumping about 900 miles an hour. They take him off to the hospital and they take me down there, too. It was minor, but I had some bite marks on me that needed washing out and bandaging.

He didn't have a heart attack. It was just the exertion. I arrested him for assault on a police officer. I got my wits back together and went and got a new shirt.

The next week, I did some follow-up on him. It turned out the guy is a county fireman. He's been out on disability for a year with the heart condition. He wanted to retire, but the county had been screwing him over on his retirement. No history of any criminal record. He was a deacon in his church, a scout leader, as fine a background as you'd ever want in a man.

I got a letter from just about every fireman in the

county asking that I not press charges against him. The district attorney calls me and wants to have a council between myself and this guy's attorney. The D.A. goes, "Hey, you've got a good case. You don't have to talk to his lawyer." But I agreed to talk to him.

His lawyer comes in and basically says, "He was despondent over this whole thing and he just flipped out. To put an arrest on his record and to disgrace him and his kids would seem unnecessary. We'd really like for you to drop the charges." The D.A. concurred.

I go off and I'm thinking. The only thing I did was respond. I could have gotten killed. I got in a fight. I got bit. I got knocked down and torn up. But what should I do? Here's the shades of gray. Here's a violation of the law and I am a police officer. I thought, "I'll go with the program if he gets professional help." The D.A. arranged something like deferred prosecution. If he got competent help, they wouldn't press charges against him. I kind of forgot about it. It was just one of those things.

About four months later, I got a card from him and his wife. He'd gotten his retirement and things had worked out. They thanked me for being, I don't know, generous, I guess. I talked to the D.A. and I said, "I'm glad everything worked out for those people. But you know, it's a funny thing. When a police officer has too much stress and cracks out, you guys prosecute the hell out of him."

CHAPTER 8

Curtains

THAT MORNING in late September 1984, the weather was changing. Fitful gusts of wind blew through the sea of blue uniforms that filled the street for six blocks at Holy Name Catholic church in Manhattan. There was a sound like distant thunder as the motorcycle contingent preceding the cortege approached. The rumbling of their pistons gave way to the slow pounding of the dirge on muffled drums. An officer standing on top of a van equipped with loudspeakers called the assembled throng to attention. Just as four thousand white-gloved hands rose in unison, a squall of thin autumn rain whipped through the crowd, sending a chill trickle down every neck.

One last time an on-duty officer told the jabbering teenagers on the corner to shut up. The scree of the pipers puling out "Amazing Grace" did the trick and the kids watched in silence as the coffin seemed to float up the steps and disappear into the church. The honor guard and the brass followed it in. The rain slowed and stopped.

"Dismissed," came the order. "Be back here in ranks at 10:40." Cigarettes materialized everywhere, ordered lines jumbled and broke over the curbs, ready to consume hundreds more gallons of coffee. The wire trash baskets up and down Amsterdam Avenue were already half full with Styrofoam cups from the first round. As circumspectly as they could, a few men looked over their shoulders and ducked into a liquor store for a pint. Others simply headed for a bar a discreet distance away for a beer and a shot. Most simply wandered around the general vicinity.

They were there to honor transit police officer Irma Lozada, the first female police officer to be killed in the line of duty in New York City. She and her partner had been working on the LL subway train in Brooklyn. As the train pulled into the Wilson Avenue Station, they saw a young man run from the train with a necklace in his hand. Officer Lozada and her partner split up to chase the suspect. She took the team's radio and her partner told her to call for backup. Then he climbed a wall and began searching the subway tracks.

It is assumed that Officer Lozada went to search the street. There was no record of a radio communication between Lozada and the district headquarters. However, transit police radios don't work well outside the subway stations; the above-ground antennae system is unreliable.

When he didn't find anyone on the tracks, Lozada's partner went to the street to look for her. He checked with the railroad clerk at the token booth to see if she'd been seen coming back to the station. He tried to contact her on another officer's radio. There was no answer. He called district headquarters and asked if she had checked in with them and then returned to headquarters himself.

Around 5 P.M., when there was still no word from Officer Lozada, a search was begun. Approximately two hours later they found her in the tall weeds of a vacant lot at Chauncey Street and Central Avenue in the Bushwick section of Brooklyn. Lozada's shield was under her body, her handcuffs were out and a necklace was lying on the ground nearby. Her .38-caliber service revolver was missing. She had been shot in the head, twice.

It wasn't the kind of heroic death most cops picture for themselves, not exactly a blaze of glory. But Officer Lozada's death was a sadly typical police death. She was doing her job. Something inadvertent or unexpected had happened. She lost control of the situation and was murdered. There's nothing glorious or glamorous about dying all alone in a vacant lot full of rubble and garbage, but it happens much more often than those romantic gunfights at the O.K. Corral which many cops envision when they daydream the endings of their personal movies.

By TEN-THIRTY the street had begun to fill again and the rain threatened to return as well. The wind was blasting harder than ever, rattling the limbs of the scrawny city trees and snapping off the leaves that had already turned brown.

The crowd of police wasn't what you'd call somber. There were smiles and even laughter punctuated by the hearty backslapping of renewed acquaintance. Informal group photos were snapped around a fire hydrant. One knot of men and women made fun of a crazy wino who was inspired by the sight of so many cops to perform a short but ecstatic dance.

But when the loudspeakers boomed, "Stand by," they formed ranks without reluctance or hesitation. They were there to do a job. They would show their respect and they would demonstrate their solidarity to the television audience. And they would keep up the barriers that hold fear at bay. They have to face the possibility of death every day. One police officer, a thousand miles away from this particular funeral, expressed the attitude of police officers this way:

"You don't really get that camaraderie. You really don't know that much about individuals. All you do is live with cops.

"I remember a line on 'Kojak' once. A cop gets killed and somebody asks, 'Does he have any kids?' Why is it that times like that is the only time people ask, 'Did he have kids?' Nobody gave a shit if he had kids when he was alive. Now he's dead and they want to know.

"When you walk in and look at the casket, you know that's now So-and-So that got killed. But it could have been any one of you. They shot at the uniform. You're sorry, but what hits you is, 'It could be me laying there, because I'm wearing the same uniform.' That's what you're really giving a few prayers about. It's not, 'I'm sorry you're laying there.' It's about, 'Whew, that could be me.' Very weird."

*

I stood in the lee of an apartment building while waiting for the last act of the funeral pageant to begin. A white-haired man had taken shelter under the overhang with me. He was wearing a maroon sport coat over a faded navy knit shirt and holding a long fat cigar that had gone out. He had been a lieutenant on the NYPD and was up from retirement in Florida, taking treatments at a medical center. He spoke with that Queens accent that gives explosive force to the consonants in a word like "perpetrator."

"You never get used to these things," he said. "What I hate most is when they play 'Taps.' Jeez, there's something about that sound. I told the wife that if something should happen to me—God forbid—don't let them play 'Taps' at the funeral. I hate it when they play that.

"Every night I was a cop, when I'd come home and climb in bed, my wife would wrap an arm around my neck and hold on to me all night long. Sometimes I thought she'd choke the shit out of me. She was worried the whole time I was on the job.

"After the second time I got hurt, she went crazy: 'You got to quit. I'll get a divorce. I can't stand it.'

" 'Look,' I told her, 'you know it's part of the job. It's what I do.' She calmed down a little, but after that I thought about it.

"This was '72. Christmas Eve, the kid was at his grandmother's and I says to my wife, 'Let's go out to eat.' We get to this nice place and I pull out this big box all wrapped up with a hell of a big bow on it and she says, 'What's that?' I told her it was her Christmas package which she was going to open at dinner. She said, no, we should wait until we got home, but I wasn't hearing any of that.

"So we sit down in this restaurant and she opens this big fucking box and all there is inside is a little envelope about six inches long.

" 'What's this?' she says.

" 'What do you think it is,' I says to her. 'My retirement papers. Effective January One. Now I don't want to hear any more of your barking.' We moved to Florida. She hated New York. Won't even come back for a visit."

At this point Officer Lozada's coffin reappeared and we stood in silence with our hands over our hearts. As the trumpeter hit the first three notes of "Taps," the ex-lieutenant whispered, "Jeez, I hate it when they play that shit."

Then the crowd broke up like kids getting out of school. Those officers who didn't have to return to duty went looking for a bar. The cops from other jurisdictions and other states were looking for a good time.

"You know what one of the biggest things is at a police funeral?" a suburban police officer said. "It's to show off police cars. 'Let's go out of state and show them what kind of patrol car we got and all the gadgets we got in it.' You go out of respect, but as soon as the funeral is over the cops begin to mingle and talk about the bad guy they just shot or the one they kicked the shit out of. Ten minutes later, every one of them is checking out the police cars from the other states. 'Man, look at that big Plymouth four-barrel.' 'Damn, look, he's got four different radios. Who the Christ does he talk to?' "

So Officer Lozada was taken to the cemetery in Queens and the rest went their separate ways. Violent ends like Officer Lozada's are the exception in police work. The ex-lieutenant's orderly retirement is the rule. Most officers put in their fifteen to twenty-five years of service and then retire to one of those Archie Bunker dreams so many of them have—to buy a fishing boat or a bar. But that doesn't mean it's easy for an officer to make it through twenty years of mental stress, emotional strain and physical punishment. Or that if he does make it, he'll be all in one piece, body and mind.

"The great danger in this job is not getting shot or stabbed. It's that you'll get fat and die of a heart attack. Or because you let your nerves eat you up, you'll have a nervous breakdown. Or you become an emotionally disturbed person," one police officer told me at the end of his interview.

"Chances are shooting and stabbing aren't going to happen to you. There's a good chance that you're going to be dragged out of your patrol car or from behind your desk dead from cardiac arrest. A good chance that you'll be a nervous wreck. A good chance that you won't be able to talk to normal people because of your own emotional problems. The rest of the shit, don't worry about.

"You talk to the new kids and they can't wait to strap that gun on their side, go out there and show the world. They're going to do a job, man. I had that feeling and it's a good feeling. But when the reality comes round, you got to worry about your sanity and making it through your career."

*

You see guys who find it very difficult to retire from the police department. It's become more than a way of life for them. It is all those toys, those gifts that he has, the authority, the specialness that he has. To give that back and go back to the real world, that's what the tremendous surrender is.

Policemen have this sense of "I don't care who you are or what you are, you're not a cop. You can be the President of the fucking United States of America or a God damn brain surgeon, but you're not a cop. I'm special. I can give you a summons and you're going to sit and listen to me. If I stop you, you may be driving a brand new Mercedes worth $50,000 and you may've done more in one afternoon than I've done in my lifetime, but for this five minutes that I have you for running that red light, you're going to sit and listen to what I have to say. I may go home to my above-ground pool and drink my beer, while you're off to drink Dom Perignon someplace. Nevertheless for that moment in our lives, I'm the boss and you're the shithead."

You go to Park Avenue to someone's apartment and they want to sit and listen to your story, especially if they've been robbed or mugged. They've seen the other face and it scared them to death. Now they see this face who is on their side and is the answer to the other face. "You're going to help me. You're going to protect me. That other person isn't going to touch me again." The guy may be a major movie star, but he wants your gun and hat and badge, because he wants to go out and kill that son of a bitch that just made him plead for his life for a stinking watch.

There are a lot of cops who have that sense of their own specialness and they don't want to give that up. When they do give it up, it's very difficult for them to function. "How am I going to go out there and listen to some shit tell me how to stack boxes? I'll kick the shit out of him. I'm not going to be able to deal with that." That's a problem.

*

I've been on the job for seventeen years and I've seen a lot of guys come and go. You know what I've never seen? I've never seen a guy quit in seventeen years.

As soon as you been on the job for four or five years and you're making good money, you can't quit. You're a high school graduate and now you're twenty-six years old. Where are you going to work and make $31,000 a year?

Now what do you do? Got to go to work, but you hate the job. Hate it. Despise it. Most of it's in your head. You just can't get up for the job any more. You don't want to hear any more people complaining. You don't want to worry about the bosses giving you complaints. You start drinking too much. You're fighting with your family because you're upset about your job, but you can't quit.

So how do you react? You might take it out on the public. You might take it out on the job itself. Some guys go out there and try to do nothing. They say, "I'll fuck this job." They just do nothing unless the sergeant actually orders them to do it. I know about them. There's people out there like this. There were a lot more years ago.

You got guys with calendars inside their lockers,

marking the days off until they can retire. Get out of this job. The job sucks.

The guy next door in mounted, he brings his horse over to you and he says, "Listen to this." He says to the horse, "Does the job suck?" The horse whinnies and shakes his head up and down. It's a big joke. All the cops go, "Hey, Billy, Billy. Bring the horse over here. Ask him. Ask him."

"Does the job suck?" The horse does his thing.

There's different approaches for these kinds of guys:

"I'm going to stay here, but I'm going to get a plum assignment someplace if it's the last thing I do."

"I'm going to stay here, but I'm going to fuck the job to death. They're not going to get anything out of me."

"I'm going to stay here, but I'll get hurt in the line of duty and get fucking three-quarters pay."

All police officers are potential lottery winners. I can win right now, there's no question about it. I go out in the radio car and I get injured so I can't work. I wouldn't swear that I knew a police officer that slammed his hand in the radio door so that he couldn't shoot the gun anymore. I wouldn't say that had happened, but it is possible that that happened.

You get three-quarters, that means you get $22,000 a year, tax free. Tax Free. For the rest of your life. Plus you're allowed to get another job making the other quarter. When you reach what would have been your twentieth year on the job, then you can make as much money as you like.

We got a captain that should hear from the civil service review board this week. He's making $63,000 a year. He's going to make over forty of that tax free. You'd have to be making eighty thousand a year to clear forty. You hear guys say, "You got three-quarters. Congratulations!"

We have the heart bill now. If I'm home and I have

a heart attack, I get three-quarters. They consider it in the line of duty whether you're at home or at work. They say the stress of the thing is job-related. But the average life expectancy for men receiving benefits of the heart bill is two years. Nobody has ever lived over ten years. So the heart bill is not the way to go three-quarters. Like the guy says, "Just take the tip off my trigger finger. Just an inch or so. I don't mind. I can't fire no more, I got to go three-quarters."

There are stories that you hear. Who's to say that they're not true. You're at home and you're painting your house. You fall off the ladder and you hurt your ankle real bad. Maybe you've got a fracture or something. If you can drag yourself to work, put yourself into a uniform and get in a radio car, the first job you get, step off the curb and fall down. It could happen. I've heard stories about guys with heavy-duty compound fractures making it in to work. Your wife even warns you when you do something dangerous around the house, "You fall down and I'm going to get a radio car here to get you to work." It's a psychological out about the job. Hey, the job sucks but I could always get three-quarters.

*

There are cops that have no business being in the police department, no business being in uniform. They're a disaster. I say to them, "You should become a garbageman. You don't want to be a cop. You're here just passing the time of day. Become a fireman. You get the same money. You're only doing it for the money."

"No, no, no," they say. "I like the gun. I like the shield. I like the authority."

These are the same men—if you call them men—that are empty people. They'll end up divorced or drunks or drug addicts. They're just wasting time. They don't enjoy it. They should do something else, for Christ sake.

346

I got a good personal friend of mine that was just like that. He was driven into the department. His wife drove him to it because of me. She seen me and thought that he should be me. He hated it. This guy used to get stomach cramps, lose clumps of hair, he was so nervous at work. It made him a wreck. Everything he did in the police department was to get himself away from police work. He tried to be a mechanic; then he tried working on the boats.

He had an incident happen to him that maybe don't happen to a hundred cops. A guy took a shot at him and missed him at close range. The guy had shot the sergeant and got him. Then he shot at my friend and hit the car right next to him. The bullet didn't hit him and he was in the hospital for two weeks. It made him so physically disabled that they put him out on three-quarters.

This guy is now the happiest mechanic you'd ever want to see. He's got grease under his nails and he's happy. He works on cars and he's smiling and laughing. Now he's no longer married to that woman. He's got a nice young wife, his pension and he's happy. Ain't that something?

*

I had a heart attack. I was out a little while with that and when I went back they put me on light duty in dispatching. I did that for three months and I was going crazy. I was stuck inside with all these machines. That was enough to make me have a heart attack right there. I was used to being on the street. So I went and talked to some people I know and got myself put back out there on patrol again. I did change and go on days though. I called it my semi-retirement. I had a few twinges, but I had the nitroglycerin pills to control that.

Then we were in the middle of the desegregation thing and that was pretty heavy. We had a stabbing at a high school one day and I was in there most of the day getting things under control and I come out and my cruiser is tipped over. All the windows are smashed, all four tires are flat. We were working extra shift and everything else. I was off for a few days' vacation in the middle of all this and I had another heart attack. I was in intensive care for about five days. Then I spent another few weeks in the hospital. It was a good one this time. That was it. I said, "There's no sense in me staying on the job with this." So I put my papers in and went out. I had a little over nineteen years in. I got out on a disability pension—the heart bill. Stress of the job and all that.

You have to go before the Civil Service Commission. I had my doctor and they send you to two more doctors, who give you the electrocardiogram and talk to you and so forth. Then you stand before the commission and they all question you. You're talking into a microphone and one'll say, "When does it bother you?"

"I got to run three floors up in apartment buildings," I'm telling them. "By the time I get up there I'm out of breath. Then I got to fight somebody."

"How often do you got to wrestle with somebody, about once a month?"

"Once a day is more like it," I say. Once a month? Jesus. Basically they want to know whether or not I can do the job any more. There was no way I could. I wasn't going to jeopardize my life for the job any more. By then my boy was finished college and I could afford to retire a little better than when I had the first one.

I didn't try to get a job like a lot of guys do. It wasn't in my nature. I didn't know if I could handle one, to tell you the truth. I get tired. If I mow the lawn, I have to do it in sections and rest in between.

My wife and I were together. I had a perfect marriage. It was just great. We'd go out to dinner once or twice a week. We had our little house down here to take care of. My wife was tremendous. Everything was grand until she died.

We got home one night about three-thirty in the morning from our best friends' twenty-fifth wedding anniversary. I kissed her goodnight. We'd had separate bedrooms since I'd worked shift work most of my life. She went to bed and I went to bed. I got up about nine the next morning. We got in late so I just leave her sleep. About noon time I go into the room and I says, "Come on, honey, get up." I grabbed her arm and she was stiff. She must have been dead from when she went in the night before, because rigor mortis had really set in hard.

I called the police and they come down. Of course they called the medical examiner. He come down and when I opened the door, he says, "Jesus, Howie, I thought it was you." He knew I had the bad heart and there was nothing wrong with my wife. It was a massive coronary. Boy, that was a jolt to me. That just corked my life. That just about done it.

*

There was no one thing that set me off. Just over a period of time it built up. I got burned out. I had eleven and a half years on. There's no incentive in the police department to do well. There really isn't. You practically have to commit murder to get fired, so you're not going to get fired. It's a typical civil service job, although I probably would not have admitted that when I was a policeman.

I had gone to school nights to get my college degree. It didn't mean a thing. There was going to be no raise. It does not help you get promoted. We have lieutenants and captains that don't have eighth-grade educations— not that they have to have more, but by the same token, if I have a college degree and the same experience, why shouldn't I have a shot at an administrative job where

I can do some good and use my education instead of just waiting through the fifteen or twenty years of normal attrition to get there? Plus the way the political air was blowing, a judge had decided that blacks and women were going to be promoted and advanced quicker than anybody else no matter what you did, so that had a lot of effect on my attitude. I decided to quit.

Now I'm working for a large chain of banks as a fraud investigator. I can truthfully say that I probably put more people in jail now than I ever did while I was on the police department. There's still the challenge of putting the pieces of an investigation puzzle together and I enjoy that.

There's a lot more freedom out here as opposed to the police department. They just give you your cases and you work on them. There's isn't any political pressure: "Drop what you're doing. We got to go take care of this group. We got to go get this guy because the chief wants it done."

If you do a good job, you are rewarded for it. I did a good job on my last case. I get three days off with pay. I'm getting taken out to dinner and I'm getting a raise. The police department can't do that. I've been here two years and I can tell you that inside of five years, I'm going to be the boss. I just know I am. I can feel it and I think I can do it. I can work for it.

*

I was on the department twenty-six years in various assignments, the last sixteen as a supervisor. One of the things that attracted me to the job in the first place was an ad in the paper that showed a picture of a police officer in uniform holding a machine gun and the words said, "Retire at 52." I made a promise to myself when I entered the police department that I would retire on my fifty-second birthday, which I did. I had how many days left to retirement written on my calendar and I started counting them off each day two years before it was going to happen. When the day fell that I was eligible for maximum retirement benefits, it was my last day. They gave me a little party. I got a leaf blower for my parting gift.

Retirement just feels great. My wife and I had purchased a house that had been vacant for a year and vandalized. I worked on the house for well over a year after I retired. I have small children. They're in the second and third grade, so that keeps you young. They like having me home as a house mom. I'm working now again part-time with an investigation service. I like it.

The good times will never be the same—the traffic man riding his motorcycle down the hall, throwing firecrackers in the building. I miss the people, but I don't miss the place. I was tired of the make-work projects that someone dreams up for the sake of seeing someone work. Monthly reports turn into weekly reports, *plus* monthly reports, and the weekly reports, of course, go in the waste basket. It was just something to keep the paper flowing. Law enforcement has changed. Attitudes have changed.

*

I was appointed in 1951. I stayed a patrolman in the department, in the exact same precinct, for thirty years. I retired in February '81. I was looking forward to it. Once I got to age fifty-five and had my years in, I just got out. With the Supreme Court decisions and everything else, you couldn't be a policeman any more. They tied your hands. The thugs in the street were dictating to you more than you could tell them what to do. In the old days, a slap on the back of the head or a good kick in the fanny did these kids a lot more good than taking them to court and giving them a tap on the wrist. They get out of the courtroom faster than you do. After a while you just do what you can. It's just something you have to put up with if you're looking for retirement.

Some of the guys went on to be security guards different places after they got out. It'd be all right punching a clock and making rounds, but carrying a gun? No, I wouldn't want it. I was never proud of that thing anyway when I had it. I was never happy with it. It never made me feel any bigger. Thank God I never had to use it in thirty years. I never had to shoot anybody.

I worked for about a year driving one of those vans for one of the express delivery companies, picking up packages and stuff. It was still dealing with the public. I always did work dealing with the public.

Then we sold our home and moved to this senior citizen community in Florida. The wife has arthritis and we thought the weather and everything would be better for her. As it turned out, it isn't. The dampness, you know. It's cheaper living down here and it's a little warmer, but that's about it. She doesn't like it because we're away from the kids.

I have no regrets. Oh, there's things maybe I could've done better. Maybe studied a little harder and made sergeant. But them things didn't happen and are all passed, so there's no sense crying about it. Once it's gone, there's nothing you can do.

*

When you're out, you're out. I was traveling out of town and I got stopped on the highway by the state police. He's getting ready to write me up and I'm telling him kind of frantically how I used to be a cop, how I worked in the city for twenty years. He looked at me like, "So, who gives a shit?"

You're saying to yourself, "But—wow—I don't belong here." You'd better make up your mind that you no longer belong, pal.

*

I know a guy who got out for the No. 1 reason that he had a lot of overtime in that year. Once you've got your years in, the pension was predicated on the amount of money you made the last year you worked. He knew he would never get that close to having that much money again. The guy decided to get out.

All he talks about now is how he made a mistake. He gets in some real depressions. He's beside himself now. He misses whatever it was he had there. Whether it was the excitement of the job, whether it was the authority, I don't know. Some guys, you take the power and distinction of being a cop away from them and they're just another Joe Schmoe out there looking for a job . . . it's degrading to them.

He's not the only guy I know like that. I've seen at least a half-dozen guys with the same problem. Very honestly, I think it's because they're not making it on the outside. It's a whole different ball game. In the job they had that umbrella of security that no matter what they did they were still a cop. A lot of guys say it's because they never had to work directly under a boss and they got to make their own decisions. I think it's just the opposite. Men find solace in the job and relative security. All of a sudden they realize, "Wow, I'm free from that now. What'll I do? I've always had 'The Job.' I had unlimited sick time. I had my medical coverage, my benefits. Who's going to take care of this?" I think guys miss the structure. You see guys who were praying twenty years to get out of the job. They take their terminal leave and try the outside for two or three months; then they try to get right back into the job.

The sad part is that now I'm seeing so many guys coming in for really menial jobs. They have gotten out of the police department and they're really not making it. I see guys with no special skills. What is a cop going to do? You walk into a company these days and tell them you're a retired detective and it's no big deal.

353

COPS

They want to know if you can run a computer or an elevator.

*

You do miss that feeling of power that no matter what you do or where you go, nobody can really do anything to you, because you're a cop.

A simple thing like driving. Once I wasn't a policeman anymore, I was so scared I was going to get a ticket. I never even thought about it before. I would drive 60, 65, maybe 70. I would bust traffic lights all the time. "I ain't going to sit here. Nobody's coming. I'm going. Somebody sees me and pulls me over, so what?"

I go into a store and see a ruckus going on; now I stay away from it. It's not my business. I don't want to get involved. Before it was, "Hey, I'll get involved. I got a gun on me and I ain't going to worry about it." Ninety percent of the policemen still on the job, whether they'll admit it or not, that's the way they feel.

I don't have that attitude any more. I have a license. I can carry a gun when I'm working, but most of the time I just don't mess with it. I forget it and leave it at home.

*

When you're in your forties and you're working with younger guys and you see them jumping over fences and stuff, you realize that it's time to go. I wasn't pressured, I wasn't really afraid. Just something inside said it was time to go. When I was twenty-two years old I could accept a lot more shit. As I got older I realized there were things I couldn't accept. For instance, I couldn't accept working with a twenty-seven-year-old boss. Don't get me wrong, I know this was my problem. But I was not totally convinced that because you passed one civil service test the police department should make you a supervisor.

About a month before I retired we had this incident. There was this girl and guy that were running together. They beat up like seventeen senior citizens and robbed them on separate occasions. The girl's father was a corrections officer and she stole his gun and gave it to her boyfriend. He proceeded to do all kinds of stickups and bang-ups with it.

I had a squeal on the guy that he was in some shithouse hotel. We were to hit the place like four o'clock in the morning. I showed the picture to the desk clerk and then grabbed him by the hair and dragged him upstairs with me so he can't call this guy on the phone. I made him show me with the passkey how all the doors work so I can get in there in a few seconds' time. The only thing he didn't tell me was the size of the room. I expected to go through the door and make like a forty-yard dash to the bed where this guy is sleeping with the girl and drag them apart.

I locate the guy's room. Now we're going to go through this door. It's not that we *think* he's got a gun. We *know* he's got a gun and he's been using it pretty well. At one point, when I put the key in the door, I said to myself, "Holy shit. I got a month to go. What if I do this now once a week? Is this really what I want to be doing? What the fuck am I doing? What the fuck am I doing here?"

If you were laying on the bed and put your arms out you would be touching both walls of this room. We crashed through the door and he did go for the gun, but it was all over in a matter of seconds, because these three gorillas ended up laying on this guy.

What the fuck am I really doing here? I enjoy it to a point. You really want to go through that door, as unlikely as that may sound, but now it's starting to seem dangerous to me. For whatever reason—I turned chicken or whatever you want to call it—I realized it was time for me to go. I retired a month later.

Twenty years to the day. Just did my time. I enjoy being out. It's rejuvenated my life. I never disliked the job. It was always good to me. It supported me and my family. I was satisfied with what I was doing, but when the time came, I felt it was right to go.

*

I was twenty-seven years old and I went to the doctor. I told him I drank a lot. He says, "I'd drink too, kid, if I had your job. But beer will never hurt you." He put me on Librium. "You shouldn't drink and take this at the same time," he did say that. So I stop the drinking and I took the Librium.

Then I couldn't sleep, so he gave me sleeping pills. When I was depressed, he gave me antidepressants. Then he gave me anti-anxiety pills. Then I was in pain, so he gave me pain pills.

I'm walking around with a bottle of pills and I'm feeling like a fucking charlatan. Here I am a cop, going to work. I'm arresting drunks and settling family disputes and my entire life is fucked up.

Instead of pulling out a flask or going around the corner into a bar to get a drink, when I'm out somewhere on the job and I feel uptight, I'd go into the bathroom and take a pill, whatever pill fit the occasion. I feel very, very phony, like garbage. I was afraid somebody would see me and find out. In fact, I used to take the bottle of pills and stuff it with cotton so they wouldn't rattle. When I had to go down to the morgue to photograph a dead body, I'd stick Vicks up my nose to get rid of the smell, light a cigar because I smoked about ten or fifteen a day—I had to compulsively always be doing something. Then I'd take two or three pills.

What I didn't know because nobody ever educated me was that I was a walking time bomb. The thought that came into my head all the time was suicide, taking my own life. I lived in fear of taking my own life. This wasn't caused through any one thing. It was a cumulative amount of stress, of handling shit over a period of time.

I didn't really know what was wrong with me, but all of a sudden that gun I carried, that went everywhere with me because I thought I had to be Mr. Macho and make all kinds of arrests, that gun became my worst enemy. I began to fear that gun. I'd photographed so many people who were dead by guns. I'd seen so many people who blew their brains out, including cops. I started to get more and more scared. The more afraid I got, the more anxiety attacks I got, the more the gun became the enemy. I was in deep depression.

It was a merry-go-round and I didn't know how to get off. I had this feeling that I was cracking up.

I was trained to use a gun. I saw cops who tried to blow their brains out and still lived because they put it to the side of their head. The oral sex, the making love to the gun is to put it in your mouth, put it inside your head so that way you don't miss. And I started to think about it an awful lot.

I lived in fear. When I was driving to a homicide to photograph the bodies and I'd have an anxiety attack and I'd panic, I've seen myself stop the car, get out, empty the gun and throw the bullets across a field. Then I felt safe. I couldn't use it on myself. Then, I'd say, "That's a lie. You can get bullets from anybody at the crime scene."

I lived that way for a couple of years and it got worse. I wouldn't bring the gun home. But as long as you worked you had to carry it. They inspected you to make sure you had the proper equipment. I used to do details at the ballpark guarding the money from the gate and I wouldn't have any bullets in my gun.

I was ashamed of that, because I felt weak. I felt not

a man. "What the fuck are you doing wearing a gun and a badge? If you feel like that, you shouldn't be on the job. You should quit." But I was more afraid of quitting the job because I got seven children and I'm the provider. Really I was afraid of what people would think of me. That's the killer, that's the real killer. To fail, to be less of a man, then I might as well kill myself. And I couldn't kill myself. I lived with it a long time.

The way I handled it was I eventually started drinking again. In other words, I just said, "Fuck it." The pills were so depressing, so I just drank, too. So now I had a dual addiction. I was a whore.

I'm sitting in my police car by myself crying, afraid somebody will see me. I didn't know what was wrong with me. It was a twelve-year period before I got this bad. I lived with this for twelve years.

I couldn't get help although I went to the doctor. I back-doored him so nobody would know. I talked about my drinking, but I couldn't tell him I thought I was cracking up. He reassured me that there was nothing wrong with me being on these pills for years and years. I would go back to him and get anything that I wanted.

Worse than that, when I would go to a drugstore or a doctor's office that had been robbed or broken into, I knew the supply and got what I wanted. It was very easy. I was a thief on top of everything else. I'm not proud of that either, but I did what I had to do to survive.

The strangest part about it was, I still made arrests—good ones. I had to prove that I was still good. I still took the best pictures. I got the best undercover work done. It didn't hurt my job performance. I'll never understand that. I didn't overreact. I didn't get complaints against me.

It came out. It came out in my home life. They're the ones that got hurt, they're the ones that paid the price. In my family life I was deteriorating. I was overparanoid with my kids. I didn't beat them with my hands, but I beat them with my mouth. My wife and I ended up in divorce. I left home for a young girl and all that kind of stuff.

We had a department chaplain, but I didn't want to talk to him, partly because I saw him as part of the administration. Plus I was convinced that I did not believe in God any more. Although I used to tell Him, "Come down off of that fucking cross, I'll put spikes in you—never mind the nails—for what you do to people out there. How dare you do this to people?" I wanted to fucking kill him. If Christ would have come in here I would have wiped him out with a shotgun. That's how much hate I had in me.

I didn't want to hurt my family. I think the only thing that stopped me from committing suicide is that I could see the faces of my kids. If I really fuck up and blow my brains out, this is going to be the biggest failure of my life, because I'm going to do this to them.

There were two guys on the job who were recovered alcoholics and they knew that I had a problem. They had tried to talk to me, but I would avoid them like the bubonic plague. But finally one day I was tired of crying, I was tired of the gun in my mouth all the time, I was tired of hurting my family and I called them. I said, "Look, take me. I don't give a shit what the fuck you do with me, just take me."

The only reason I called them was because I knew they could be trusted and they were cops like me. I wouldn't go to anyone else. I wouldn't go to God Himself if he came on Earth. I wouldn't go to a shrink. Shrinks to me were the fucking cuckoos. I'd gone into their offices and taken clients out that they were saying, "Get this nut out of here." I'd taken mental patients who were runaways back to the hospitals and seen how they were treated there. They were treated bad. If I went there, I'd be treated the same way. So, where do I go?

What they did was, these guys put me in the hospital and dried me out, got all the shit out of my system. Once I got sober, I went to Alcoholics Anonymous. I didn't like it. But I started to learn stuff about fears and anxiety. I started to see cops and reporters that I'd been in the front lines with. That made me feel better. "We knew you were having a bad problem, but nobody could talk to you," they said. "You were really bad. We were worried about you." I found out that my case wasn't unique. I wasn't alone any more.

It happens a lot to cops. They're driving around out there in their car, just crying and crying, not knowing what's wrong with them. They can't admit it. The people that are burned out are the people that care, the people that want to help and do a good job. I noticed that a lot of policemen don't have AA to go to. They're not alcoholic, maybe they don't even drink. Yet they have the same problems—fear, anxiety, ulcers, stress.

If you go to a crime scene and look at the faces, you will see the fear right on their faces. You don't see anybody smiling. People will laugh, but that's just a release from the tension. You see death, trauma, stress. I thought about my macho image and how deadly it was.

Me and another cop I sobered up with, we said, "What can we do about it? Let's get up and talk about it, get up in front of a bunch of cops and tell them how we feel."

It's scary, getting up in front of a bunch of cops and telling them how you were scared, how you thought about suicide and how you drank because you were weak. "They're going to laugh us out of the room."

But we did it anyway. They didn't laugh. Nobody laughed. They wanted to know more.

*

The job changed me. You begin to lose your perspective as to what is right and what is wrong. I'm not trying to blame the job for what I did, understand me? But you see so much that is alien to your background. You see drug use, prostitution, violence. Your moral judgments get kind of twisted around and you say, "Well, this is wrong, but it's not very wrong. I see guys get away with a lot worse than this every day." I got very weird.

I got jammed up. I got caught screwing an underage girl. It got shoved under my wife's nose. My wife said, "That's it. Goodbye." The job said, "You know, maybe it would be a good idea if you quit . . . before we fire you." Everything went down the tubes. Everything was destroyed and what's the way out? Your whole livelihood is beyond your reach. No job, no pension, no family. I came very, very close to committing suicide on more than one occasion. I sat in the backroom of the station with two of my guns in my hands, wondering if I could pull both triggers at the same time. A lot of guys go that way.

*

Mounted cop, notorious fucking drunk, an old-timer. He refused to spend his uniform allowance on his uniform, so consequently he very seldom gets out of the saddle, because his pants got no seat. Nobody fucked with him. The sergeant might give him a slash if he scratched one day—maybe, maybe not. The sergeant only saw him twice in the eight hours, going out and coming in. They don't call him on no radio run. It's a major sin to give an old fart like that a run.

He was doing the eight-to-four shift. He showed up so hung over that he was still drunk. It's broad daylight in midtown Manhattan. There was fucking people running all over the place and he was out on that Godforsaken nag. There's only one way to level off and that's to get the hair of the dog that bit him.

He spied a bar, but he knew he couldn't leave the horse parked outside. If the boss came by and saw the animal without a rider, he'd know something was afoot. But he was a slick old-timer. The doors to the basement that swing up out of the sidewalk are open and he's got this horse that will go anywhere he tells it to go, so he walks the horse down the stairs into the basement.

He stayed in there for four hours. Now he was past the level point again and out of his head. At this point, he felt that he could cope. His sense of responsibility returned and he decided to get out there on the street. He lifts the sidewalk grating and there's his horse laying on the basement floor. It weighed 1,700 pounds and it was dead as a doornail. It was confined and hot down there. The horse had swished around and inadvertently knocked the smoke stack off the heating unit. He had asphyxiated himself.

What could he do? Certainly he'll be guilty if anybody finds the horse down there. He had to get the horse up on the street so that it can have died on the curb. Then he could have said, "I don't know what happened. Who the fuck knows? The damn horse laid down in front of this bar and died on me." But the thing weighs so much that the whole bar couldn't lift it even if they were so inclined.

The bartender was smart. He said, "We call my friend with a tow truck, we put the winch on the horse and we winch the horse right up. You're set." Great idea. They went back inside the bar to have another shot while he made the call.

The tow truck came. The cop went out and opened up the doors. The truck backs up with his ass end on the sidewalk, consequently blocking all traffic. Now he had a huge traffic jam working. After about two minutes everybody's honking their horns. This of course attracted the attention of all the pedestrians. They came over to investigate what a tow truck could possibly be winching up out of a basement.

Ba-boom! Trouble. Now the old-timer has got ninety-nine ASPCA workers on his case and was being attacked by hundreds of New York animal lovers. Here's this poor dead horse and there's the owner, the cop, barfing his guts out on the sidewalk. That was his last day. He ended up on the farm taking the cure for booze.

*

Somebody knew. Somebody had to know as crazy as this guy was. His partner or his sergeant or somebody who worked with him saw that he was going crazy and should have tried to get him help. But that's not the way it usually works out. The guy who came to us at IAD was an officer who just happened to meet this cop in a bar they both frequented off-duty. They became casual friends over about a year. It had become quite apparent that this guy had all kinds of problems with narcotics in the form of pills. He was also paranoid, probably schizophrenic.

The wife of the cop who came to us was a pharmacist and the guy was always pushing to get Quaaludes from her. Of course that was wrong and he should have reported it, but he didn't think it was that dangerous at the time. But then the guy had begun to offer him weapons in exchange for 'ludes and at that point he came to us.

We recorded some telephone calls between the two of them. I listened to the recordings and I knew the guy was scary, not evil, just sick and screwed up. You could hear it in his voice. He said, "I don't want to get caught with this shit. I wouldn't do this with anybody else, I know you're a straight guy. You're probably nervous. I know I am. Here's what we'll do: We'll arrive at a motel that we will jointly agree on only at the last minute so there's no chance of setting each other up.

When we get to the room, we will both immediately strip so we'll know that we're not wearing wires. Then we'll make the exchange."

I said to my partner, "This guy is on the edge. We've got to confine this situation. He's liable to do something. Let the thing go down in a closed room like he wants. We'll bug it so he never finds the bug. He'll do the deal, walk out into the hallway and we'll grab him. That's it."

Our superiors didn't want to pop for the hotel room. They say, "We'll pick an open spot. We'll wire our car. We pull up and he gets in our car. The exchange will be recorded. We can videotape the thing from hidden vans. Then we converge on him when he starts to get out of the car."

I thought, "No fucking way."

The meeting was held in Queens near the Triborough Bridge. The quarry pulls up to a spot and our guy pulls up beside him and was just about to say, "Hop in my car," when a citizen comes out of nowhere walking a God damn dog. The guy we're after takes a look and he says, "I think he's a fucking cop." He's freaking on us. "Listen, do the deal right now. Throw me the pills, throw them. I don't have the guns with me, but for good faith here's money." He's got two grand with him and he throws the two grand into the car window. "Give it to me now, man, give it to me now!"

Our guy throws a jar of 500 fucking 'ludes into his car. The dummies have started to converge on him so he knows for sure what's up. The race is on. This guy is running amok. He obviously has no regard for his own life and doesn't give a fuck for nobody else.

He ran across Queens Boulevard nonstop, not a hesitation. We were right behind him and I was shitting in my pants. I thought, "I'm dead. I'm fucking dead." And I was driving. He wings the bottle of pills out the window, all over a residential street in Queens, runs a couple of more blocks and finally crashes his little Volkswagen into a double-parked car.

I see him fidgeting around and I just know that he's going for his service revolver. I'm with this really ballsy lieutenant. I said, "Tony, I think he's going for his gun. He's moving in that car and I think he's after his piece. Be careful." I no sooner got that out than up comes the fucking gun and he is crazed.

"I'm not going with you guys," he says. "You're IAD, right? I'm not going with you guys."

The lieutenant did the talking. We held everybody back. He sat there and we kept hoping that we can get him. The lieutenant tried everything. "Look, you fucked up. It ain't the end of the world. It's no big deal. You're still a cop and we're cops. You're one of us. Number one, you don't want to do what you're doing here. You want to shoot me? I'm like you. I promise you, we'll get you help. You got a problem with these God damn pills. It ain't a criminal thing."

"It's over," the guy says. "The job's over, everything is over." He takes his shield out, he looks at me and he just threw it at me. He said, "That's it. I ain't going with you guys." He opened the door and made us back up. He kneeled down. He took the gun and put it to his temple and he blew his brains out. Right there. I never seen anybody bleed so much in my life. It was like a geyser.

We went to his house afterwards and there was a suicide note on the bed.

*

This guy said to me once, "I don't feel sorry for cops that get killed. That's why they take the job. There's no reason to make any special ceremony or burial."

I couldn't really let myself go, so I just tried to ignore this guy. But this is the attitude you run into all the time. "You took the job. It's part of your job to get killed." It's not. "It's part of your job to get beaten up." It's not.

You take this job to protect people and to help them. I may go out there and get my ass kicked or get shot. That might come with the job, but it's not my job to die. People think that's your job, that it comes with the money. Nobody takes a $30,000-a-year job to die. You'd be crazy.

*

I made an arrest that night. I brought the guy in and I was processing him upstairs. Our man at the desk downstairs heard on the radio that there was a 10–13—which is assist patrolman. You could be doing anything, but the minute you hear 10–13, you drop everything and you go. Then it came over, "Cop shot."

I don't remember who I was with, but we jump in a car and go down to the scene. When we get there, there's a lot of cops and people milling around. They say a cop got shot. I'm looking and I see a little bit of blood on the street.

"Who got hit?" I says.

"Mikey."

We started going through the motions, trying to get names and witnesses. In the back of my mind, I think, "Flesh wound, just a nick."

We're there for maybe ten, fifteen minutes and I said, "Let's go up to the hospital and see how he's doing." So we go up.

At that particular time, since we were working the street, we were in and out of the hospital all the time. The nurses up there were all about our age. The relationship with them was, they were a lot like us. They had the same mental outlook on life. They saw the aftermath. They caught the abuse from some of these people we were trying to help. So they had a very similar job to the one we had.

We walked right up to the emergency room and the nurses we knew very well were working. When you go in, there's swinging doors and a preparation type of an operating room with four beds. If it's a rush thing, they'll work on them right there. Otherwise, they get them ready and take them up to the OR.

When we walk in there, I saw that not only was Mikey shot, but the sergeant that was with him was shot. They were both laying on the table cracked open. You could see their lungs.

The sergeant was a boss. I didn't socialize with him. But Mikey, he was over to the house. He was separated from his wife, so there wasn't that real family type of thing. But he'd come over by himself and we'd have a few drinks. He was getting back with his wife. I looked at him and it was like . . . how personal can you get when you see a guy's insides.

I looked over at one of the nurses, Ann, and she was crying. Another of the nurses just made a gesture like, "It's over." Neither one of them made it.

I just walked out of there, mad as hell. I didn't cry. Other cops in the precinct had been killed, but I didn't have the relationship with them. Just, "Hey, how you doing?" type of thing. It wasn't like the reality hit till this time.

We worked about three days straight, the whole unit. We went out and terrorized the shooting galleries. "What happened? Who did it?"

The detectives—I can see their point of view now, because I'm at their level—they weren't giving us any information. We could give them everything we had, but they weren't giving us anything. You feel frustrated, because what we wanted was more or less revenge. Now when I work on a homicide case, I know I want the information from the street cops, but I don't give them everything that I have, because you don't want them jumping the gun. Maybe the case isn't ready yet. There's a whole procedure you follow because you don't want to lose it in court.

What happened was, the guys that killed them had been doing bank stickups. Mikey and the sergeant pulled up on a car that was double-parked and got out to tell them to move the car, maybe issue the guy a summons. One guy was coming out of the tenement and saw them. He killed both of them.

They tell me Mikey was laying there in the street— that's the part that gets you—laying in all this garbage, just strangers around him. He was saying, "Call my people. Call my people." I don't know if he meant us as his people or his family. You don't know what goes through his mind when a guy dies.

Everyday you spend thirty hours thinking, "Jeez, I'd hate to die in this shit." Then when you come back to home, this isn't the greatest place in the world, but it's like a little oasis, where I can come and chill out for a few days and then go back into it.

*

I had to go to court that day, so I didn't work the same shift. By the time it actually happened, I was off-duty. My partner was killed.

His name was Mikey. Mikey had grown up in a very bad neighborhood. One of the strongest experiences of his life was when he was badly beaten up by a policeman. But he was the good guy and I was the bad guy. He was not as aggressive as I was. I was the prick. My job was not to trust anybody. His job was to give a person the benefit of the doubt.

He had hands, the largest fucking hands I've ever seen. One time we chased a guy down the street and Mikey finally got within arm's reach of him, but not close enough to get a good grip on him. Mikey swatted him on the side of the head, picked the guy up off his feet and knocked him into a hallway. He was very good with his hands and never felt the compulsion to use a gun.

That night he was working with our immediate boss, who was a sergeant—a very nice guy, very tough, but easygoing. A car was double-parked up the block, so Mikey got out of the car and went to tell the guy to move his vehicle. Any time you do that, it's just a matter of course to ask to see the driver's license and registration. Unbeknownst to Mikey, the guy had done like four stickups and had killed somebody. Mikey walked up to the car, the guy shot him, shot him twice.

Mikey and the sergeant were in a substitute car that was provided by motor transport. It wasn't a regular precinct radio car and it didn't have a radio in it. To open the passenger door you had to turn in the seat and kick the door open with both your feet. By the time the sergeant was able to climb out of the car, the guy shot him, too. Then he turned around and put two more in Mikey.

As soon as the initial shock rolled over me, I took two weeks' vacation. I didn't want to be under the direct authority of the police department. By this time, we knew who the guy was who killed Mikey. We thought we knew where this guy was holed up.

The apartment door was right across from a stairway. I sat up the stairs looking at the door. Lived on bologna sandwiches and whiskey for two weeks. I don't think I slept two hours a night. I just sat there with my palms on my knees with my gun out. I was going to kill him. All I could think of was, "You're going to kill somebody in cold blood. Can you really do this?"

I was prepared to wait as long as it took. Finally somebody came in and said, "Hey, look, we got the wrong place." As luck would have it, the guy wasn't in that apartment. So, I never had to deal with that for real. If nothing else, it taught me that to go out and kill somebody in cold blood requires a special person.

I felt very guilty about Mikey's death. He was a very positive person. At that point, I wasn't. I felt guilty for being alive, guilty for surviving, guilty for not being there to protect him.

Under the circumstances, I probably would have been the one to go to the car, if I'd been there. If I didn't have my gun out, I would have sure as hell had it loose. Since I was more suspicious and cynical than Mikey, I always had my gun ready.

Anyway, my first official day back at work, don't you know, I was assigned to that same car. About the next six months after that, I teamed up with another guy— good guy. Finally Jack grabbed me one day after six months and said, "Look, if you want to commit suicide, that's your business. But do it on your own time. Don't drive when I'm with you."

What I'd been doing without realizing it was jumping into situations that clearly mandated caution and some degree of force and I was doing it empty-handed. I wanted somebody to kill me. I got help after that, because when he said what he did, I realized he was right. I was acting crazy. Because of my own emotional thing, I was likely to hurt this guy, Jack.

On the anniversary of his death every year, I go up to the cemetery. It's one of those new cemeteries. They don't use headstones any more, just plaques in the ground. They don't want to have to mow around the memorials. It seems like if you're dead you should be able to inconvenience people. Every year I go up there and cut the weeds away. Nobody's going to walk on that grave. I'll break their fucking ankle.

Sometime within a year after the killing took place, I was working with my new partner in a radio car. It was nasty out, cold and misty. This Spanish woman was trying to hail a cab and she was very pregnant. It had been quiet and just because it seemed appropriate, we stopped and said, "In your condition, I wouldn't be standing out here in the rain. What's the matter? Are you ready to deliver?"

"No, no," she says. "I just have to go see my gynecologist. I got a few pains and I thought maybe I ought to have him check it out."

"Where's your husband?"

"Oh, he's at work right now." The long and the short of it was, we put her in the radio car and gave her a lift up to the hospital. She said, "Would you do me a favor? I haven't been able to reach him, but I'm supposed to tell the district attorney where I am at all times."

"What do you mean?

"I'm a witness to something and they have to know."

"What is that?" I asked her.

"I saw the guy kill two cops."

She was the principal witness to Mikey's killing. She came forward on her own with a description of the guy who did the shooting. She stuck her neck out, didn't even ask us for anything. With all the people pushing to the head of the line, she wanted nothing from anybody. She could have really asked us for anything and we would have done our damnedest to give it to her. She was just doing the right thing.

It's people who keep you in this game. Long after you're completely disaffected with society as a whole, the majority of people you encounter, you always think of those few good people. They're too fucking honest to be prosperous, just too fucking good. They're really the only thing that makes this life worth it.